Interdependence in a
World of Unequals

Also of Interest

*Debt and the Less Developed Countries, edited by Jonathan David Aronson

*Threat to Development: Pitfalls of the New International Economic Order, William Loehr and John P. Powelson

OPEC, the Gulf, and the World Petroleum Market, Fereidun Fesharaki, Harrison Brown, Corazon M. Siddayo, Toufiq A. Siddiqi, Kirk R. Smith, and Kim Woodard

The Arab-African Connection: Political and Economic Realities, Victor T. Le Vine and Timothy W. Luke

Western Economies in Transition: Structural Change and Adjustment Policies in Industrial Countries, edited by Irving Leveson and Jimmy W. Wheeler

Science and Technology in a Changing International Order: The United Nations Conference on Science and Technology for Development, edited by Volker Rittberger

Managing Development Programs: The Lessons of Success, Samuel Paul

Implementing Development Assistance: European Approaches to Basic Needs, Steven H. Arnold

Development Financing: A Framework for International Financial Cooperation, Salah Al-Shaikhly

The Economics of New Technology in Developing Countries, Frances Stewart and Geoffrey James

*International Financial Cooperation, Frances Stewart and Arjun Sengupta

Food, Development, and Politics in the Middle East, Marvin G. Weinbaum

Migration and the Labor Market in Developing Countries, edited by R. H. Sabot

Local Politics and Development in the Middle East, edited by Louis J. Cantori and Iliya Harik

Managing Renewable Natural Resources in Developing Countries, edited by Charles W. Howe

*Managing Development in the Third World, Coralie Bryant and Louise G. White

*Alternative Futures for Africa, edited by Timothy M. Shaw

*Available in hardcover and paperback.

Westview Special Studies in Social, Economic, and Political Development

Interdependence in a World of Unequals: African-Arab-OECD Economic Cooperation for Development
edited by Dunstan M. Wai

The accumulation of surplus petrofunds by some Arab countries, far exceeding the present absorptive capacities of their economies, has given rise to the idea of a major new development effort in sub-Saharan Africa, financed by Arab surpluses and supported by OECD technology and expertise. The guiding principle in the idea of a tripartite partnership is that, given a proper allocation of responsibilities among the three regional participants, cooperation would benefit all parties. The Arab countries, it is argued, would gain experience in management and in the acquisition of technology as a result of increased transactions with Western industrialized countries. Funds from the Arab countries would catalyze accelerated development in sub-Saharan Africa and would provide a desirable alternative to OECD-intermediated flows of capital and trade between Africa and the Arab world; this could help reduce Africa's dependence on the OECD countries for technology, expertise, financing, and markets. And finally, the OECD members would benefit politically from an effective development effort involving their response to initiatives taken by the South, and would gain economically by increasing their exports as African and Arab absorptive capacities rose and by continuing to exercise management functions in the context of development.

To further explore the potential of this triangular cooperation, a group of experts from Africa, the Arab Middle East, Western Europe, and North America held a conference at the Rockefeller Foundation conference center in Bellagio, Italy, in May 1980. In their discussions--the basis of this book--they identified and analyzed a wide range of problems and issues involved. They concluded that the central issue is whether trilateral projects of appropriate design for the African setting can be identified and implemented through arrangements that ensure an equitable and effective distribution of responsibilities, risks, and benefits among the participants, with due regard for the existing profound asymmetries in triangular economic relations.

Dunstan M. Wai was a fellow of the Woodrow Wilson International Center for Scholars in 1981. He also has been research consultant to International Relations Division, Rockefeller Foundation, and consultant to the Special Unit for Technical Cooperation Among Developing Countries, United Nations. He is author of *The African-Arab Conflict in the Sudan* (1980), editor and coauthor of *The Southern Sudan and the Problem of National Integration* (1973), and has contributed articles to numerous books and periodicals.

To
Mason Willrich
innovator and initiator

Interdependence in a World of Unequals

African-Arab-OECD Economic Cooperation for Development

edited by Dunstan M. Wai

Westview Press / Boulder, Colorado

Westview Special Studies in Social, Economic, and Political Development

Copyright © 1982 by Westview Press, Inc.

Published in 1982 in the United States of America by
    Westview Press, Inc.
    5500 Central Avenue
    Boulder, Colorado 80301
    Frederick A. Praeger, President and Publisher

Library of Congress Catalog Card Number 82-050601
ISBN 0-86531-363-6

Printed and bound in the United States of America.

Contents

viii

Tables

Acknowledgments

The chapters in this book are only some of the papers that were especially written for and presented at a conference on "African-Arab-OECD Triangular Cooperation" at Bellagio, Lake Como, Italy. The conference was sponsored by the International Relations Division of the Rockefeller Foundation, and its preparation received the support and encouragement of many persons. I am thankful to the Rockefeller Foundation for its financial support of the conference, and I am indebted to Dr. Mason Willrich (formerly director of the International Relations Division), Dr. Edwin A. Deagle, Jr., and Dr. John J. Stremlau for their friendship, intellectual encouragement, and unfailing enthusiasm in supporting my research activities during my tenure at the foundation as a visiting research fellow. Special thanks must also go to Mrs. Karen S. Noonan, whose help in organizing the conference was truly indispensable. I should also like to express my thanks to Mary Ryan, consultant for publications, for editing the papers for the conference and for helping to prepare the manuscript for publication. Jackie Bassett, Maureen Gillen, Geraldine Mannion, and Maria Ramos were all in varying degrees helpful in my research project, which has contributed to this book. I am also grateful to Francis Nyirjesy for his assistance in my research on African-Arab relations.

Finally, I would like to express my gratitude to all colleagues and friends who commented on the papers at Bellagio. In particular, I would like to thank Ambassador Tahsheen Basheer of the United Arab Republic of Egypt, Dr. Michael A. Samuels (vice-president for international affairs of the U.S. Chamber of Commerce), Professor Abbas Alnasrawi (University of Vermont), Dr. Charles Odidi-Okidi (Nairobi University), Mr. Basheer Ben Basheer el Haskoury of the Arab Monetary Funds (UAE), Peter Kok (Khartoum University), and Dr. Shimshon Zelniker (University of Tel Aviv). These persons and others not mentioned here helped shape the success of the Bellagio symposium that yielded this book.

Dunstan M. Wai

1
Introduction: African-Arab-OECD Triangular Cooperation

Dunstan M. Wai

The idea of triangular cooperation among African, Arab, and member countries of the Organisation for Economic Co-operation and Development (OECD) is based on three assumptions. First, a number of African countries have enormous investment potential for improving their agricultural production, for both domestic consumption and foreign trade, whereas others have mineral resources that could be more substantially developed. But these countries lack capital, technology, and trained manpower--all necessary for the development of their natural resources. Second, some Arab oil-producing and oil-exporting countries have surplus petrofunds--buying power--but lack other resources such as agricultural potential, the development of which would increase their capacity to diversify their economies and to absorb the petrofunds domestically. Third, some OECD members possess technology, trained manpower, banking facilities for recycling the Arab petrofunds, purchasing power, and marketing expertise.

From these assumptions flows the hypothesis that a tripartite partnership in development among African, Arab, and OECD countries would promote complementary linkages between resource bases and development processes, thereby increasing trade and income to the benefit of all regions. Such a relationship would require each participating group of countries to contribute the essential resources, labor, finance, and technology as well as to become involved in all stages of the project, starting from the investment idea, project formulation, appraisal, and implementation, up to and including operation and management.

How feasible is such cooperation? Is it possible for the African and Arab countries to embark on a comprehensive program of economic cooperation with Western industrialized countries, notwithstanding their ideological and political differences and unequal power at the international level? The primary focus of this volume is on the prospects, and the lack of them, for the use of Arab petrofunds and OECD technology and expertise

1

in African economic development. A variety of related issues, ranging from political and economic convergencies and asymmetrical relationships to enduring cultural influences that bear on contemporary relations among the three regions, are covered. The volume also examines the African resource base and constraints to development of these resources; the present financial flows (concessionary and nonconcessionary) from the rich Arab countries and the Western industrialized economies to sub-Saharan Africa; and the types of legal framework, initiatives, measures, mechanisms, and institutions that could help to overcome the constraints and promote triangular cooperation.

I will briefly explain in this chapter the basis for the rapidly evolving relationships among African natural resources, Arab petrofunds, and foreign technology and expertise: in other words, the rationale for triangular cooperation.

AFRICAN RESOURCES AND DEVELOPMENT NEEDS

The enormous resources of raw materials in sub-Saharan Africa were well known prior to, and in fact prompted, European colonization. Imports of cobalt, manganese, phosphates, tin, and vanadium from African countries supply the European Economic Community (EEC) with more than 80 percent of total consumption needs in each category. Bauxite, iron ore, and copper, found in abundance in Africa, are also imported in great quantities by OECD countries. Furthermore, African countries supply approximately 50 percent of the world's phosphate minerals (Japan and the United States are completely dependent on phosphate imports). Thus minerals resource development in Africa has great potential as a source of revenue for African countries. (Africa's consumption of these metal ores is very low; therefore they are available for export.)

The agricultural potential of most sub-Saharan African countries is impressive. More than 80 percent of the economically active population in Africa is involved in the agricultural sector; an only slightly smaller percentage participates in growing cash crops. At least up to the 1970s Africa produced about 77 percent of world production of cocoa beans, 34 percent of palm oil, 64 percent of peanut oil and 53 percent of the nuts themselves, and 32 percent of cotton. These crops are not essential agricultural commodities for Arab countries; however, many African countries can also produce such essential food commodities as sugar, rice, and cereals in addition to vegetable oil. Coffee, tea, and tobacco, which are imported in large quantities by Arab countries, are grown and exported by some African countries.

The agricultural potential of many African countries

has been restricted because they were and still are producing export crops for metropolitan European countries.
Thus, at present Africa is unable to meet all its food
demands, partly because of the priority given to export
crops (coffee, cocoa, tea, cotton, sugar, oil crops, and
fruits) and partly because of low agricultural labor
productivity. Markets for agricultural exports in Arab
countries could provide new sources for export trade and
stimulate production of a variety of agricultural commodities that have previously been grown in small quantities. Development assistance from the Organization of
Arab Oil Producing and Exporting Countries (OAPEC) could
focus on increasing production of rice, sugar, maize,
wheat, millet, and sorghum--all traditional subsistence
crops.

The infrastructures of African countries are not yet
developed. They have weak administrative capacities
(which hinder agricultural development), inadequate socioeconomic structures, insufficient investment in infrastructures, poor institutions for providing extension,
credit, and marketing, and a paucity of skilled manpower.

Thus, Africa needs capital, technology, and skilled
manpower for economic development. Its development goals
should take into account the felt needs of the people in
the rural areas but should not neglect other productive
sectors of the economy. These goals can be pursued by
both gaining self-reliance and encouraging foreign investments.

ARAB OIL RESOURCES AND PETROFUNDS

At present the Arab oil-producing countries (Algeria, Iraq, Kuwait, Libya, Qatar, Saudi Arabia, and
United Arab Emirates) have enormous reserves of oil, and
their production far surpasses that of all the other
OPEC members combined.

Since the "quantum leaps" of oil prices, the OAPEC
countries have accumulated billions of dollars (Table
1.1).

By the end of the World Bank's fiscal year, June
1977, OAPEC members held about $2.3 billion of the
bank's loans and notes, representing approximately 12.5
percent of its total obligations. They made subscrip-
tions of $517.2 million to the bank's capital. The Arab
boost to the International Monetary Fund (IMF) was reflected in Saudi Arabia's pledge of $2.5 billion for the
so-called Witteveen Facility, designed to raise the
credit available to IMF members by $10 billion.

These facts emphasize the availability of Arab oil
revenues, which continue to exceed the absorptive
capacities of their economies (here I refer to Saudi
Arabia, Kuwait, and the United Arab Emirates). The
infrastructures of the Arab oil-producing countries are
grossly inadequate, and given their sparse population

TABLE 1.1

MAJOR ARAB OIL PRODUCERS AND EXPORTING COUNTRIES, OIL RESERVES
AND REVENUES

Country	Estimated population	Oil reserves (Billion barrels)	Oil revenues ($ billion)
Saudi Arabia	7 million	165.7	36.7 (1978)
Kuwait	1.2 million	66.2	9.5 (1978)
Bahrain	0.28 million	0.25	0.45 (1978)
Qatar	0.2 million	4	2.2 (1978)
Abu Dhabi } Dubai }	0.88 million	30 1.3	} 8.7 (1978) }

SOURCE: Financial Times, January 22, 1980.

and size (especially Saudi Arabia and Oman), it would be
extremely costly to develop these countries. The climate
is so harsh that it takes a "great toll in depreciation
of machinery and structures."[1] In addition, the supply
of skills is extremely limited. These countries also
lack adequate agricultural resources and depend heavily
on food imports as well as technology from the OECD countries. Some, particularly Saudi Arabia, Kuwait, the
United Arab Emirates, and Qatar, lack almost all other
natural resources, including the most important of all,
fresh water.

Nevertheless, oil revenues have given the Arabs purchasing power that in the past was almost a complete
monopoly of the industrialized countries. They have invested billions of dollars in Western countries, mainly
in the United Kingdom and the United States.

In the last four years, the capital-surplus Arab
countries have realized the necessity of creating depend-
able sources of food and raw materials for Arab investors.
It was then thought conceivable that "food" could be used
as a weapon against them, just as they used oil against
the West following the Arab-Israeli war of 1973. Arab
development priorities also require the use of petrofunds
for aid to spur domestic economic development, for
example, to widen markets for domestic industries,
especially petrochemicals. On the political level, Arab
financial aid increases their influence in the recipient
countries and in international institutions (the U.N.,
the Food and Agriculture Organization [FAO], the World
Bank, the IMF, and the U.N. Conference on Trade and
Development [UNCTAD]), counter-balances both Western and
Eastern bloc influences in the poor countries (particularly in Black Africa), and may enhance Third World
solidarity. Therefore it is no surprise that committed

Arab aid represents a very high percentage of the gross national product (GNP) of the donor countries.[2]

Total Organization of Petroleum Exporting Countries (OPEC) surpluses invested worldwide were estimated at $168 billion by the end of 1978.[3] Of this figure, Arab surpluses amounted to $145-150 billion. But most of the OPEC investments were in the international markets, as shown in Table 1.2.

Africa offers many opportunities for Arab investors. Although both the African and Arab states have weak infrastructures that must be developed, they also have different resources and developmental needs. All African states, except Nigeria, Angola, and Gabon, lack oil resources and all depend on oil imports for agricultural development. The Arab oil states (particularly the Asian Arab countries), however, need to import most of their food products. According to Ray Vicker, "the Arab countries imported $1.7 billion of agricultural commodities in 1970, nearly $7 billion in 1975 and about $8 billion in 1976. In 1976, they imported 3.5 million tons of wheat, 400,000 tons of rice, 258,000 tons of barley, 156,000 tons of legumes such as lentils and 149,000 tons of millet, a type of grain. Imports of nearly all these items are still rising."[4] Yet, it is reckoned that domestic agricultural production in Arab lands is likely to increase at only about 4 percent a year in the 1980s. Meanwhile, food requirements are expected to grow rapidly because of population pressures and growth, increasing urbanization and industrialization, rising incomes, and rising living standards. Vicker further noted that experts forecast that "demand is likely to grow at a rate of 3 percent to 4 percent for cereals, 4 percent to 5 percent annually for fruits and vegetables and as much as 5 percent to 7 percent a year for meat, eggs, milk, sugar, fats and oils." All of these products are expected to be imported from OECD countries--for instance, beef from Australia, lamb from New Zealand, fish from Scandinavia, and wheat, rice, and potatoes from the United States.

Tropical Africa could become a source of some of the countries' food imports. There could, therefore, be economic complementarity in the fields of food and petrofunds between the Africans and the Arabs. So far, both parties have agreed in principle to supply their respective markets on a priority basis, as much as possible.

OECD MEMBER COUNTRIES AND
MULTILATERAL FINANCIAL INSTITUTIONS

The OECD consists of several European countries as well as the United States, Canada, Japan, Australia, and New Zealand. It is a loose organization of the industrialized countries of the capitalist world. For a long time they have had an almost complete monopoly of both

TABLE 1.2
ESTIMATES OF DISTRIBUTION OF OPEC INVESTMENTS, END OF 1978
(BILLION DOLLARS)

Financial investments in the international markets	60
Financial and direct investments in the U.S.	42
Financial and direct investments in other industrial countries	32
Loans and aid to Third World countries	18
Others (including Eastern bloc)	4
Financial contributions to international development institutions	12
TOTAL	168

Source: OAPEC Bulletin, January 1980, p. 17.

technological and purchasing power. Their banking institutions control and monitor the flow of capital around
the world, and they own the transnational corporations
that dominate and control investments and trade in the
free enterprise world. The oil companies that have been
involved in oil exploration and exploitation in the
Middle East and in selling oil to the rest of the world
are owned by shareholders from OECD countries. It is
needless to emphasize further the economic and political
power of the OECD countries and their worldwide influence. Suffice it to note that they constitute a
dominant voice in the international financial institu-
tions--the IMF and the World Bank.

Some OECD members have had links with Africa and the
Arab Middle East for more than two centuries. These
traditional ties have undergone different levels of
transformation. For our purposes, the most important
are (1) the acknowledgment by both African and Arab
countries that they need OECD technology and manpower
to make the most of the geological, technological, and
economic potential of their respective regions, and (2)
the realization by OECD countries of the immense investment opportunities available in African and Arab countries. The Development Assistance Committee (DAC), an
OECD agency, has been the main source of "development
aid" to the Third World and compares favorably with
the OPEC countries in the amount of aid given.

Contributions to cofinanced projects in sub-Saharan
Africa by multilateral financial institutions more than
doubled between 1974 and 1979. The World Bank has been
by far the most active party in multiparticipant

projects, contributing $4.2 billion and participating in more than half the projects. The European Economic Community (EEC) participates by channeling funds through the European Development Fund (EDF) and also through its Special Action account in the form of grants. Cofinancing arrangements among DAC members, Arab aid agencies, and international financial institutions have been increasing. Very few studies, however, have been done with particular reference to sub-Saharan Africa.

RATIONALE FOR TRIANGULAR COOPERATION

This volume attempts to show that the potential of African raw materials, the availability of Arab oil revenues, and the need for OECD technology and trained manpower could serve the economic interests of all parties. Several related factors provide the rationale for such cooperation in development based on comparative advantage.

First, the availability of financial capital from the Arab countries for African agricultural development will attract OECD technology. The application of "appropriate" technology will both stimulate local food production and increase production of cash crops.

Second, the Arabs now import vast amounts of food from the West, and therefore African food exports produced with Arab petrofunds (aid and investments) will diversify Arab sources of food imports.

Third, development of the African agricultural sector (with high yields) will depend on improvement of the infrastructures of African societies. Adequate attention must be given to building infrastructures and administrative capacities as prerequisites to modernization of the agricultural sector.

Fourth, African development in the mining sector will be accelerated because of the OECD demands for African minerals and because of the Arab enthusiasm for investing in the mineral sector.

Fifth, triangular cooperation will spur domestic economic development in Arab oil-producing countries as Arab financial investment in Africa increases markets for certain domestic industries, among them petrochemicals. This will also reduce African and Arab dependence on OECD petrochemical products.

Sixth, triangular cooperation will expand and create new African markets for OECD services and technology; it will secure continuing access for OECD members to African raw materials.

Seventh, African-Arab and OECD collaboration in joint development projects will provide employment opportunities for all parties.

Eighth, the flow of trade among all three areas will be greatly increased. It may also induce inter-African trade and inter-Arab trade, particularly if the

Organization of African Unity (OAU) and the Arab League can establish institutionalized relationships with the various regional economic organizations in Africa (e.g., ECA, ECOWAS).

Ninth, the OECD countries will have the opportunity to cultivate new ties and strengthen their traditional ones with Africa and the Arab Middle East. All three regions will increase their levels of interactions and consequently, through their interlinked economic interests, will gain leverage to apply on each other in international issues.

Tenth, the basic philosophy and objective of the Arab oil producers is to increase the flow of development assistance, but not to substitute it for traditional sources of finance. The Arabs prefer to elicit a long-term involvement by multinational companies from OECD countries in the operation of the African development projects financed by their money. On the other hand, the OECD countries feel that the Arabs should provide the bulk of finance for the African development projects, while OECD countries would provide project appraisal, token participation, and technological know-how and equipment. However, the Arab and African countries accept third-party involvement in their economic transactions (besides needing the technology and foreign expertise). Consequent diversification of African sources of financial and technological aid might keep neocolonial cleavages from developing and at the same time enhance interdependence.

Although the idea of triangular cooperation among Africa, the Arab Middle East, and the OECD countries is attractive, there are some precautionary measures that must be taken. The OECD-Arab participation in the triangular relationship must be carefully coordinated and scrutinized to keep Africa from becoming a dumping ground for OECD products and technology, in a process facilitated by Arab petrofunds. Care must therefore be taken to secure the technology needed for local African conditions and circumstances. African and Arab countries must try to acquire training in technology to reduce their external dependency. Hence, Africans and Arabs must avoid passivity while the OECD countries sell them inappropriate technology.

African countries must be able to choose development projects suited to their developmental needs. On the other hand, these must be economically viable projects that also address food needs. Triangular cooperation must loosen, not reinforce, the ties of dependency. It must not be used to promote economic and political structures that may be desirable to the donors but undesirable to the recipients. All three parties must, therefore, agree on contractual terms that will facilitate and regulate the cooperation.

It must be realized that Arab investment and aid are in all probability transitory phenomena. First, oil is not an everlasting resource, and therefore Arab aid is not permanent. Second, an increase in the absorptive capacity of the Arab donors will lead them to use more petrofunds internally, and the nature of the triangular relationships will undergo change.

It is now clear that in relations between the OECD and the Arab capital-surplus nations, the latter would like to be treated as equal partners in world economic management. Now that they are less dependent upon the OECD area for financial capital, they seek to exercise their new power, especially in financial institutions such as the IMF, the International Bank for Reconstruction and Development (IBRD), and the private investment sector. It is not yet clear what impact OECD-African relations on the one hand and OECD-OAPEC relations on the other will have on African-Arab-OECD triangular cooperation.

This book is divided into three parts. In Part 1, Professor Ali Mazrui analyzes seven triads (location, acculturation, pigmentation, stratification, confrontation, allegiance, and dissent) that have conditioned relations among Africa, Europe, and the Arab world. He explores interregional identities, tensions, and mechanisms of positive interdependence with clarity and verve. The impact of arms transfers from the OECD countries to Africa and the Arab Middle East on the development process in these two regions is comprehensively covered by Robin Luckham. He argues persuasively that whereas there is a discernible connection between the problems of development and the issues of international security, it is farfetched, if not illusory, to assume that the security pursued by the great powers is correlative to the security of African and Arab peoples.

In Part 2, Suleiman Kiggundu, Ernest Wilson, and Frank Ocwieja examine and discuss, respectively, Africa's natural resource base, oil bills, and patterns of trade between and among the three regions. Kiggundu provides a comprehensive survey of Africa's natural resources and discusses how and to what extent these have so far been utilized. He suggests what Africa can contribute to the tripartite economic partnership envisioned in this book.

Ernest Wilson traces and analyzes the adverse effects of the ever-rising oil bills on African development. He suggests that energy provides the connecting tissue in African-Arab-OECD relations in the post-1973 period and examines possible mechanisms for alleviating the agony of the non-oil-producing African countries. Frank Ocwieja's chapter on patterns of trade argues that whereas trade between Africa and the industrialized economies on the one hand and between the Arab world and the OECD countries on the other has greatly expanded in the last decade, the nature and pattern of trade between Africa and the Arab world are still narrow in scope.

According to Ocwieja, the impact of colonial history on
the interactions of the three groupings of economies
through trade remains pervasive. Present and future
trade patterns among the three regions are examined.
    In Part 3 of this volume, there are three chapters
on Arab petrofunds and a legal framework for triangular
cooperation. Kamal Hossain and Michael Lyall provide a
critical assessment of financial flows from the Arab oil-
producing and oil-exporting countries to sub-Saharan
Africa. The criteria for the terms of disbursement of
Arab petrofunds to Africa and present investment patterns
by OECD countries in Africa are examined. What are the
likely trends of such investments? What is the nature
and extent of private or other nonconcessional Arab
capital flows to Africa? How do Arab concessional aid
flows rank as a percentage of the overall resource flow
to Africa? The authors in this section explore these
questions in detail and suggest various ways of enhancing
a meaningful tripartite economic relationship. A. O.
Adede's chapter suggests a legal framework for establishing tripartite economic transactions among African, Arab,
and OECD countries. He cogently discusses the legal
framework for investment and for transnational lending.
He also examines bilateral agreements for economic and
technical cooperation between the African and the
industrialized countries, on the one hand, and similar
agreements between African states and the other members
of the Third World, on the other hand. These discussions provide the background for the type of legal
framework that should facilitate economic and financial
transactions between and among African, Arab, and
OECD regions.
    A tripartite partnership in development could pro-
vide an attractive framework for reducing asymmetries in
triangular economic relations. The new financial means
of the OAPEC countries, and their firm grasp on the
supply and price of energy resources, have given them
considerable leverage vis-à-vis the OECD countries.
Whether they will ultimately seek accommodation with the
existing international economic order or demand fundamental changes in its structure remains to be seen.
However, at present their immediate concern is to gain
experience in managing financial and commercial investments, to acquire the technological means for industrial
development, to lessen their dependence on OECD expertise, and consequently, to reduce the scope of their
vulnerability in the context of interdependence. Given
their present low absorptive capacity and the immediate
and growing availability of surplus funds, it is conceivable that their long-term development strategies
might best be served by investments in sub-Saharan Africa
in conjunction with Third World and OECD technology
suppliers and management experts.
    The critical determination to be made, however, is

whether a tripartite partnership is really viable with respect to African economic development. As the chapters indicate, there are complementarities between Africa's enormous resource base and the investment needs and industrialization strategies of the OAPEC countries. Yet a realization of Africa's productive potential, and the establishment of mutually beneficial trade links between the two regions, require massive financial inflows, comprehensive reforms of African domestic institutions, a reordering of development priorities, and a fundamental redefinition of external dependencies so that self-sufficient growth can begin to lead African societies out of absolute poverty toward a more reciprocal relationship with the developed world. At issue, therefore, is whether trilateral projects, appropriately designed for the African setting, can be identified and implemented through arrangements that ensure an equitable and effective distribution of risks, responsibilities, and benefits among the regional participants.

Such an undertaking would clearly depend on the availability of a wide range of incentives and mechanisms for cooperation as well as on the compatibility between the benefits sought by each region and the development needs of the African host societies. On the one hand, constraints peculiar to the African institutional and socioeconomic setting, as well as disharmony within the African and Arab regions, could undermine a comprehensive effort of sufficient magnitude to produce concrete results, particularly as the cost-benefit calculations of Arab financiers have stressed immediate benefits and failed to incorporate a commitment to the rehabilitation of Africa's socioeconomic structures. To the extent that the Arabs are seeking investments in countries that are potentially "high absorbers," the fragility of African national and regional institutions could discourage an expanded investment effort. Furthermore, the lack of skilled manpower in both Africa and the Arab world means that OECD participants would play a key role in organizing cooperative structures and processes. Arab financiers may be unwilling to embark upon a partnership in which innovative interregional strategies are to be designed and managed to a large extent by non-Arab parties.

On the other hand, Arab and OECD initiatives could lead to profitable investments in Africa without by the same token increasing self-sufficiency and prosperity in the African host countries. In other words, it would be possible for Arab financing and demand to catalyze a partnership in exploitation by reinforcing Africa's dependencies and deformed production priorities as a result of increased penetration of domestic markets by OECD multinational companies. This unfavorable result could occur even without conscious volition on the part of Arab and OECD participants; careless design of projects and inept coordination by African national and

regional institutions could jeopardize the desired
development impact of trilateral projects.

But given the new international position of the
OAPEC countries and the increased vulnerability of the
OECD members to manipulations of energy supplies and
prices, it is likely that the latter group would accede
to certain basic demands of the oil producers, demands
that of necessity relate to North-South issues such as
technology transfer and the "unraveling" of the OECD aid
and investment packages. Both Arabs and Africans wish
to increase the flow of information, supplies, and expertise to their regions and to exercise control over the
use of their resources. But to what extent would
arrangements inspired by Arab-OECD interdependence
facilitate African economic development?

It is argued that the Arab capital-surplus states
need the partnership of countries where investment opportunities abound in order to achieve their own bargaining
objectives vis-à-vis the industrialized world. Yet as
their own absorptive capacity increases, they might
completely cease to identify with the dependency experi-
ences of the Third World, and this could be reflected in
the operations and policies of new "trilateral" development organizations. On the other hand, it is possible
that the comparative advantage of the OAPEC countries in
energy-intensive industries is so strong that they will
always constitute a major source of finance for developing African and Arab complementarities. In any case,
given the different needs and unequal power of these two
regions, the only desirable outcome of a cooperative
development strategy would be a situation in which
Africans and Arabs both will have gained leverage in the
international economy, each group according to its own
peculiar needs.

One must also consider the extent to which African
and Arab world views can be reconciled through economic
interaction. The Arab states are most immediately concerned with penetrating the international economy on the
basis of their energy resources and buying power, whereas
the African countries and the rest of the non-oil-
producing and -exporting countries (NOPEC) are feebly
attempting to restructure the existing economic order
in the context of the "North-South Dialogue." The OAPEC
countries have enjoyed the admiration and support of the
Third World, and yet they have failed to respond to the
urgency of North-South issues in their oil-pricing
policies and in their foreign investments. They are becoming increasingly identified with the North, having
cooperated with OECD strategies for recycling petrofund
surpluses. Massive arms purchases and formidable investments in OECD markets characterize the new relationships
brought about by the oil boom. When one examines the
record of Arab-African relations in the 1970s, a record
that is to a large extent consistent with the aims of Pan-

Arabism as well as compatible with the security concerns
of the OECD countries, it becomes apparent that the
African countries must carefully weigh the risks of increased transactions with Arab and OECD parties. A
tripartite partnership can be based neither on illusory
notions of African-Arab solidarity or ideological
affinities nor on a claim of altruism on the part of OECD
participants. It must rather be governed by the principle of the mutuality of interests of all parties and be
based "less on power and status, more on justice and
contract; less discretionary, more governed by fair and
open rules."[5] If we fall short of those goals, the
cooperation will be skewed, and unequal exchanges will
continue unabated.

NOTES

    1. Ray Vicker, in the Wall Street Journal, June 26, 1978.
    2. For instance, the following Arab countries provided a very
high percentage of their gross national product for aid to non-oil-
producing developing countries: Qatar, 11.98 percent; United Arab
Emirates, 10.9 percent; Kuwait, 5.03 percent; Saudi Arabia, 5.02
percent.
    3. OAPEC Bulletin, January 1980.
    4. Wall Street Journal, June 26, 1978.
    5. North-South: A Program for Survival (The Report of the
Independent Commission on International Development Issues under
the Chairmanship of Willy Brandt) (Cambridge, Mass.: M.I.T. Press,
1980), p. 35.

Part 1

Geopolitics and Arms Transfers

2
Eurafrica, Eurabia, and African-Arab Relations: The Tensions of Tripolarity

Ali A. Mazrui

The tripolar world of Europe, Africa, and Arab countries has a number of asymmetries. Economically Europe and the Arab countries do constitute a regional subsystem. The flow of commodities, capital, technology, and to some extent labor is sufficiently regular to constitute a systemic pattern. The concept of Eurabia--linking Europe with the lands of the Arabs--is therefore systemically coherent.

What about the relations between Africa and Europe? Here, too, there is pattern and regularity. The whole colonial experience had forged African economies in Europe's image. Trade, investment, and aid have together created structures of uneven interdependence between Africa and Europe. Those two regions together do constitute an international subsystem. The concept of Eurafrica --signifying a special relationship between those two continents--is therefore also systemically coherent.

What about relations between Africa and the Arab world? Is there sufficient pattern or regularity in economic relations to convert the two regions into an international subsystem? The answer in this case is less clear-cut. The two regions of Africa and the Arab world are overlapping categories. North Africa is of course overwhelmingly Arab in population, although it is also an integral part of African realities. Politically Africa and the Arab world have been strengthening their links. There are also overlapping institutions and organizations, including the OAU. But in the economic sphere, interactions between the two regions are still either modest or irregular. The concept of Afrabia is therefore inchoate and premature at the present moment.

The triangle connecting Europe, Africa, and the Arab world has two thick and sure lines, connecting Europe with Africa on one side and Europe with the Arab world on the other. But the third line between Africa and the Arab world is, at least in the economic domain, still thin and uncertain. The question for the future concerns, among other things, how best to complete and even out this particular eternal triangle.

Curiously enough, the process by which this triangular exercise is to be accomplished does itself involve other triangles or triads. These are sometimes cultural in nature, sometimes economic, sometimes political and diplomatic. The tripolar world of the Arabs, the Africans, and the Europeans lies in the shadows of a history that is almost an echo of the Christian doctrine of three in one and one in three.

In this chapter I will address myself especially to seven triads that have conditioned relations between Africa, Europe, and the Arab world.

THE TRIAD OF LOCATION

In a novel I wrote more than ten years ago, set in the Hereafter, I referred to "the Curse of the Trinity." A Nigerian poet had been put on trial in the Hereafter for deciding he was an Ibo first and an artist second, thus betraying poetry and dying for Biafra. The trial was conducted before nine Elders of After-Africa, where all dead Africans go. On the day of judgment men and women, drawn from all the centuries of Africa's human existence, sat there in the Grand Stadium, attentively awaiting the considered wisdom of the Elders after hearing all the evidence. The Elder on the fifth throne first explained what it was that had influenced the Council of Grand Trials to decide on making a special case of the poet Christopher Okigbo and the Nigerian civil war. "It occurred to us that this whole tragedy was once again the Curse of the Trinity unfolding itself in the drama of Africa's existence. Let us remind ourselves, Oh fellow citizens of After-Africa, of the meaning of the Curse of the Trinity in relation to this old continent of ours."[1] The Elder on the fifth throne continued to explain that the Christian story of three in one and one in three had in part been a prophecy about Africa, and in part a postmortem on Africa. At the structural level there was the Trinity as the basis of Africa's geography--the Tropic of Capricorn, the Equator, the Tropic of Cancer. Of all the continents of the world only Africa was central enough to be traversed by all the three basic latitudes. The Equator almost cut the African continent into two halves--such was the centrality of Africa to the global scheme of things.

Since then I have further developed this triad of location. Of the three ancient continents of Asia, Africa, and Europe, Africa has often played the role of a link, and sometimes a mediator, between the Occident and the Orient. In history it has never been quite clear whether Africa was indeed part of the Orient or whether it should be included in the universe of the Occidentals.

So ambivalent has the status of this continent been that its northern portion, North Africa, has changed identity a number of times across the centuries. At one time North Africa was an extension of Europe. This goes back to the days of Carthage, Hellenic colonization and, later, the Roman Empire. The concept of Europe was at best in the making at that time. In the words of historians R. R. Palmer and Joel Colton: "There was really no Europe in ancient times. In the Roman Empire we may see a Mediterranean world, or even a West and an East in the Latin-and-Greek-speaking portions. But the West included parts of Africa as well as of Europe. . . ."[2]

Even as late as the seventeenth century the idea that the landmass south of the Mediterranean was something distinct from the landmass north of it was still a proposition that was difficult to comprehend. The great American Africanist, Melville Herskovits, once reminded us that the Geographer Royal of France, writing in 1656, described Africa as "a peninsula so large that it comprises the third part, and this the most southerly, of our continent."[3]

This old proposition that North Africa was the southern part of Europe had its last desperate fling in the modern world in France's attempt to keep Algeria as part of France. The myth that Algeria was the southern portion of France tore the French nation apart in the 1950s, created the crisis that brought Charles de Gaulle into power in 1958, and maintained tensions between the right and the left in France until Algeria's independence in 1962. This bid to maintain Algeria as the southern portion of a major European nation had taken place at a time when in other respects North Africa had become substantially an extension of Asia. From the seventh century onward the gradual Islamization and Arabization of North Africa helped to prepare the ground for redirecting North Africa's links more firmly toward West Asia, without necessarily ending residual interaction with South Europe. The Arabs themselves had become a bi-continental people, traversing both Africa and Asia. By the twentieth century the majority of the Arab people were in fact within the African continent, although the majority of Arab states by the last quarter of the twentieth century were in West Asia.

If in some respects and at certain periods in history North Africa has virtually been the southern extension of Europe, and if since the Muslim conquest it has been the western extension of Asia, it has all along also remained the northern portion of Africa. The greatest theater of interaction between Europe, Africa, and the Arab world has been the Mediterranean coastline of the African continent.

For reasons of both geographic contiguities and

historical continuities one would have expected the
structural relations between the Africanness of North
Africa and its Arabness to be closer than between its
Arabness and its European orientation. But so great has
been the impact of European imperialism on North Africa
that the European orientation is deeper than the African.

THE TRIAD OF ACCULTURATION

The second basic triad concerns three civilizations--
Western civilization, Islamic civilization, and the
interrelated cultures and civilizations of Africa south
of the Sahara.
Religion is one aspect of these civilizations. Here
again there are dissimilarities in the three regions that
we are examining. Europe is in a sense religiously
homogeneous. Where people are still religious in Europe,
they are far and away most likely to be Christian, although the denomination may vary. Similarly, the Arab
world is basically homogeneous in the religious sense.
The overwhelming majority of Arabs are Muslim. Even in
Lebanon the demographic balance has now shifted in favor
of Muslims.
But unlike both Europe and the Arab world, Africa
is religiously heterogeneous. The continent has not only
its own indigenous traditional religions; it has also
accommodated different versions of both Christianity and
Islam. Kwame Nkrumah reminded us about these three parts
of the soul of Africa:

> African society has one segment which comprises
> our traditional way of life; it has a second
> segment which is filled by the presence of the
> Islamic tradition in Africa; it has a final
> segment which represents the infiltration of
> the Christian tradition and culture of
> Western Europe into Africa, using colonialism
> and neocolonialism as its primary vehicles.
> These different segments are animated by
> competing ideologies. [4]

The original intrusion of Islam was mainly through
North Africa, although there is some evidence of Muslims
arriving in the Horn of Africa almost from the beginning
of the Muslim era. Two processes of acculturation got
under way fairly early--Islamization and Arabization. I
use the term Islamization here to denote conversion to
Islam as a religion. I use the term Arabization to
imply the process of becoming an Arab through linguistic
socialization. The majority of Egyptians today are not
former migrants from the Arabian peninsula; they are de-
scendants of people who were in Egypt from the days of
the Pharaohs. The Muslim conquest of Egypt in the
seventh century did not result in either the expulsion

or the liquidation of the population of ancient Egypt. What the Muslim conquerors did over time was gradually to transmit not only their religion but also their language and identity to the conquered people. In time, Islamized Egyptians came to think of themselves as Arabs.

Curiously enough, where only the language was transmitted, but not the religion, the recipients did not become fully Arab. This is the case of the Copts in Egypt. Over the centuries they became Arabic speakers but not Muslims. They therefore fell short of becoming fully Arab. What this demonstrated is that Arabization as a process could not be fully consummated without Islamization.

The twin processes also occurred in Libya, Northern Sudan, and the Maghreb. The majority of the inhabitants in these parts of Africa gradually witnessed a change in self-identity--and saw themselves as Arabs.

In West Africa, on the other hand, the process was mainly that of Islamization--the conversion to the religion of Islam without necessarily indigenizing the Arabic language. Although North Africa could not become fully Arab without adopting Islam, West Africa could become Muslim without Arabizing its identity.

Somalia, in a cultural sense, falls somewhere between North Africa and West Africa. The Somalis are as Muslim as, say, the emir of Kano in Northern Nigeria and Anwar Sadat in Egypt. But the Somalis are less Arabized than Anwar Sadat was and more Arabized than the emir.

But although the Arabic language has not been indigenized in places like Northern Nigeria and Tanzania, the language has had a profound effect on some indigenous languages in both West and East Africa. Indeed, the most important indigenous languages in the African continent are probably Kiswahili in East Africa and Hausa in West Africa--both languages that have been deeply influenced by both Arabic and Islam. In the case of Kiswahili, even the name of the language is derived from the Arabic word "coast." And up to one-fifth of the basic vocabulary of Kiswahili is also derived from Arabic. Of course the structure of the language is still Bantu--but Arabic is to Kiswahili what Latin is to the English language, a source of great enrichment in vocabulary.

But how was Kiswahili to be written? At first, along the coast of East Africa, written Kiswahili used the Arabic alphabet. Some of the earliest documents available in Kiswahili are indeed in Arabic script. But then European imperialism came to East Africa, and new approaches to literacy were in time adopted. Kiswahili came to be written in the Roman alphabet. In fact, given the nature of the sounds of Kiswahili, this author believes that the Roman alphabet is more efficient for Kiswahili than the Arabic script. But it is illustrative of the triad of cultures in East Africa that this major Bantu language should have had to choose between the

alphabet of the Arabs and the alphabet of Western Europe
to express its African self in writing.

The triad of cultures now also increasingly emerges
from further changes in the language. More and more
words of European languages, especially English, are
entering Kiswahili as loan words. These coexist and
sometimes compete with words of Arabic derivation on one
side and words drawn from indigenous languages on the
other.

In some African countries even the political culture
sometimes reflects that historic interplay between and
among the three civilizations we are examining. The
British policy of indirect rule and its aftermath are
particularly interesting from this point of view.
Britain's colonial policy of indirect rule was born out
of a marriage between Islam and the Anglo-Irish philoso-
pher, Edmund Burke. In a sense the legacy of Edmund
Burke is what British political culture is all about.
As a rule of political prudence Burke advised: "Neither
entirely nor at once depart from antiquity. If a society
does aspire to change direction, it would be a mistake
to do it either totally or in one sudden move." Political prudence, according to Burke, requires political
sensitivity to history. As he put it again: "People
will not look forward to posterity who never look backward to their ancestors."[5]

British political culture is a reflection in part of
this broad political philosophy. The British are
reluctant to turn their back on antiquity either entirely
or at once. So they maintain ancient institutions and
modernize them as they go along, and they are slower to
modify traditional habits than many of their peers.

This same Burkean gradualism in British domestic
political culture came to influence British colonial
policy. Indirect rule was based on a Burkean principle
of gradualism. Many colonial policymakers felt con-
vinced that you could not persuade Africans to look forward to posterity unless you respected their tendency to
look backward to their ancestors.

But British indirect rule assumed the presence of
defined institutions in African societies, rooted in the
history of those societies. And yet many African
societies were relatively decentralized, without the
statelike institutions of authority that the British
would have preferred to use for purposes of governing.
Where was indirect rule to find its paradigmatic formulation? Lord Lugard, the architect of Britain's policy of
indirect rule, found those institutions in the emirates
of Northern Nigeria. The legacy of Islam in Northern
Nigeria, implanted several centuries before the British
took over, provided a fertile ground for the implementation of the legacy of Edmund Burke in a colonial setting.
Lugard found a "well-organized fiscal system, a definite
code of land tenure, a regular scheme of local rule

through district Heads, and a trained judiciary administering the tenets of the Muhammedan law."[6]
   The British used the institutions they found for
their own purposes. The native institutions of Northern
Nigeria, if used properly by the new conquerors from
Europe, could ensure that the people there were "neither
entirely pushed nor at once pressured into turning their
backs on their own antiquity."[7] A colonial doctrine was
born within the wedlock of Burkean philosophy and
Nigerian Islam.
   The consequences of British colonial policies in
places like Nigeria are of course still unfolding. Some
are good and some evil. Some have been disruptive and
some moderating and civilizing. What is clear in Nigeria
is precisely the dramatic interplay of three civiliza-
tions--the culture and technology of Europe, the culture
and religion of the Arabs, the culture and personality
of Africa.
   What should be remembered is the basic asymmetry
in the relations among these three civilizations. The
Europeans and the Arabs have both lent to each other and
borrowed from each other. Europe today uses the Arabic
numerals, and uses words like algebra, amalgam, and
chemistry borrowed from Arabic and Islamic science. On
the other hand, the world of the Arabs in the last two
centuries has been considerably conditioned and influenced by the science and technology of the Western
world. Intellectually and scientifically it is possible
to argue that the cultural interchange between Europe
and the Arab world has been basically reciprocal.
   What about the cultural relationship between Europe
and Africa or between Africa and the Arab world? In
these two areas there is considerable unevenness. Although the religion of the Arabs is in the process of
converting nearly a third of the population of black
Africa, the religions of black Africa have had little
influence on the Arabs. Similarly, while the Arabic
language has profoundly conditioned such African media
as Kiswahili and Hausa, the languages of Africa have made
little reciprocal impact on mainstream Arabic.
   A similar unevenness is evident in Africa's relationship with Europe. European Christianity has made
impressively rapid progress in black Africa in a single
century. Indeed, Christianity now is virtually an Afro-
Western religion--since all Christian nations are either
in the Western world or in Africa. Asia has millions of
Christians, but almost everywhere Christianity in Asia
is a minority religion, with the exception of the
Philippines. But in Africa, within a few decades, whole
societies have come to regard themselves as Christian.
In contrast, African traditional religions are not only
despised in the Western world; they are often also
despised by the newly Christianized Africans.
   Linguistically, Europe's impact on Africa has also

been colossal, considering the brevity of European
colonial rule. Almost everywhere in Africa south of the
Sahara the natives who have acquired competence in
European languages exercise disproportionate political
influence and enjoy disproportionate prestige. The
official language in most black African countries is a
European language. Where parliaments still exist, the
language of discourse is a European language. Indeed,
the continent itself identifies the different countries
partly in terms of whether they are English-speaking,
French-speaking, and now Portuguese-speaking. In contrast, Africa has exercised little linguistic influence
on Europe. Once again the relationship is decidedly
asymmetrical.

The two main policy issues that emerge from the
triad of acculturation are, first, the problem of synthesizing the three civilizations within Africa and,
second, the problem of reciprocating the penetration of
Africa by the other two civilizations.

Nkrumah put the first problem of internal African
synthesis at its most ambitious. As he formulated it:

> With true independence regained . . . a new
> harmony needs to be forged, a harmony that
> will allow the combined presence of traditional
> Africa, Islamic Africa, and Euro-Christian
> Africa, so that this presence is in tune with
> the original humanist principles underlying
> African society. Our society is not the old
> society, but a new society enlarged by Islamic
> and Euro-Christian influences. A new emergent
> ideology is therefore required, an ideology
> which can solidify in a philosophical state-
> ment, but at the same time an ideology which
> will not abandon the original humanist prin-
> ciples of Africa.[8]

The idea of synthesizing the Western heritage, the
Islamic civilization, and African cultures appears not
only ambitious but perhaps unnecessary. What is
necessary is a broad modus vivendi as a basis of co-
existence and interaction among the three cultures--the
foundations of a more balanced tripartite heritage.
In Nkrumah's words again:

> Practice without thought is blind: thought
> without practice is empty. The three segments
> of African society . . . co-exist uneasily; the
> principles animating them are often in conflict
> with one another. . . . What is to be done
> then? I have stressed that the two other seg-
> ments, in order to be rightly seen, must be
> accommodated only as experiences of the
> traditional African society. If we fail to

do this our society will be racked by the most
malignant schizophrenia.[9]

As for the task of redressing the balance of influence between Europe and Africa and also between the
Arab world and Africa, this to some extent hinges on a
process that I have christened counterpenetration.
Africa has for too long been penetrated by others without attempting counterpenetration in return. Over the
centuries the continent has been invaded from outside by
foreign travelers, traders, slave-dealers, explorers,
missionaries, colonizers, and teachers. Africans have
often been passive receivers rather than active inter-
ventionists. The question that arises is how the process
of acculturation can be reciprocated. As Africa gets
increasingly Westernized, is there a chance that one day
the West might be to some extent Africanized?

Apart from the influence of such artists as Picasso,
the most important transmission belt of African culture
into the Western world has been the black population of
the United States. The black American impact on the
musical culture of the United States especially has had
worldwide reverberations. Black America in this sense is
a crucial instrument of Africa's cultural counterpenetration into the Western world. Young people from Vancouver
to Rio de Janeiro, from New York to Tokyo, from London to
Belgrade, have often danced to jazz tunes that bear the
unmistakable stamp of the black experience in the Western
diaspora.

But what about former black slaves in the Arab
world? Why did not people of African ancestry imported
into places like Saudi Arabia become in turn transmission
belts of African culture deep into the heritage of Islam?

One reason might well be Islam's profound distrust
of certain art forms, including the performing arts.
Although Western civilization and African cultures gave
instrumental music a role to play even in prayer and
worship, Islam as a religion tended to keep instrumental
music at bay, while putting some value on the human voice
for recitation of the Qur'an and hymns.

The first great muezzin of Islam was a man of
African ancestry--Bilal. He seems to have had a powerful voice. In my imagination I tend to see Bilal as
the Paul Robeson of Mecca and Medina. Here was this
black Muslim, equipped with a vibrant voice and a considerable personal presence. The voice was used not to
sing "Ol' Man River" but to summon believers to prayer
in the very first years of Islam.

The constraints that Islam imposed on artistic
culture not only narrowed the areas of creativity of the
Arabs themselves, in areas where Islamic orthodoxy pre-
vailed, but also significantly reduced the potentialities
of Africa's counterpenetration into Islamic culture.
What Africa had to offer to the Muslim world often lay in

precisely those areas where the Muslim world was austere
and puritanical. Africa's genius for rhythm and dance,
the obsession with the drum, did not entirely miss the
Arab world. Some elements of counterpenetration did take
place in spite of the haughty puritanism of Islamic
orthodoxy. Nevertheless, the contribution was not as
striking as Africa's impact on America's musical culture
on the opposite side of the globe.

The search has to continue for greater balance,
greater mutuality of influence, between African civilization on one side and the civilizations of Europe and the
Arab world on the other.

THE TRIAD OF PIGMENTATION

The third salient triad in relations between Europe,
Africa, and the Arab world concerns issues of race and
color. Technically the Arabs are part of the Semitic
races, the Europeans part of the Caucasian, and the
black Africans are deemed to be Negroid. Three "racial
stocks" seem to be involved in the triangle of Africa,
Europe, and the Arab world.

Historically, there was once again an important
asymmetry in relations among these three peoples. Both
the Europeans and the Arabs once raided black Africa for
slaves and exported them to different regions under their
control. But there was no instance of black Africans
counterraiding either Europe or the Arab world for
retaliatory enslavement. Europeans and Arabs were
slavers and slave traders. Black Africans were primarily
slaves, although parts of the African continent did
perpetuate domestic slavery of an indigenous kind.

Between the European slave trade and the Arab slave
trade there were some basic differences. The European
slave trade in the modern period was much more race-
specific, and even Afrocentric, than the Arab slave trade
was. In other words, in the modern period, Europe had
decided that the people most deserving of enslavement were
those who were furthest away from Europeans in pigmentation or color of skin. Theoretically Europe could have
invaded India for slaves, or the Middle East, or China,
or indeed the Amerindian civilizations of the Americas.
But for a variety of reasons, from the sixteenth century
onward Europeans decided that the most deserving of
enslavement of all people were in fact the black people.

In contrast, the Arab slave trade right into the
twentieth century has continued to be racially ambivalent.
According to the Arab system, white slaves were not a
contradiction in terms. The traffic in slaves looked to
the Near East, to Europe, to Asia, to the Arab world itself, as well as to Africa, for slaves. In the last
three hundred years the bulk of the male slaves who went
into the Arab world were perhaps from Africa, although
figures are very difficult to compute. However, it is

possible that the majority of female slaves during the
same period came from outside black Africa.

Aristotle had once suggested that some people were
born to be slaves, while others were destined to be
masters. Modern Europeans until the nineteenth century
interpreted this to mean that some races were born to be
slaves and others to be civilizing conquerors. However,
the Arabs were seemingly accepting of Aristotle's position that some people might indeed have been destined to
be slaves, but the Arabs rejected the proposition that the
dividing line between slave and master was in terms of
skin color and racial origin. Arab slave trade was pig-
mentationally diverse, a multicolored phenomenon.
European slave trade in the modern period was overwhelmingly targeted at the black peoples.

With regard to the interplay between slavery and
sexuality the two "master" races also had divergent
inclinations. One interesting contrast from this point
of view is between the eunuch culture in Middle Eastern
slavery on one side, and the stud culture in Western
slavery on the other. Middle Eastern cultures were in-
clined to overprotect their free women. If male slaves
were to guard these women, how could temptation be controlled? One brutal answer was to make the male slaves
incapable of "abusing" the women sexually. These specific
males were therefore sexually mutilated as part of the
process of preserving the chastity and dignity of the
harem. What should be noted is that the custom of
eunuchs is a product of Middle Eastern folk culture and
is not sanctioned by Islam as a system of laws.

While Middle Easterners were making their male slaves
incapable of sexually abusing their free women, Westerners
were converting some of their male slaves into special
studs to help produce good specimens. In North America
especially, good strong male slaves were specially
commanded to mate with diverse female slaves with a view
to producing more highly marketable stock. The be-
ginnings of eugenics in the Western world, in the field
of human breeding, lie in the special utilization of
strong "Negro" specimens as breeding studs. Among the
factors that in the twentieth century have led to black
excellence in sports and athletics in the United States
might conceivably be counted the special breeding system
that U.S. slavery sometimes encouraged. Indeed, by the
early nineteenth century, some plantations in the South
had become primarily "nigger farms"--in which the main
concern had shifted from producing cotton to producing
physically more attractive slaves.

What all this means is that Middle Eastern slavery
included in its culture the brutalities of eunuchry.
The masculinity of the male slaves was so distrusted
that, when the slave was put in charge of a free harem,
that masculinity had first to be destroyed. On the other
hand, Western slave trade included in its culture the

crudities of eugenics--the masculinity of the male slaves was sometimes so admired that a market value was put on it, and the potency of the man used for purposes of procreating more marketable progeny. Morally, it is difficult to be sure which was a greater insult to the male slave--destroying his capacity to produce children or forcing him to produce children for sale. On balance, the male slave in the Arab world was as badly off as the male slave in the West.

What about the state of the female slaves? On this issue Arab slavery was on the whole morally superior at least to the slavery of the Anglo-Saxons. Under Islamic law a slave woman who is sexually used by her master moves upward halfway toward freedom, and any children she might have with the master become absolutely free. In contrast, children produced as a result of mating between the master and his women slaves in the United States were themselves slaves. Alex Haley's character Chicken George, in Roots, was the child of a white master who raped one of his slave girls. Therefore Chicken George became a slave. His own father later sold him to a British slaver who took Chicken George beyond the seas. Under Islamic law, such a situation would have been indefensible. Chicken George, whose father was a free man and owner of his mother, would himself have been legally free.

This is linked to wider systems of lineage in the three civilizations of Africa, the Muslim world, and Europe. They encompass the rules of "miscegenation"-- mating and procreating across racial lines. I distinguish among four systems of "miscegenation" in respect of lineage and descent of the children.

In a system of descending miscegenation, the offspring of a racially mixed parenthood is relegated to the status of the less-privileged parent. Thus, in the United States a child who has one parent black and the other white is categorized as black, regardless of whether it was the father or the mother who was black. The child descends to the status of the less privileged parent.

In contrast, Semitic civilizations observe a system of qualified ascending miscegenation. A child of racially mixed parenthood can move upward to the status of the more privileged parent, depending upon whether the parent who is more privileged is the mother or the father. Thus, in Israel, if the mother is Jewish the child is Jewish. The child ascends to the status of the mother in a society where Jews have a privileged position. In the Arab world, on the other hand, it is the father who decides the lineage. If the father is Arab the child is Arab--virtually regardless of the race or nationality of the mother. The child thus ascends to the status of the father.

That is one reason why the Arab world has such a multicolored composition. It includes white Arabs from

Syria and Lebanon, brown Arabs of the Hadhramout and the Yemens, and the black Arabs of the Sudan. Indeed, the Sudan itself is an interesting laboratory of this principle of ascending miscegenation. In purely racial terms the so-called Arabized North is, on balance, more Negroid than Semitic. The balance of the races in the North is in favor of the blacks, but because of the lineage system, and of cultural and linguistic assimilation, the cultural balance in the North is in favor of Arabism. The remaining one-third of the Sudan is indisputably Negroid. What remains to be seen is whether this portion of the Sudan also will in time become Arabized as a result of both racial intermingling and general acculturation. In the latter process the principle of ascending miscegenation so characteristic of the Arabs would constitute a major aspect of the racial transition.

The third system of racial mixture important in Africa is <u>divergent miscegenation</u>. Under this lineage, a product of racially mixed parenthood constitutes a separate group. Thus a child with one parent black and the other white becomes classified as a third category. A particularly important illustration in Africa is the Cape Coloureds of the Republic of South Africa. This is a community consisting of people of mixed racial origin. For the time being they are deemed to be neither white nor African. In the United States they would be classified as black, but officially in South Africa they are not now so classified.

On the contrary, their fate could go in either direction as the situation in the republic polarizes. The great majority of the Coloured population in South Africa are culturally Afrikaners. In other words, the white part of their ancestry is predominantly from the whites known as Afrikaners. The native language of the great majority of the Coloureds is Afrikaans--the language of the Afrikaners. Some reformers in South Africa have suggested that the Coloureds should be reclassified and considered as Afrikaners. If this was accepted, the Coloureds would in fact be beneficiaries of ascending miscegenation, becoming part of the privileged class. In the struggle of the whites against Africans this would increase the number of those who are classified as, in some sense, white. And in the electoral struggle between Afrikaans-speaking and English-speaking whites the ascent of the Cape Coloureds to Afrikanerdom would double the number of Afrikaans-speaking whites in their rivalry with the Anglophones.

On the other hand, many Coloureds in South Africa have recently been in rebellion against white privilege and power. Some of them have even begun to identify themselves with the Africans. Indeed, a few analysts of the South African situation have started a redefinition of the vocabulary of racial analysis in South Africa. For such analysis the term <u>blacks</u> in South Africa should now mean not merely Africans but also Coloureds or people of mixed origin. This analysis would transform the lineage system of South Africa into something similar to the situation in the United States. There are even some analysts who would recommend the inclusion of people of Indian origin under the rubric of black.

The term African would refer to that section of the black population that is totally indigenous and racially unmixed.

It remains to be seen whether such a new vocabulary of the racial politics of South Africa will gain credence and replace the present one that differentiates between blacks, whites, Coloureds, and Indians. If the racial polarization of South Africa really gets under way, the people of mixed parenthood may indeed be forced to choose among ascending miscegenation, descending miscegenation, and divergent miscegenation.

Elsewhere in the African continent the interplay between ascent and descent has sometimes coincided with the period after independence and the period before. The first military coup in black Africa took place in Togo in 1963. The founder-president, Sylvanus Olympio, was assassinated in January 1963, and a man of racially mixed ancestry took over as head of state of Togo. Before independence, when Africans were the less privileged race, the categorization of this particular individual as an African was a case of descending miscegenation. But in 1963, when he assumed supreme authority as head of an independent African state, the racial ancestry had in this case become an instance of ascending miscegenation. Part of his parenthood was African. Therefore he was African himself. Therefore he had a right to assume supreme command in an African state.

In 1979, a similar situation seemed discernible for a while in Ghana. A soldier of mixed racial parenthood (Scottish to some extent) staged a coup against a military government. He then proceeded to execute three former presidents of Ghana, all of them much more purely African than he was. He succeeded in doing this in a manner that won him acclaim from millions of "pure Africans." Thus a product of mixed parenthood in independent Ghana as late as 1979 could be deemed to be so acceptable as an African that he could even execute former African presidents of the same country with impunity. Before independence this would have been a case of descending miscegenation. In the independent West African state of 1979 it was a striking case of ascending miscegenation.

Although in reality the basic systems of lineage and miscegenation do themselves constitute a triad (descending, ascending, and divergent) there is a residual fourth category, which we might call ambivalent miscegenation. Under this category a child of mixed parenthood could move up or down, following either the more privileged or

the less, depending upon a number of indicators. Sometimes the indicator could be class-related; if the "half-
caste" was economically poor, he just mingled with the
blacks and became black. On the other hand, if he became
economically prosperous he could mingle with the whites
and become white.

A second indicator is the shade of skin color itself. If the "half-caste" was quite fair in appearance
he could enter the white circuit, although everybody in
that circuit knew that his parenthood was mixed. On the
other hand, if that child was pretty dark, he might drift
into the universe of the black population.

A third indicator after economics and skin shade is
education and culture. Two brothers with identical
parents could be racially designated differently. The
highly educated surgeon, even if his color was dark,
could to all intents and purposes live as a white man.
On the other hand, his brother--working as a trade
unionist at the docks, or relegated to the ghettos--might
live as a black man although he was a shade fairer than
his sibling.

Within Africa itself ambivalent miscegenation is
more discernible in Portuguese-speaking Africa than any-
where else, although at least as strong in some societies
is the divergent phenomenon of mulattoes in Latin Africa.

THE TRIAD OF STRATIFICATION

Issues of race and racism in our tripolar world
would have included questions of rank and the pecking
order. In the modern period, partly because of their
technological power, the Europeans have successfully
managed to lay claim to the highest positions in international ranking. Africans on the whole have usually
been condemned to the bottom position--while the Arabs
have sometimes been almost white in the privileges they
have enjoyed and sometimes been almost black in the
exploitation and humiliation to which they have been
subjected.

But stratification is not simply a question of race;
it is more often a question of class and status. In
postcolonial Africa the three most important classes have
been the peasantry, the new bourgeoisie, and the emerging proletariat. Numerically the peasants are the most
important--they constitute the majority of the population
in most African countries. But in terms of power the new
bourgeoisie, almost by definition, has managed to amass
a disproportionate share.

But what is this new bourgeoisie in Africa and to
what extent is it a product of the impact of Europeans
and Arabs upon the continent? It is not often realized
that class formation in Africa is not simply a matter of
economics; it is also an outgrowth of culture. Class
formation is not simply a question of "who owns what?"

but also a question of "who knows what?" Among the areas
of knowledge that have been particularly important in
African stratification is knowledge of European languages.
In one African country after another the imported imperial language is the official language of the nation--
used by a small elite at the top to conduct the central
political and diplomatic business of the society. In
most African countries, people cannot become members of
parliament unless they have a command of the relevant
European language in the country. For the acquisition of
ultimate political power in an average black African
country, the only alternative to competence in European
verbal skills is relative command over imported Western
military hardware. The latter basis of power is what
all military coups in Africa are all about. To penetrate the citadels of political power in an African
country one must have a good command of either the barrel
of the gun or the flow of words.

Europe's impact on the Arab world in the cultural
sphere is less consistent than Europe's impact on Africa.
Although countries like Algeria are still struggling to
find the right balance between the role of Arabic, the
role of French, and the role of the Berber language, the
Arab world as a whole has managed to escape black
Africa's fate of conducting the most important national
business in a European language. The Arabs have
succeeded in retaining Arabic as the primary instrument
of national politics and administration. The fact that
the Arab world is, by definition, much more linguistically
homogeneous than black Africa can claim to be is certainly
an important part of the explanation.

What about the impact of Arab culture on the stratification systems of black Africa? In those African countries that are primarily Muslim there is indeed a tendency toward a stratified triad of cultures. More often
than not, those who are Westernized still have disproportionate influence and power. Second in importance
from this point of view are those who are substantially
Islamized. At the bottom of the pyramid of power and
influence are the purer indigenes--the local "natives"
who have not been assimilated into an alien culture.

What should be borne in mind is that Islamization
and Westernization often compete for the top positions
of influence in such black African countries as Senegal,
Mali, and even Nigeria. On balance those who were
Westernized tend to have the best chances in the system,
but by no means invariably. Those who are within the
Islamic power structure in Northern Nigeria or Senegal
are sometimes as powerful as anybody else within the
system.

Throughout Africa there are occasions when the
three cultures (indigenous, Islamic, and Western) are
associated with specific occupations. A certain level
of Westernization is often associated with white collar

work. An African child who completes secondary education in a Western-style institution is often reluctant to consider any job that is not white collar. If the parents had made sacrifices to enable a child to complete secondary education, they in turn would feel betrayed if the child did not do his best to get a clerical job, instead of helping with the farm at home. Westernization carries occupational expectations that sometimes make young Africans prefer unemployment and social redundancy rather than an "inappropriate" job outside the culture of offices.

Islamization, on the other hand, has often been associated with trade rather than white collar work. Migrant Hausa traders in West Africa and Kiswahili-speakers on trading routes in East Africa are part of this association of Islam with commerce on foot.

In religiously heterogeneous African countries, it has also made sense to leave the business of meat selling and butchery to Muslims. Since Muslim customers insist on a particular way of killing the cow or the goat if the meat is to be halal (legitimate as diet), and African Christians and followers of African religions are neutral on how the animal is killed, it is only common sense to let the Muslim part of the population take care of the business of butchery and meat distribution. This has certainly tended to be the pattern in Eastern Africa. In Uganda, under the political leadership of Benedicto Kiwanuka at the beginning of the 1960s, the principle of a Muslim monopoly of the meat trade was temporarily repudiated by the government. But since then the Muslims have reasserted their control of a disproportionate share of the meat trade.

As for those Africans who have not been assimilated into either Western or Islamic culture, it is easier to refer to occupations from which they are excluded than to specific occupations with which they are associated. Africans who are completely non-Westernized are very un-likely to enter the general field of white collar pro-fessions. Africans who are neither Westernized nor Islamized are unlikely to become administrators or bureaucrats. The great majority of such Africans are peasant farmers, but many have also become traders and some have been recruited into the newly emerging proletarian class.

But stratification is not merely at the national level or the level of the class designation of individu-als. Stratification is also an international phenomenon. Whole societies can be classified and ranked.

Ahmed Sékou Touré, president of Guinea (Conakry), has sometimes referred to Africa as "a continent of the proletarian peoples." Touré's view is different from the view that sometimes sees Africa as "a classless conti-nent." A "proletarian Africa" is virtually a class in itself--a class within a global system of stratification.

Julius K. Nyerere also has been sensitive to the
fact that wealth differentials are not simply between
individuals but also between societies. As Nyerere put
it in the year of Tanganyika's independence:

> Karl Marx felt there was an inevitable clash
> between the rich of one society and the poor
> of that society. In that, I believe, Karl Marx
> was right. But today it is the international
> scene which is going to have a greater impact
> on the lives of individuals [in Tanganyika]
> than what is happening within Tanganyika. . . .
> And when you look at the international scene,
> you must admit that the world is divided be-
> tween the "haves" and "have nots." . . . And
> don't forget that the rich countries of the
> world today may be found on both sides of the
> division between "Capitalist" and "Socialist"
> countries.[10]

If black Africa is basically part of the "have nots"
of the world, and the Europeans are part of the "haves,"
where do the Arabs fit in? If Africa is part of a
global proletariat, and Europe indisputably part of the
global bourgeoisie, to what global class do the Arabs
belong?

Until oil wealth affected the destiny of some of the
Arab states, it was easy to think of the Arab world as
part of the "have nots" in the economic sense. Indeed,
until the 1970s the terms underdeveloped countries and
poor countries were almost interchangeable.

But the emergence of oil power has shattered the
easy equation. Virtually all Third World countries are
still technically underdeveloped, but only some of them
are now poor. South Yemen and Tanzania are still good
illustrations of the old equation. They are both poor
and underdeveloped. But since the 1970s it has become
difficult to think of Saudi Arabia as a "poor country."
This is one of the best-endowed countries in the world
in oil wealth and dollar reserves, yet at the same time
one of the least developed.

We said earlier that class formation within African
societies was often a matter of "who knows what" rather
than a matter of "who owns what." The question that now
arises is whether the international stratification system
is based on know-how (especially technology) or on wealth.

The concept of the Third World is normally associ-
ated with technical underdevelopment rather than dollar
reserves in the bank. There is therefore the First
World of technically advanced capitalist countries (the
West and Japan); then there is the Second World of
technically advanced socialist countries (the Soviet
Union and its European allies); and lastly there is the
Third World of technically underdeveloped countries of

Africa, Asia, and Latin America. The stratification here is decidedly in terms of modern and developmental know-how rather than in terms of idle petrodollars languishing in Swiss banks. Under this technological definition, the Arab countries and black Africa belong to the same global class.

But if one adopted a system of global stratification based on the per capita income of societies, Saudi Arabia would belong to a decidedly different class from Tanzania. What should be remembered is that Nigeria would belong to a higher class than North Yemen. And Kuwait and Saudi Arabia would both belong to a higher class than Great Britain.

On balance, a global stratification based on income per head of population is less credible than a global stratification based on technical development and know-how. Under the latter structure Egyptians, Nigerians, Tanzanians, and the ordinary people of Saudi Arabia are all part of an exploited and underdeveloped stratum of an international pyramid of privilege and power.

It is of course possible to think in terms of a Fourth World. Under this scheme the Third World would consist of those countries that are technically under-developed but at the same time resource-rich. The term Fourth World would be reserved for those countries that are both technically underdeveloped and resource-poor. Saudi Arabia and Nigeria would thus become part of the Third World, while Tanzania and South Yemen would be classified as members of the Fourth World.

There are two or three objections to this sub-division, some political and some intellectual. Politically it can be asserted that the whole technique of separating resource-poor underdeveloped countries from resource-rich underdeveloped countries is a device of the North to turn underdeveloped countries against each other. It is the old technique of "divide and rule."

Secondly, using resources as a way of defining the world's global system makes the system appear more fluid than it really is. Niger lacked uranium a decade ago and has since discovered it. Has Niger really shifted in international affiliations? The copper market was booming a few years ago and has drastically declined. Did Zambia really belong to a higher class a few years ago than it does now? If the Western powers succeeded in developing alternative sources of energy, and the world had a surplus of oil, would OPEC members really undergo downward social mobility in class terms?

The trouble with stratifying the world in terms of mineral resources is that we would need to reclassify countries every time there is an oil strike in a partic-ular society in the South or every time commodity prices on the world market rise or fall dramatically. In reality the global stratification system is much less flexible and more obstinate than this kind of analysis would imply. There is not enough structure at the global level in a class system based on income per head of population, drawn from a fluctuating or perishable commodity.

If Saudi dollars are languishing in Western banks, instead of being used to transform Saudi society, one reason could be Saudi Arabia's incapacity to absorb that wealth. There is a technical gap that requires more than the availability of dollars to fill it. If Saudi Arabia's oil has to be used in the streets of Tokyo and Philadelphia and is inadequately utilized for the internal industrial development of Saudi Arabia, one reason might be the preexistent technological underdevelopment of the society.

Perhaps at the global level, as well as in internal domestic arrangements in formerly colonized countries, class formation is decidedly not merely a question of "who owns what"--but is ultimately a consequence of "who knows what." The North's leadership in technology guarantees it leadership in power for at least the rest of this century. In that sense the Arabs and the black Africans are in the same boat--and their boat is definitely not the flagship.

A TRIAD OF CONFRONTATIONS

So far we have discussed direct relations between Europeans, Africans, and Arabs. In the long run perhaps these are the most important relations. What should be remembered constantly is the influence of other parties on these tripartite contacts.

In the political domain, a major variable has been the role of adversaries of each of these regions. As far as Western Europe is concerned, the most important political adversary is the Soviet Union. As far as the Arab world is concerned, the adversary that commands the greatest hostility is still Israel. As far as black Africa is concerned, the remaining symbol of racial humiliation on the continent is the white-dominated Republic of South Africa. In other words, each of our three regions has one particularly visible adversary. Its own relations with that adversary have had repercussions in its relations with the other two regions.

The Soviet Union has been an imperialist power in Europe, a liberating force in Africa, and a force with a mixed record in Asia. In Europe the USSR allowed itself to be heir to both the Czarist and the Nazi empires. What the Czars acquired territorially and incorporated into the body politic of Russia, the new Communist regime after 1917 retained. What the Nazis occupied in the course of World War II and the Soviet troops ostensibly liberated, the Soviet Union continued to dominate. Soviet allies in Eastern Europe are mainly countries that had once been under the Nazi yoke--and now remain under

Soviet hegemony.

But in Africa the Soviet rule has been--whatever the motives of Moscow--basically liberating. The liberation of countries like Zimbabwe, Angola, and Mozambique would have taken at least a generation longer to accomplish if the Soviet Union had not supported the liberation fighters with weapons and other forms of assistance. No Western government would have provided to African liberation fighters the scale of military support that they received from the Soviet Union. And elsewhere on the African continent the political and diplomatic rivalries between the West and the Soviet Union have been major contributors to the decolonization process. The West's commitment to decolonization needed the impetus of Soviet rivalry in the quest for friends in Africa.

As for the Soviet Union's record in Asia, this has been mixed. It has included the constructive role of helping Vietnam defeat its Western imperialist enemies. On the other hand, the Soviet role in Asia has also in-cluded acquiring new territory. Among the more blatant imperialist roles that the Soviet Union has played recent-ly has been its role in the invasion of Afghanistan. On balance Soviet occupation of Afghanistan is strikingly reminiscent of the Italian occupation of Abyssinia (Ethiopia) in 1935. Both Afghanistan and Abyssinia were relatively backward societies that had nevertheless managed to maintain a degree of ferocious independence across the centuries. Some of their institutions were feudal and outmoded, yet they seemed to retain legitimacy for a while in their own populations. But Abyssinia was then crushed by the Italians, and Afghanistan by the Russians.

However, most African leaders have been relatively mild in their condemnation of Soviet intervention in Afghanistan--even though it is a massive retrograde step in the history of imperialism in the second half of the twentieth century. One reason why African leaders have been relatively insensitive on the issue of Afghanistan is simply the record of the Soviet Union in helping African liberation. While Westerners have been slow to recognize the rights of blacks in Southern Africa, the Soviets have been in the forefront of sympathetic support for many years.

The second critical adversary involved in this drama is Israel as an adversary of the Arabs. If the West has been strengthening the Republic of South Africa econom-ically, Israel may have been strengthening it militarily. Speculation about Israel's military relations with South Africa has focused on two aspects--counterinsurgency and nuclear power. The Israelis have been singularly successful in virtually every battle they have fought with Palestinian insurgents. Israel as a country may one day lose the war for its survival, but for the time being Israel has managed to win the battles. This posture of heroic and lonely battles against "terrorism" has inspired many whites in Southern Africa. Diehard Afrikaners in the Republic of South Africa are sometimes both anti-Semitic and pro-Israel. They dislike their own Jews domestically while strongly admiring Israel's glories of heroic isolation. As a result the Pretoria government has sought to learn from the Israelis the techniques of counterinsurgency and antiterrorism.

The second major military area of collaboration between Israel and South Africa is nuclear collaboration. When in September 1979 the United States announced that a nuclear device had been exploded not far from Southern Africa, the immediate suspicion was that the Republic of South Africa had at last gone nuclear. South Africa vigorously denied this. The United States then hesitated on its own evidence and allegedly seemed unsure. Subsequent speculation seemed to indicate that if there was a nuclear explosion, it might have been primarily Israel's with the support of South Africa, rather than South Africa's with the support of Israel. If the explosion was primarily Israel's, Washington had additional reasons for suddenly pretending it was not sure if any nuclear device had exploded at all. Washington's fear of nuclear proliferation becomes even stronger in the case of proliferation in the Middle East. Has a conspiracy of silence developed to disguise Israel's nuclear capability? Is South Africa an ally in all this?

In the last ten years the broader politics of black Africa have certainly intermingled with the politics of the Middle East. One aspect of this intermingling has been the growing cordiality between Israel and South Africa. It would not be correct to say that Israel has drawn nearer to South Africa only because the majority of black African states decided to break off relations with Israel in 1973. There was already evidence of very rapid increase in trade and economic cooperation between the two countries well before the outbreak of the October War. Again, before black Africa broke off relations, Israel had decided to raise the level of its representation in Pretoria, and Ambassador Michael Michael was designated. This trend antedated black Africa's severance of relations and therefore was clearly independent of it. Nevertheless, the outbreak of the October War and Africa's decision to declare its solidarity with the Arabs against Israel provided an additional linkage between the politics of the Middle East and the politics of Africa.

Some Western and African commentators have suggested that the Arabs owed the Africans financial and economic reciprocity—that in return for African support over Israel the Arabs should extend greater economic and financial support to African development. There is certainly a compelling case for Arab contributions to African development, but the case should not depend

primarily on African support for the Arabs in their
confrontation with Israel. In exchange for that African
support, the Arabs should maintain and increase their own
support for African liberation in Southern Africa. Indeed, the Arabs had been substantially supportive of the
African cause in Southern Africa at least a decade before
the majority of African states discovered that there was
a Palestinian cause worthy of their moral interest. The
relevant modus vivendi in African-Arab politics is the
mutual recognition of each other's primary adversaries--
African support against Israel in exchange for Arab
support against white minority rule in South Africa.

As for that third adversary, the Soviet Union, it
encountered certain setbacks in the Arab world in the
1970s. Not long after the death of Nasser, Egypt
drifted out of the Soviet sphere of influence. This was
a major reversal in the Soviet Union's diplomatic
offensive in the Arab world. And although Egypt would
not have had the modest success it had in the October War
of 1973 without Soviet support, the trend throughout the
1970s was toward widening the gap between Cairo and
Moscow.

Then, on the Western extremity of the Mediterranean
world, another event seemed to open a new opportunity for
the Soviet Union when a historic military coup took place
on the Iberian peninsula. This was the coup in Lisbon in
April 1974. The overthrow of the legacy of fascism soon
resulted in the collapse of the Portuguese Empire. The
Soviet Union had a new opportunity to compensate for
losses in the Arab world. Marxist regimes seemed to be
on the horizon in Portuguese-speaking Africa. Henry
Kissinger woke up one day to discover a "Soviet threat"
in a previously undisputed "Western sphere of influence."
The West sat up at last and took the issue of residual
liberation in Southern Africa much more seriously than
it had ever done before. The Soviet Union as a super-
power had to some extent compensated in Southern Africa
for the serious setback it had suffered in North Africa
when Egypt expelled the Russian advisers and later
repudiated the treaty of friendship between the two
countries.

The politics of linkage had once again brought together three different confrontations--the West versus
the USSR, the Arabs versus Israel, and the Africans in
opposition to white minority rule in the southern portion
of their continent.

THE GLOBAL CONTEXT: A TRIAD OF ALLEGIANCE

Many of the triads discussed above have had an
ideological component. In both Africa and the Arab world
there is a good deal of ideological fluidity--partly because of the impact of European ideas. Governments and
the intelligentsia are, on the one hand, sensitive to the

need for authenticity and autonomy and, on the other,
responsive to the spell of Western-derived systems of
thought--especially liberal capitalism, socialism, and
nationalism.
Underlying the ideological fluidity in Africa and
the Arab world are the dynamics of three forms of loyalty
--to the individual, to the group, and to the nation.
Loyalty to the individual creates a predisposition toward
liberalism. Loyalty to the nation can sometimes become a
form of nationalism. As for group loyalties, these range
from ethnicity to class solidarity. The latter sometimes
leads to debates about the comparative relevance of
liberal capitalism and socialism.
The African and Arab response to European colonialism included elements of all three forms of loyalty--
individual loyalty, group solidarity, and national
allegiance. Particularly potent as a force against
colonialism was African and Arab nationalism.
But is not nationalism inward-looking and tending
toward isolating these peoples? That depends upon the
type of nationalism. Both Pan-Africanism and Pan-
Arabism are major regional movements involving many countries. They also tend to have a built-in global
consciousness, if only of a defensive kind. Pan-
Africanism and Pan-Arabism are in part a response to an
unfavorable distribution of power in the world. Both
movements include an antiimperialist tradition and an
ambivalent attitude toward the Western world.
Pan-Africanism and Pan-Arabism have found institutional expression in the OAU and the League of Arab
States, respectively. The league has been in disarray
since 1977 because of the Sadat peace initiative and the
consequent isolation of Egypt in the Arab world. But
that debate itself is probably a product of nationalism
at two levels. Was the Sadat initiative partly a child
of Egyptian nationalism? Was it a child of Egyptian
weariness at having to pay the price of Arab leadership?
Is there a continuing basic clash between Egyptian and
Arab nationalism?
In addition to these clashes between national and
transnational loyalties, there are the subnational
conflicts in both Africa and the Arab world. Sometimes
these are also forms of nationalism. Nigeria fought a
civil war because of Ibo nationalism. And Uganda continues to be centrally affected by the nationalism of
the Baganda.
But where does Europe fit into all this? For one
thing the nation-state system is itself a child of
Western diplomatic history and Western statecraft. The
legacy of the Treaty of Westphalia of 1648, when sovereign statehood was inaugurated, has now been globalized.
Concepts of nationalism, sovereignty, statehood, and
liberty on the world scene have never been the same
again. The rhetoric and paradigm of nationalism in both

the Arab world and Africa in the twentieth century have shown the marks of the European impact. Another effect of Europe's influence on our tripartite concerns is that it has helped to reduce the danger of a clash between Pan-Africanism and Pan-Arabism. As I indicated, the Arab slave trade still casts its shadow on African perceptions of the contemporary Arab world. But the legacy of shared European imperialism and the continuing economic hegemony of the Western world have, on the whole, continued to give Pan-Africanism and Pan-Arabism a semblance of comradeship-in-arms against Northern hegemony.

Not that tensions are entirely absent from African-Arab relations. The OAU, OPEC, and the League of Arab States have overlapping memberships. The African states have sometimes attempted to turn the OAU into a lever to extract _economic_ benefits from the oil-rich Arabs and their allies. The Arab states have at times attempted to turn the OAU into a lever to extract _political_ benefits from black Africans, especially on the issue of Israel.

As for OPEC, it is both admired and resented in much of the Third World. It is admired as an instance of the Third World's potential power; OPEC is the most powerful instrument that the Third World has produced in the twentieth century. But OPEC is also resented by poorer Third World countries for being inadequately sensitive to the catastrophic impact of oil prices on many of the economies of the Third World.

In black Africa OPEC is sometimes popularly equated with the Arab world. And yet the most important Arab member of OPEC is more opposed to high oil prices than is the most important black African member of OPEC. Saudi Arabia is more of a price "dove" in OPEC than is Nigeria; Nigeria is more of a price "hawk" than Abu Dhabi.

But in the ultimate analysis, what makes African-Arab solidarity survive is a continuing and growing awareness by the two regions that they both continue to be dominated by the North.

This brings us to the fourth variety of nationalism. We have so far discussed state-specific nationalism (like Egyptian nationalism), regionwide nationalism (like Pan-Arabism) and substate forms of nationalism (like Ibo, Ganda, and Kurdish brands of nationalism). What has been emerging more recently is what one might call _hemispheric nationalism_. The Third World has been evolving a level of solidarity that is partly a form of nationalism across three continents and partly a form of class consciousness on the global scale. It manifests itself most sharply within the U.N. system--from UNCTAD sessions to the general conferences of the United Nations Educational, Scientific and Cultural Organization (UNESCO), from special economic sessions of the U.N.

General Assembly to the search for a New International
Information Order.
We need to place these developments within a global,
overlapping systemic triad--the wider state system, the
U.N. system, and the system of transnational, nongovernmental movements and trends. In the twentieth century
the wider state system has been fostering global
ethnicity. The idea of the nation-state has on the one
hand resulted in such transnational movements as Pan-
Africanism, eager one day to produce a United States of
Africa. It has also produced Pan-Arabism, with endless
experiments in federations and confederations. But the
same idea of the nation-state has inspired substate
units--such as the Ibo, Kurds, and some Welsh-speaking
Welsh nationalists--that have dreamt about forming their
own nation-states. Centrifugal and centripetal varie-
ties of nationalism in this context are what global
ethnicity within the first system of nation-states is
all about.
The second global system is that of the United
Nations. My thesis here is that the second system
generates the nearest thing to global class consciousness that we have witnessed so far. The United Nations
converts the whole world into an arena of scarce resources. The United Nations also provides the forum of
debate and the battlefield of at least political confrontation. In such a situation of global sociology
the possibilities of perceiving planetary resources as
being subject to distributive justice are enhanced; they
are sometimes even maximized.
What all this means is that the U.N. system is in
a sense the most important "proletarianizing" factor on
the global scene. It helps to enable poor societies to
sense their predicament in a planetary context. Hence
the emerging Third World solidarity--however fragile--
in the U.N. system.
In this context the Arabs and Africans find themselves part of the underprivileged "class" of the
world--even when the Arabs are rich in dollars. Why
should they not be rich in their own currencies? Because the monetary system of the world has a stratified
system of exchange--dinars, for example, are not valued
independently but only in relation to dollars. There is
a pecking order of currencies. There is also a pecking
order of technology. Higher development amid energy
deficit is more powerful than energy surplus in the
midst of primitive technology.
The third global system of transnational, private,
nongovernmental movements and institutions unfortunately
is predominantly Northern, made up especially of North-
Western movements like independent trade unions, peace
research movements, transnational corporations, and
liberal movements on human rights. Many of these movements (although not all) are instances of globalized

individualism and planetary private initiatives.
What all this means is that the first system of
Westphalia--the nation-state--has been promoting forms
of global ethnicity. The second system of the United
Nations has been promoting global class consciousness,
ranging from UNCTAD debates to those of special economic
sessions of the General Assembly. The third system of
transnational nongovernmental movements includes a
tendency toward globalized individualism and planetary
private initiatives.

Europe is strong on this last ideological tendency--
leaning toward individualism, private enterprise, and
human rights. This is the heritage of liberalism. The
Arab world and Africa are strong in this period of history
on the rights of groups. Arabs and Africans are also
strong, as new converts to Westphalia, on the rights of
nation-states.

The struggle for the future is to convert Arabs,
Africans, and Europeans to planetary concerns. How can
we create the context for planetary interchange and
global cooperation? It may well be that an intermediate
stage is a triad of dissent. Let us now turn to this
triad.

THE GLOBAL CONTEXT: A TRIAD OF DISSENT

But even beyond the specific national adversaries
of each of our regions, there are the broader social
forces at work in the world as a whole. The historical
context, as intimated earlier, includes the rise of the
West into global hegemony. Western technology, culture,
and power began to conquer much of the world. Western
ideas, languages, systems of education, modes of engineering and production, patterns of consumption, and even
rules of behavior began to penetrate societies originally
vastly different from those of the West.

What has emerged in recent times are three major
challenges to Western hegemony--the challenges of Marxism,
Islam, and nationalism in the Third World. This is the
global triad of dissent.

Marxism's main attack is on the West's economic
hegemony. The Marxist paradigm highlights economic
factors and traces power to the fountainhead of basic
production. The attack on capitalism and economic
imperialism is an inevitable outgrowth of the paradigm.
The Islamic challenge, on the other hand, is directed
more at the West's cultural hegemony than at its economic
domination. The revolution in Iran is the epitome of
this cultural challenge. The nationalism of the Third
World started off as being aimed primarily at the West's
political hegemony. The anticolonial movements were
seeking to enter the arena of Western-style diplomacy--
from flags to diplomatic immunity, from national anthems
to membership in the United Nations.

The question arises whether Third World nationalism will learn from Marxism and seriously challenge Western economic hegemony. The question also arises whether Third World nationalism will learn from Islam and begin to challenge the West's cultural hegemony. Africa and the Arab world are two of the arenas where these battles of dissent are being fought out. Europe, on the other hand, is part of the dominating presence of the Western world as a whole.

In the quest for equity at the global level, the other triads discussed raise policy issues. I mentioned that Europe's relations with the Arab world are structural, and so are Europe's relations with Africa. What are not as yet adequately structured are the relations between the Arabs and the Africans on their own. The triangle needs to be completed. The Arabs have had three major roles in their relations with Africa across the centuries. They have been accomplices in Africa's enslavement and exploitation in the past, allies in Africa's liberation from the Western world more recently, and potential partners in Africa's development. The completion of the triangle may require an expansion of the role of the Arabs as partners in development in the years ahead.

With regard to the triad of acculturation, we noted that the penetration has been from Europe into Africa much more than from Africa into Europe. It has also been from the Arab world into Africa much more than from Africa into the Arab world. The policy issues that arise for the future are whether this asymmetry is inevitable, or whether a process of Africa's counter-penetration into Europe and the Arab world can in fact be inaugurated at a new level. Such counterpenetration by Africa could take cultural, economic, or political forms. A fusion of economic and political counter-penetration can take place when an African country succeeds in converting a particular commodity from a basis of great dependency upon Europe into an instrument of political leverage. Oil was once primarily a basis of dependency; it has now become an instrument of power and influence in the hands of those who possess it. Niger discovered uranium—but its dependency upon France did not lessen very significantly. It is conceivable that Niger could transform its uranium resources into a basis of countervailing power.

With regard to the Arab world, there has been some counterpenetration of the Gulf by Swahili culture in the last twenty years. Many East Africans, especially from Zanzibar, went looking for jobs or political refuge in the Gulf States after the Zanzibar revolution in 1964. Some of these Swahili-speaking East Africans hold important jobs in Oman, Abu Dhabi, and even some towns in Saudi Arabia. One can overhear a conversation in Kiswahili in the Hilton Hotel in Abu Dhabi or in the streets of Muscat. This is a form of counterpenetration, and East Africa should facilitate it.

The triad of pigmentation may be the most finite of them all. A revolution in the Republic of South Africa could occur within the next generation. And racism as an institutionalized phenomenon may in any case be on the way out of human history. In the decades ahead Arabs, Africans, and Europeans will probably quarrel less and less on issues of race and color and more on issues of resources and jobs. The basic policy issue here therefore is to promote those forces that are battling against racism. The Arabs should go beyond diplomatic support for movements against apartheid and commit greater economic resources to the tasks of liberation. Greater pressures on Western oil companies to stop or reduce the illicit flow of oil to the Republic of South Africa would also be a major contribution to the fight against institutionalized racism.

It would also make sense to revive the battle of denouncing Zionism as a form of racism. Zionism started off with religious and nationalist connotations, but it has developed into a racial ideology. Indeed, its insistence on separating the Jews into a distinct Jewish state is very similar ideologically to the commitment by apartheid to create a separate homeland for each cultural group in South Africa. Israel was created as a kind of "Bantustein." The Arabs and Africans should not be "terrorized" by Western governments and media into giving up the struggle against the racial aspects of Zionism.

But more long-lasting than issues of race are issues of stratification and class formation. The domestic triad of stratification--peasantry, bourgeoisie, and proletariat in Africa especially--is bound to undergo significant changes in the rest of the century. The proletariat will grow, and so will the bourgeoisie. The persistent question is whether the peasantry will succeed in protecting its economic interests and enhancing its political participation as Africa undergoes the twin processes of proletarianization and embourgoisement.

As for the triad of international stratification, the Muslim world has become part of the vanguard of dissent. Although Islam's main preoccupation is indeed cultural, particular Muslim countries vary in the foci of their efforts. As we indicated, Algeria took the lead in the struggle for a New International Economic Order. It is feasible to argue that militant Iran and militant Libya are both involved in challenging the foundations of traditional international law and aspire to create a new international legal order.

NOTES

1. Ali Mazrui, The Trial of Christopher Okigbo (London:

Heinemann Educational Books, 1971), p. 135.

2. See R. R. Palmer in collaboration with Joel Colton, A History of the Modern World, 2d ed. (New York: Knopf, 1962), p. 13. This issue is also discussed in the Introduction to Ali Mazrui, The African Condition: A Political Diagnosis (London: Heinemann Educational Books; New York: Cambridge University Press, 1980) (the B.B.C. Reith Lectures), pp. ix-x.

3. See Herskovits's contribution to Wellesley College Symposium on Africa (Wellesley, Mass.: Wellesley College, 1960), p. 16.

4. Kwame Nkrumah, Consciencism: Philosophy and Ideology for Decolonization and Development with Particular Reference to the African Revolution (London: Heinemann Educational Books, 1964), pp. 69-71.

5. Edmund Burke, Works, Vol. 4, Reflections on the Revolution in France (1790) (London: World's Classic Edition, 1907), p. 109.

6. Hugh, Lord Hailey, An African Survey, rev. ed. (London: Oxford University Press, 1957), pp. 453-454.

7. This doctrinal marriage is also discussed in Mazrui, The African Condition, pp. 97-99.

8. Nkrumah, Consciencism, p. 70.

9. Ibid, p. 78.

10. Julius Nyerere, "The Second Scramble," a speech delivered at the opening of the World Assembly of Youth Seminar in Dar es Salaam, 1961.

3
African-Arab-OECD Military Relations: The Recycling of Imperialism

Robin Luckham

INTRODUCTION: COOPERATION OR DISENGAGEMENT?

The theme of this book is African-Arab-OECD trilateral cooperation. Yet it is being written during a
period of rising international conflict in Africa and the
Middle East, itself a consequence of the struggle for
power and resources among the dominant world powers.
The beneficent triangle of Arab petrofunds, OECD
technology, and African-Arab development, confronts a
contradictory triangle of Arab petrofunds, North
Atlantic Treaty Organization (NATO) (and Warsaw Pact)
arms supplies, and African and Arab conflict.
If we are to discuss cooperation realistically in
such a context we must not disregard its Janus face.
For cooperation can polarize as much as it brings together, nowhere more so than in military relationships.
Military cooperation between African and Arab countries
and their Western suppliers of arms pulls them into the
Cold War, impedes cooperation with the socialist countries, and aggravates internal conflict in the two
regions themselves.
What could one say were the benefits and who were
the beneficiaries of collaboration between Morocco,
Mauritania, and France in the war against the Polisario
Front in the Western Sahara? Or of the Joint Afro-
Franco-American interventions against the insurgencies in
the Shaba region of Zaire in 1977 and 1978? Or for that
matter of Russo-Cubo-Ethiopian military cooperation in
the wars in the Ogaden and Eritrea? Does acceptance by
Oman, Somalia, and Kenya of U.S. military and economic
aid in exchange for military facilities constitute a
case of cooperation or of collaboration, in the pejora-
tive sense of that term? Have the Camp David agreements
brought peace any closer, or have they merely divided
the Arab world and made it more difficult to achieve a
just settlement in Palestine? Cooperation in war as in
peace is not a politically innocent topic; it can create
losers as well as beneficiaries. Moreover, cooperation
can alter the very structure of social relationships. It

can bring undesirable as well as desirable social transformations, dependence as well as interdependence. In particular the recycling of petrofunds into weapons diverts resources from alternative uses and distorts social and economic structures, both within countries that buy arms and within those that sell them.

There is of course a close connection between the problems of development and the issues of international security. Development in Africa and the Middle East is impossible without security, at least in the minimal sense of freedom from war, disaster, and famine. But security in this sense can easily become confused with the stability of existing social arrangements, the power of established ruling classes, and a whole series of blocks to national and international development.

And further, the security the great powers pursue cannot be assumed to coincide with the security of African and Arab ruling classes, still less that of the people they govern. Indeed, this is just what impels many Arab and African governments to purchase weapons. Yet, as I shall argue below, such purchases must be self-defeating, because arms can be acquired only by entering into new kinds of international dependence--the more so because the powers that sell weapons and provide military assistance are recycling not merely Arab petrofunds, but also their own vanishing hegemony.

The question that must hence be asked is how much it is cooperation with the major powers that Arab and African countries require and how much disengagement and cooperation among themselves, for example, to prevent the kind of military buildup now occurring in the Indian Ocean. Disengagement need not, of course, exclude development cooperation with the OECD (nor for that matter with the Council of Mutual Economic Assistance [COMECON]). But it would be compatible only so far as such cooperation could be separated from the requirements of NATO security and Western hegemony.

PETROMILITARISM

Since the 1973 oil price rise and the Yom Kippur War, the barrel of the gun has seemed inextricably connected to the barrel of oil.[1] A substantial proportion of the major arms sales agreements concluded by the countries of the industrial North between 1974 and 1977 were with Arab and African members of OPEC. Military transfers to the two regions accelerated sharply after 1973, rising faster than those to any other part of the Third World. The Middle East is now by far the world's largest importer of arms, and Africa comes fourth after East Asia and Europe, well ahead of both Latin America and South Asia. Between them the two regions account for almost half the international trade in weapons and about two-thirds of that with the Third World. Furthermore,

the largest importers of arms are (with certain significant exceptions like Israel, Syria, Egypt, and South
Africa) the members of OPEC. In the period 1973-1977 the
oil producers purchased about two-thirds of the arms
transferred to the Middle East and almost half those
transferred to Africa.

The major arms exporters have viewed the sale of
weapons not only as a way of reestablishing political
relationships with the Arab countries after the Yom
Kippur War, but also as a convenient means of reinte-
grating their petrofunds into the circuits of the international economy. For weapons have certain characteristics as commodities that facilitate the rapid international transfer of value. They tend to have high (and
rapidly increasing) unit costs. Spare capacity in the
arms industries has tended to increase. Weapons are
relatively easily transferred as a "package" that includes the required training and support services; this
both increases their price and makes them easier to absorb
than many other kinds of capital equipment. And they
have the convenient property of increasing their own
demand by contributing to arms races. Nevertheless, the
scale of military recycling should not be exaggerated.
Sales to the Middle Eastern and African members of OPEC
between 1973 and 1977 were 24 and 32 percent of total U.S.
and European Common Market arms exports, respectively.
Moreover, military sales have constituted a relatively
small (and possibly declining) fraction of the total
exports of the OECD, even when allowance is made for
their underestimation in the standard statistical
sources. Their direct balance-of-payments contribution
has thus been relatively small, certainly less than that
of the flow of Arab funds into Western financial markets
or into transfers of nonmilitary technology.

A second set of linkages has arisen through which
the more radical members of OPEC have spent petrofunds
on weapons from the socialist countries, which in turn
have used these funds to acquire grain and technology
from the West. Slightly less than one-third of the
OPEC countries' military imports came from Warsaw
Pact countries (mostly from the Soviet Union), making up
roughly one-fifth of total Warsaw Pact arms trade.
Weapons constitute around one-tenth of the Soviet Union's
exports, a considerably larger proportion of total
foreign trade than for any of the major Western exporters. However, the contribution of the arms trade
to the USSR's balance of payments is almost impossible
to estimate. It seems reasonable to assume that the
greater part of the weapons sold to members of OPEC are
exchanged for hard currency. Nevertheless, the amounts
involved are not large, no more than about 2 percent of
total Soviet exports. And they are no doubt offset by
the foreign exchange costs of the Soviet Union's military
presence in the non-OPEC countries, which OPEC arms

purchases in effect help to subsidize.

The share of arms transfers in the trade flows of the OPEC countries themselves (and of those of their Arab and African neighbors) has been distinctly greater than that of the corresponding flows in the total trade of the industrial North. Weapons made up approximately 7 percent of OPEC's total imports between 1973 and 1977 (and roughly one-third of its imports of capital goods)-- less than for the Middle East as a whole but very much greater than the corresponding figures for the developed countries and for the non-OPEC countries of Africa.

Nevertheless, the holders of petrofunds have varied greatly in their appetite for military goods. Some, like Libya and Saudi Arabia, with surpluses greatly in excess of immediate development needs, have spent a correspondingly high proportion on weapons. Others, like Algeria, with smaller reserves relative to population, have deliberately restrained military spending, despite the temporary availability of funds, in order to invest these surpluses in their industrial base. In yet others, the dynamics of oil and weapons have changed from one period to the next. Nigeria, for example, experienced during the 1967-1969 civil war a period of rapid military growth, accelerated by oil revenues, but by no means determined by them. This was followed by a brief pause, after which military spending again expanded during the oil boom of the early 1970s (even farther than when the country was engaged in hostilities). This military spending declined during the preparation for civilian government in the late 1970s, but aided by oil revenues that have again increased, it has been restimulated by the civilian government that took office in 1979. Finally, there have been considerable variations in the import content of military spending. A substantial proportion of Nigeria's military expenditures, for example, were on barracks and higher salaries for a military establishment greatly increased in size by the civil war. Hence its military imports have been lower than one would predict on the basis of expenditures alone. Conversely, Libya, whose armed forces are numerically smaller, has been a very large importer of military goods because of its stockpiling of equipment for use elsewhere in the Arab world and Africa.

As the latter suggests, another factor to be taken into account is the contribution of OPEC countries to the arming of their allies and clients in Africa and the Middle East--thus the military import of the Arab frontline states; Egypt (prior to Camp David), Jordan, and Syria have been in differing degrees subsidized by their OPEC neighbors. The Arab Organisation for Industrialisation (AOI), which was to have created an Arab armaments-production complex, would have been based on Gulf petrofunds, Egyptian skills, and (for the most part) OECD technology. Libya has played an important, although

somewhat erratic, role as military provider for Arab
confrontation states, African clients (notoriously
Idi Amin), and liberation movements on both continents.
Petrofunds from other OPEC members have also found their
way to liberation movements in Palestine, Northern Africa,
and the Horn, and (in smaller quantities) Southern
Africa.

A further set of interconnections has operated
through the negative effects of high petroleum prices on
the balance of payments of the non-oil-producing countries. To the extent that this has hastened the crises
of underdevelopment, it has also sharpened conflict, increased the number of repressive (often military) regimes,
and resulted in a higher proportion of each country's
scarce resources being spent on the military. During the
decade 1966-1976 the military expenditures of all but
four of the non-OPEC countries in Africa and of all the
non-OPEC Middle East countries increased in real terms;
in two-thirds of the African and all but one of the
Middle Eastern countries military spending increased as
a proportion of the gross domestic product. In some
cases the increases compare with those in OPEC, although
for the most part they are not as large.

To be sure, high oil prices are only one of the
factors that contribute to the economic crises faced by
the non-OPEC countries. There are other reasons for high
military spending, the highest being experienced by the
confrontation states in the Middle East and in Southern
Africa. Nevertheless, there remains enough evidence to
support the seemingly paradoxical conclusion that whereas
the inflow of petrofunds has accelerated armament in the
oil-surplus countries, their outflow has also increased
it in countries with an oil deficit.

Some of the adjustments made by these non-OPEC
countries to the rise in the oil price, including their
military expenditures, have in turn been financed by
petrofunds re-lent through the international financial
system. It is no longer the practice, to be sure, for
impecunious governments to finance their weapons directly
by going to the international banks. But there are a
number of indirect linkages. The availability of petrofunds in financial markets probably increases the ability
of Western governments to offer lines of government-to-
government credit to support arms exports. At the same
time, petrofunds re-lent through the Eurocurrency market
have provided a number of non-OPEC developing countries
with temporary balance-of-payments relief, making foreign
exchange available for weapons that would otherwise have
had to be spent on other imports or debt repayments.

Such relief, however, has been largely confined to
those few countries with easy access to international
financial markets. Indeed, the OPEC countries themselves
(especially those like Algeria and Nigeria with small
reserves relative to their population and development

programs) have been among the biggest African and Middle
Eastern borrowers. Only a handful of other countries--
notably Egypt, Zaire, Kenya, and South Africa--have been
able to borrow enough to have a significant effect on
their military outlays. Of these it is probably South
Africa that has benefited most from the recycling of
petrofunds through the international financial system.
In the early 1970s, South Africa's military expansion was
in some measure cushioned from the effect of the oil
price increases by foreign borrowing and IMF standby
credits. However, in the latter part of the decade the
movement into gold by (among others) Arab holders of
petrofunds, and the dramatic increase in the gold price,
ended South Africa's balance-of-payments difficulties,
coinciding with the development of greater self-sufficiency in military production.

WEAPONS AND THE RECYCLING OF IMPERIALISM

The preceding section suggests that although petrofunds have been connected with arms sales in multiple
and often contradictory ways, their direct contribution
to the resolution of the economic crisis facing the OECD
countries themselves has been relatively limited. Arms
transfers have been important less for ensuring the
economic viability of Western capitalism than for protecting the political conditions of that viability. In
the first place, they have underwritten Western arms
production and hence subsidized Western security.
Second, they have been used to cement political alliances
with Arab and African ruling classes, thus protecting
raw material supplies, markets, and investments.
It became apparent in the early 1970s that the arms
industries of the West were in major difficulties that
resulted in the cancellation of major weapons systems,
brought a number of arms and aerospace firms close to
bankruptcy, and led to a series of proposals to
rationalize arms production on a multinational basis,
especially in Europe. These developments were partly the
result of political changes, including the withdrawal of
the United States from a global role after Vietnam and
the decrease in its military expenditures. They were
also, however, rooted in longer-run trends in arms production, with its tendency to create ever more complex,
capital-intensive, and costly weapons, the development
of which no one military producer could afford without
access to external markets.
An increasing proportion of arms production has been
exported, not only from Europe, where the defense industries have been dependent on exports since the 1950s,
but also from the United States, where domestic requirements had broadly sufficed to fill the order books of the
arms industries until the late 1960s (even though the
United States remained the world's largest exporter for

most of the postwar period).
There was also a shift toward the supply of weapons,
services, and software on commercial terms, rather than
under military aid programs. The proportion of U.S. arms
transfers financed by security assistance grants and
credits declined from almost 90 percent in the 1950s and
early 1960s to well under 50 percent by the mid-1970s.
At the same time, recipients of arms were increasingly
pulled into the entire cycle of weapons development, production, sales, and maintenance. As a congressional
report on U.S. Arms Policies in the Persian Gulf and Red
Sea Areas puts it:

> The nature and extent of American participation
> in selling equipment and services has often been
> determined by surveys conducted by the Depart-
> ment of Defense of local military establish-
> ments. . . . What has tended to occur is a
> chain reaction. Surveys may often go beyond
> general preconceptions of needs and amplify
> and redirect them. They lead to requests for
> arms mentioned in the surveys; requests are
> granted in part, if not in total; deliveries
> are scheduled; training starts; U.S. military
> presence increases; deliveries start; follow-
> on maintenance and service contracts for de-
> fense contractors develop. The cycle has
> followed the same pattern in at least Iran,
> Saudi Arabia, and Kuwait.[2]

During the early 1970s the political formula for
U.S. arms transfers was supplied by the Nixon Doctrine[3]
(renamed the Guam Doctrine in post-Watergate U.S. government publications). In brief this doctrine stated that
the United States could no longer ensure the security of
clients and allies in the Third World by intervening
directly on their behalf as it had in Korea and Vietnam.
Instead, in what seemed a parody of fashionable development rhetoric, the latter were to be encouraged to be
more "self-reliant." In a happy coincidence of politics
and profit they would be sold the arms with which to
provide their own security. At the same time the
doctrine permitted the United States to put a good face
on its imperial decline and on the isolationism character-
izing its foreign policy after Vietnam.
When President Carter took office in 1976 he
committed the U.S. administration to a major military
reduction, including a cut in arms sales and in U.S.
interventions in the Third World.[4] Arms limitation soon
succumbed, however, to the revival of the Cold War. This
delayed conclusion of the SALT II (Strategic Arms
Limitation Talks) agreement and resulted in NATO's
decision to increase real military expenditures by 3 percent annually to match alleged Soviet expansion.

Furthermore there were major increases in arms sales in
the Third World (at least when due allowance is made for
Iran's cancellation of its huge orders after the 1978-1979
revolution). Without doubt, the renewal of Western
military expansion was encouraged by strong domestic
pressures from within the defense establishments and arms
industries. For although the latter were not the only
influence, they had a decisive effect on how the "threat"
posed by the USSR's military programs was perceived.

The effects of the West's rearmament on that of the
Third World have, however, been complex. On the one
hand, the increase in the West's own military spending
may have reduced the pressure to export weapons in order
to keep the defense industries viable. On the other
hand, the crisis within these industries has deepened
with every increase in the cost and complexity of new
generations of weapons.

One reason for this predicament is the very success
of Third World energy producers in securing the redistribution of world power and resources through OPEC. That
success, however, complements trends within capitalism
itself--including the global spread of the multinational
corporation, the growth of the Eurocurrency market, and
the international cumulation of inflation and balance-of-
payments difficulties--which have weakened the Western
economies and made them more vulnerable to changes
occurring in the Third World. The default of a country
like Zaire, which is heavily indebted to the Eurocurrency
market (and is also a producer of strategic raw materials), could send ripples through the international financial system, especially if it became the signal for other
debtors to default. More upheavals in the Middle East
comparable to the Iranian revolution and the Iraq-Iran war[5]
could bring forward the economic crisis that is already
spreading through the international economy.

At the same time, political changes have undermined
the assumptions on which the accommodation with economically strategic regions in the Third World has been
based: that stable alliances cemented by the transfer of
arms can in fact be established with local ruling
classes and that it is possible through such alliances
to manage regional conflict or, at the least, to ensure
that such conflict does not seriously damage Western
interests. The downfall of the emperor of Ethiopia and
that of the shah of Iran, together with other political
events, have made it obvious that the weapons transferred
to a country's ruling class guarantee neither its military
effectiveness nor its political stability.

Furthermore, the political leverage that weapons
have provided the Western powers is uncertain, even as it
pertains to the ruling classes with whom they are most
closely associated. Although Saudi Arabia, for example,
has remained a voice of moderation in OPEC, this is more
the result of its large oil reserves and its financial

stake in the West than of specific Western pressures.
U.S. attempts to draw Saudi Arabia away from the Arab
states and obtain its support for the Camp David agreements have signally failed. At the same time, the U.S.
compact with Sadat has cut Egypt off from the petrofunds
that would otherwise have financed its industrialization
and weapons, has made the regime itself more fragile,
and has greatly reduced its influence in the Arab world.
    Such attempts by Western powers to engineer regional
security are inherently problematic because they violate
the desire for national self-determination shared by the
ruling classes of even the more conservative Arab and
African states--all the more so because the contradictions these attempts seek to overcome--like the struggle
with Palestine, the liberation of South Africa, or the
nationality problems in the Horn of Africa--are too deep-
rooted to be managed from outside. Moreover, in the two
former conflicts the Western powers are incapacitated by
their commitments to Israel and white South Africa,
respectively. Sociologically both are extensions of the
West. Neither can easily be abandoned: Israel, because
of (among other things) its unique position in the
political process of the United States; South Africa,
because of the importance of its gold and other raw
materials, the level of Western investment in its economy,
and its significance in Western geostrategy. However much
the Western powers may distance themselves, their
incestuous ties with the two countries are a serious
obstacle to their relationships with Arab and black
African states.
    Yet the Western powers do not seem to have drawn
the obvious conclusions from the failure of arms sales to
protect their interests. One of the U.S. government's
first responses to the fall of the shah of Iran was to
increase weapons deliveries to Saudi Arabia and the Gulf.
Sadat's rift with other Arab leaders following the Camp
David agreements accelerated the replacement of Egypt's
Soviet weapons with U.S. hardware. Morocco's military
failure in the war in the Western Sahara, and Mauritania's
decision to withdraw, resulted in a reduction of French
military support but also in a major increase in U.S.
arms, not unconnected with King Hassan's support for U.S.
policy initiatives in the Middle East. And the Western
powers reacted to the Ethiopian revolution and the subsequent Soviet and Cuban aid to the military regime by
authorizing military exports to the Sudan, Kenya, and,
more recently, Somalia (although to be sure they resisted
the temptation of supplying the latter during the Ogaden
war).
    The European countries as well as the United States
have reacted to the crisis of hegemony by supplying more
weapons, although the figures suggest significant differences. The combined arms trade of the European Common
Market countries approaches that of the United States or

the Warsaw Pact countries in value, especially if
allowance is made for its underestimation in the standard statistical sources. However, because of their
narrower national military markets, the profitability of
European weapons industries is, if anything, more difficult to maintain. Thus a higher proportion of total
military production is exported and the Europeans have
tended to pursue the petrodollar markets more aggressive-
ly than either the United States or the USSR. The
proportion of European arms exports reaching OPEC countries in Africa and the Middle East is about one-third,
representing up to one-tenth of total military production.
Moreover, the Common Market countries have been the
largest suppliers of arms to sub-Saharan Africa, reflect-
ing neocolonial links with black Africa (especially
those with France), as well as French and Italian sales
to South Africa (until officially terminated in 1977
after the imposition of the U.N. embargo). On the other
hand, they have supplied substantially less than either
the United States or the USSR to non-OPEC countries in
the Middle East, where the Arab-Israeli conflict has
induced a pattern of supply more closely geared to the
conflicts between the superpowers.

Arms transfers have also reflected the disarray
in Western security policies that has arisen from
divisions between the United States and its European
allies (and among the latter themselves) over a range
of issues. The first issue has been how to handle the
growing power of OPEC--whether the OECD countries should
adopt a common strategy under U.S. leadership in order to
confront the threat to their interests or whether they
should accept the reality of OPEC and make the best of
the situation by establishing bilateral military and
economic relations with OPEC members of the kind now
being built up by France. Second, there is the question
of relations with the radical Arab confrontation states--
whether to follow the Camp David strategy of trying to
isolate them from their more conservative neighbors or
whether to keep open the channels of political communication by selling them technology and weapons. Third, there
is the problem of nuclear proliferation, with European
countries like West Germany and France sometimes being
prepared to support their own industries by exporting
nuclear technology, and the United States attempting
(with relatively little success) to impose restraints.
Finally, there is the question whether problems of
Western arms production are best resolved by joint
decisions on procurement within the framework of NATO
(almost certainly to the disadvantage of European
manufacturers) or by European coproduction ventures.
Coproduction has tended to inflate the development and
production costs of weapons, but it becomes more viable
to the extent that the Europeans can find foreign markets,
especially in OPEC. The interimperial rivalries around

these issues are linked and make it difficult to
establish a coordinated NATO-OECD approach to arms
transfers or to the protection of Western interests in
Africa and the Middle East.

INTERVENTION FOR WAR; INTERVENTION FOR PEACE

The crisis in Western hegemony has produced two
seemingly opposed trends: first, a revival of direct
military intervention by the major powers in the affairs
of the two regions, and second, a number of major
Western initiatives to encourage negotiated settlement
of conflicts. In certain respects these policies might
be regarded as alternatives both to each other and to the
transfer of arms to local ruling classes. But at the
same time they form part of the same contradictory unity
established by the disintegration and reassertion of
Western power and interests.

In the 1970s there was a gradual rehabilitation of
the idea that direct military intervention in the
affairs of another country is internationally legitimate.
Soon after the 1973 oil crisis the U.S. administration
and Congress began openly to discuss the pros and cons of
armed invasion to keep oil flowing from the Gulf if there
were a crisis in the Middle East. In the terminology of
U.S. security doctrine, the U.S. military has prepared
for "one and a half wars," one in Western Europe, half
in the Third World. Half a war may indeed understate the
current position, for the revolution in Iran (and taking
of U.S. diplomatic hostages) and the Soviet invasion of
Afghanistan have legitimized a reorganization of and increase in the U.S.'s Rapid Deployment Forces and the
acquisition of (in exchange for military and economic
aid) military facilities in Egypt, Oman, Kenya, and
Somalia to facilitate operations in the Gulf and Indian
Ocean. Thus far the United States has made little use of
such facilities, except to stage the abortive attempt to
rescue the hostages in Iran. Yet the U.S. military
buildup clearly increases the danger that a dispute such
as might occur if Iran carried through its threat to
close the Gulf to the shipment of oil would escalate into
a major military conflict.

In Africa a disproportionate share of the burden of
maintaining Western hegemony has been borne by the
French. Their strategy of military couverture à distance
temporarily declined in the late 1960s but was revived
again in the mid-1970s. France played a major role in
supplying, organizing, and indeed fighting the wars
against the National Liberation Front (FROLINAT) in Chad
and Polisario in the Western Sahara. It was the major
partner in the joint interventions of European and conservative African countries that rescued General Mobutu's
crumbling regime from the uprisings that took place in
the Shaba Province of Zaire in 1977 and 1978. And it

organized the coup that overthrew General-Emperor Bokassa
in the Central African Republic in 1979. Nevertheless,
the failures of the counterinsurgencies in Chad and the
Western Sahara (from direct participation in which France
has withdrawn) have exposed the limits of French power.
And France has not been entirely happy about being cast
in the role of "NATO's gendarme in Africa,"[6] even less so
because of the possible opportunities foregone in terms
of sales of technology and military goods to radical OPEC
states like Algeria and Libya.

The desire for negotiated settlement of the major
conflicts in the two regions springs from the same
motivations that have led the powers to supply arms and
mobilize their armed forces for intervention: not a
disinterested concern with peace or a simple drive for
hegemony so much as a concern about the disruption that
major regional conflict could create in Western finances
and supplies of energy and raw materials. The middle and
late 1970s saw a veritable spate of Western initiatives,
including the Kissinger negotiations in Southern Africa
and the Middle East, the Camp David agreements, the five-
power attempt to sponsor a settlement in Namibia, and the
Commonwealth proposals that led to independence in
Zimbabwe. Nevertheless, the results have been meager,
the only real success being the settlement in Zimbabwe,
where the high cost of protracted guerrilla war gave both
sides a strong interest in a solution. There is little
evidence, however, that the West's diplomacy has had any
effect on the flow of armaments, which in some instances
may indeed have been accelerated by defective peace,
as after Camp David.

ILLUSIONS OF THE COLD WAR

Those who would justify the West's armament of
Africa argue that it is necessitated by the Soviet
Union's "surge towards globalism,"[7] just as those who
would justify the Soviet Union's arms supplies no doubt
refer to the military activities of the capitalist countries. I wish to argue, however, that arms transfers
have been determined by factors that are separable from,
although to be sure influenced by, the conflict between
East and West. The recycling of petrofunds, the requirements of arms production, and the vulnerability of the
Western economies to conditions in Africa and the Middle
East are all factors that spring from the logic of the
Western system itself.

The Cold War provides a set of ideological re-
flexes through which the dominant classes of the Western
countries (and also by a parallel, although somewhat
different, process, those of the Communist bloc) can
justify the pursuit of their interests in the Third World.
It clearly suits them to explain the current economic
recession to their electorates in terms not of failures

in their own economic policies, for which they would be held responsible, but of oil and insecurity in the Middle East. In the same manner, it is easier to justify the increasing Western military presence east and south of Suez, not as a reply to the upsurge of legitimate nationalist feeling against Western economic and political control, but as a response to the Soviet threat.

Of course, this does not mean that the greater military activity of the socialist countries in Africa and the Middle East is entirely a figment of capitalist imagination. From the mid-1950s the USSR has played a major part in accelerating the transfer of arms to both regions, following the breakdown of colonial and neocolonial security arrangements. It was the largest supplier of arms to the Middle East for much of the 1960s and (according to the arms trade statistics) is currently the largest supplier to Africa. The socialist military presence in the latter region was more significant in the latter half of the 1970s than at any time in the past, involving not only the transfer of arms, but also the use of Soviet and Cuban personnel in military support roles, especially in Angola and Ethiopia.

The great bulk of Soviet arms transfers have been to countries whose ruling classes could at the time of the transfer be regarded as "progressive," or "socialist": to Egypt, Iraq, and Syria in the Middle East and to Libya, Algeria, Somalia, Ethiopia, Angola, and Mozambique in Africa. It is clear that the USSR and its military bureaucracy have powerful vested interests in the Cold War. And arms sales, although not a necessity of production in the same way as in the West, are clearly sustained by the Soviet version of the arms economy.

Nevertheless, the Cold War rhetoric of the West has undoubtedly exaggerated the importance of the socialist countries' military activity in the Third World. The growth of Soviet military ties with Africa must be considered in relation to the United States's relatively more favorable position in the Middle East. Furthermore, the role of the European members of NATO in both regions tends to be understated in published arms transfer statistics. France's weapons transfers to Africa in the 1970s were comparable to those of the Soviet Union, at least until the latter years of the decade. In both the Middle East and Africa, the combined arms exports of the members of NATO remain considerably larger than those of the socialist bloc.

Moreover, the ability of the socialist countries to control events is too readily exaggerated. They have won considerable support in Africa as a result of their assistance to the frontline states and liberation movements. Yet the revolutions in Southern Africa, Ethiopia, Chad, and the Western Sahara were homemade, arising out of the contradictions created by colonialism and underdevelopment. To be sure, in Angola Soviet and Cuban advisers and equipment have been crucial for the survival of the revolution, but they were needed in the first place only because of the joint Central Intelligence Agency (CIA)-South African destabilization and invasion of 1975-1976.

Rivalries within the socialist camp have made socialist assistance less effective than it might other-wise have been. For instance, such rivalries resulted in the Soviets' providing weapons and instruction to the Zimbabwe Independence People's Revolutionary Army (ZIPRA) rather than the Zimbabwe African National Liberation Army (ZANLA); this has contributed to the coolness of Mugabe's government toward the Soviet Union after in-dependence. It was Somalia's intransigence in invading the Ogaden against Soviet advice--not the USSR's "expansionism"--that ultimately induced the latter to provide Ethiopia with arms and military assistance in the Ogaden and Eritrea. In Ethiopia, as in Afghanistan, the Soviets have been pulled deeper and deeper into murderous and costly conflicts, which surely harm their interests as much as they advance them.

Socialist arms transfers have sharpened regional arms races (as in the Horn of Africa) by virtue simply of the fact that more weapons are on the market, these weapons being less easily controlled by any one dominant supplier. By the same token, however, they have widened the options of the purchasers and made it easier for them to pursue policies independent of or opposed to Western interests. The sole exceptions have been among the more conservative Francophone states and in the Arab Emirates, the ruling classes of which have depended on Western military support for their very existence.

Despite this pluralization of the sources of military power at the continental level, there has been a clear tendency for the supply of weapons to individual coun-tries to become polarized, to a much greater extent than international trade or development assistance. All but a few countries in either region obtained the major pro-portion of their weapons (i.e., more than three-quarters) from within a single bloc, roughly a third of them from a single supplier. Nevertheless, such figures tend to overstate the polarization between the superpowers and to understate the heterogeneity of national military markets. Because they are based on five-year aggregates (over the period 1973-1977), they conceal the facts that a significant minority of countries (notably Egypt, Ethiopia, Somalia, and Iran) have broken with previously dominant suppliers too recently to have had much effect on the figures and that a number of other countries like Libya, Iraq, and Guinea are deliberately setting out to diversify their sources of military supply.

Further, there is no necessary correspondence be-tween a country's weapons and its politics. Few of the recipients of socialist arms (probably only Afghanistan, Democratic Yemen, and, less certainly, Ethiopia) can be said to have become client members of the socialist bloc itself. Of the remainder, the majority (but by no means all) pursue socialist or state-capitalist development paths, but more as a result of their national needs and circumstances than of any external pressure. There is no doubt that Soviet, Czechoslovakian, Cuban, or Chinese weapons have made it easier to chart a course of economic and political independence from the West. But most recipients of socialist weapons (including the more radical members of OPEC) remain firmly tied to the international economy. Indeed, one may argue that they present a much less serious threat to regional security or to the functioning of capitalism than some of the West's own less stable client regimes--such as that of the late shah of Iran or the current governments of Morocco, Egypt, and Zaire.

PETROFUNDS AND REGIONAL SECURITY

There may be a perverse rationality in the way the countries of the industrial North recycle petrofunds and maintain their own uncertain hegemony by selling arma-ments. But this certainly does not sufficiently explain why the ruling classes of oil-surplus states should spend their petrofunds on weapons, still less why those oil-deficit countries should do so, as they represent real opportunities foregone in terms of both consumption and development.

Weapons are no ordinary commodity traded in the market. They are simultaneously a special form of capital and a claim to power, not creating values, but rather enabling those who control organized force to appropriate values. They embody the assumptions that for a quantity of money one can buy a stock of military hard-ware with a known capacity related in a measurable way to military power; the greater the investment in military capital, the greater the power of those who control it, relative to other investors in weapons.

Such assumptions are seldom tested, and when they are the evidence is far from conclusive. There are situations in which the sheer quantity of military fire-power may be decisive, and there are others in which it most definitely is not. The disintegration of the shah of Iran's large military machine during the Iranian revolution, the collapse of General Idi Amin's army before the Tanzanian forces in 1979, despite hardware supplied by the USSR and Libya, and the failure of capital-intensive methods of warfare against the popular revolutions in former Portuguese Africa, Chad, Zimbabwe, and the Western Sahara are instances of the latter.

Nevertheless, countries that acquire large inven-tories of weapons clearly are seldom restrained by such thoughts. One of the main reasons is that in a world of arms races and military balances, armaments continue to be an internationally recognized claim to power, having become part of the ideology through which power is allocated in the international system.

Petrofunds are invested in weapons in order to acquire the right to participate in major decisions about international security to which the OPEC countries feel their economic resources entitle them. For the Arab members of OPEC there is the added incentive that they believe such an investment would also increase their ability to compel a just solution to the problem of Palestine.

In their pursuit of military power, however, the OPEC countries face two major obstacles. First, the superpowers have a monopoly of nuclear weapons, which protects their claim to a privileged position in world politics. These powers have maintained a sharp distinction between conventional weapons--whose transfer to the Third World they have permitted and indeed encouraged--and nuclear weapons, whose transfer has been prevented by an entire superstructure of international controls, organized around the Non-Proliferation Treaty and, in addition, guarded directly by the powers themselves.

Despite the real dangers of nuclear proliferation, it has become ever harder for the powers to make their monopoly seem legitimate, the more so because the existing safeguards do not set limits to their own nuclear armories. The nuclear balance of terror and the quantitative arms limitation organized around it, such as the SALT agreements, have served only to accelerate qualitative innovation in the methods of destruction. Further, they have increased nonnuclear competition between the powers, including the expansion in their conventional forces and the transfer of weapons to the Third World.

Hence, there are real incentives for Third World countries to go nuclear, especially in Africa and the Middle East, because the only countries thus far to obtain technology of a kind that would bring nuclear weapons within their grasp are Israel and South Africa. Some OPEC countries have already established their own facilities for the peaceful production of nuclear energy, and others are in the process of so doing. There have been several reports of individual countries, such as Libya, clandestinely seeking to obtain their own nuclear weapons. None of the black African countries have yet gone nuclear. Nigeria, however, is to acquire nuclear technology for peaceful purposes; its policy-makers are openly canvassing their desire for nuclear weapons.

The second obstacle that impedes the transformation of OPEC weapons into internationally valid claims for power is the fact that they have to be acquired in the international arms market, for the most part from the major powers themselves. That Israel and South Africa are the only significant arms producers in the two regions adds still greater force to the arguments for local arms production.

However, the difficulties of such production, including the shortage of technical skills, the lack of horizontal linkages with civilian industry, and the narrowness of markets, are formidable. The establishment of the AOI in 1975 as a joint venture of Egypt, Saudi Arabia, Qatar, and the United Arab Emirates (UAE) was the only systematic attempt to overcome such difficulties. The oil surpluses of the three latter countries would have been used to manufacture weapons in Egypt, although such manufacture would have been confined almost exclusively to production under license of NATO weapons (including, for instance, the Franco-German Alphajet, versions of the Mirage, British Swingfire antitank missiles, Westland helicopters, and American Motors jeeps). However, the project has been virtually abandoned because of the fissures between the Arab countries opened up by the Israel-Egypt peace treaty. The only other country to have attempted to build a weapons industry of its own was Iran, where the shah's government embarked on coproduction ventures with a number of U.S. defense contractors--for example, with Bell Helicopters to produce helicopter gunships to equip an army aviation force modeled on that of the United States in Vietnam--all of which have been abandoned.

Even if arms manufacture were to be organized on a significant scale, it would face several drawbacks. Studies of Third World arms production suggest that it has had little effect on the cost of weapons (sometimes actually increasing it); that dependence on the major arms suppliers (for licenses, technology, and parts) has not been much diminished; that relatively few countries have acquired the capacity to carry out R&D and design their own weapons; and that the "spinoff" effects on civilian industrialization are limited by the specialized nature and high import content of much military production.[8]

Hence, the thrust of petromilitary expansion is still toward acquiring larger numbers of complex conventional armaments from external suppliers. The costs of these weapons have continued to rise, and their destructiveness has become such that the threshold between nuclear and conventional weapons has been disappearing, thus loosening the constraints against the transfer of nuclear weapons. It is conceivable that the oil-surplus countries may eventually advance their claims to participate in major decisions about international security through the sheer accumulation of firepower, although their economic bargaining power is much more likely to improve their international position.

The main effects, however, of the accumulation of

armaments have been on the distribution of regional,
rather than global, military power. Distinct quantitative and qualitative differences have begun to emerge
between the militarily better-equipped states and their
less well-armed neighbors. Estimates ranking the countries of Africa and the Middle East in terms of a very
crude index of armament, based on the sophistication of
equipment and the size of armed forces, should be treated
with great caution, as it is impossible to give all the
dimensions of military force their correct weight.
Moreover, such estimates embody the ideology of the
military balance criticized earlier, that the accumulation of weapons corresponds to true military strength,
notwithstanding the many examples to the contrary.

Nevertheless, there are differences within each
region that cannot be ignored--between those states like
Iran, Egypt, Israel, or South Africa that possess all or
nearly all the technological elements of modern conventional military power, thus being equipped for a sub-
imperial role; those able to operate at a regional level
and to wage conventional war against their neighbors;
those equipped purely for the defense of national fron-
tiers and internal security; and those that are militarily peripheral, with small armies and few, if any,
sophisticated weapons.

Such differences correlate with variations in
military spending. Yet the association is by no means
perfect, because, among other reasons, the weapons
acquisition of some countries--such as Somalia, Ethiopia,
or the two Yemens--has been heavily subsidized by major
powers and that of others--such as Egypt, Jordan, or
North Yemen--by their oil-producing neighbors.

One result of these differences is that the more
powerful countries are increasingly capable of playing a
military role in the affairs of their neighbors. There
have been several recent instances, some but by no means
all petrofunded: for example, the participation (before
the revolution) of Iran in "counterinsurgency" in its
smaller neighbors in the Gulf; the annexation of former
Spanish Sahara by Morocco and Mauritania and their war
against Polisario; the use of Libyan petrodollars to
fund liberation movements throughout Africa and the
Middle East and to finance military ventures in Uganda
and Chad; Tanzania's participation in the overthrow of
Amin in Uganda; and proxy intervention by Morocco,
Senegal, and other Francophone countries on behalf of the
Western powers in Zaire in 1978.

In each region, however, there have occurred major
arms buildups (in Palestine, Southern Africa, and the
Horn) in which the main oil exporters have not been the
direct protagonists. To be sure, OPEC countries have
funded arms purchases by Arab confrontation states and
revolutionary movements (and to a lesser extent the
liberation movements in the Horn and Southern Africa).

Yet they have given this assistance in a context in which the major powers have contributed still more heavily to the military buildup. To overemphasize the importance of any single factor like petrofunds is to run the risk of becoming parti pris, in that it would be hard to propose unilateral reduction in the petrofunding of the confrontation states and liberation movements without seeming to take sides.

The same is perhaps not true of the warfare between Iraq and Iran in the early 1980s. Petroleum has financed the stockpiling (and now destruction) of weapons by both countries. Oil fields and transport routes have been at stake. Nevertheless, the problems at issue had previously been negotiable, having been to all appearances settled by the agreement of 1975 as a result of the arbitration of OPEC itself. The agreement was undermined by two major new developments. First, the Iranian revolution posed a major new threat to the state structures and ruling classes of the neighboring Gulf and Arab states, regardless of whether they were theoretically under conservative or (like Iraq) socialist regimes. Second, the current international conjuncture of confrontation between the major powers in the Gulf has created a climate of insecurity in the region (even though it is unlikely that either power directly instigated the Iraqi invasion).

Security in such a dynamically evolving context as the present-day Middle East and Africa cannot be conceived abstractly. It must be judged in terms of substantive criteria--such as disengagement from rivalries between the powers, the removal of international obstacles impeding development, and the resolution of the basic injustices (like those in Palestine and South Africa) that are the origin of conflict in the first place. A case can be made that petrofunds have positively contributed to security in the latter sense, not so much by adding to the armed strength of the OPEC countries as by reinforcing their economic bargaining power and that of the various Third World coalitions to which they belong.

This does not, however, detract from the argument that the sheer accumulation of weapons may not be the most efficient way of ensuring regional security or of bringing the struggles in Palestine and South Africa to a successful and just conclusion. There is no doubt that a number of Arab and African governments have used the conflicts occurring in their regions to legitimize military spending programs, which in reality have had relatively little relevance to their security. Moreover, the benefits of armament have seldom been measured against its costs in terms of external dependence on international suppliers and of their effect on the economic and political structures of the purchasers.

In principle, African and Arab countries would be

better able to afford such costs if they could provide
for their security jointly. In practice, both international and regional imperialism have prevented such
cooperation. The breakdown of Arab plans for joint
weapons production (the contribution of which to regional
security was in any case uncertain) has already been
mentioned. The proposals put forward at the United
Nations for a "Zone of Peace" in the Indian Ocean have
become a dead letter, not least because of decisions by
certain states in the region to permit the establishment
of foreign military facilities and bases. Likewise,
none of the proposals to create an African peacekeeping
force has been successful. Of the two practical efforts
to put such a force into operation, one (the OAU peacekeeping force in Chad) failed because of lack of finance
and interest from OAU member states; the other (the
inter-African force that "kept peace" in the Shaba
Province of Zaire after the 1978 rebellion) was in
effect a proxy force for the West. [9]

ARMAMENTS, STATE POWER, AND DEVELOPMENT

As I have already argued, the military effectiveness of weapons bears only a tenuous relationship to
their cost and complexity. Although their accumulation
supports claims to international status, such claims are
of uncertain validity, being undermined by dependence
on the international suppliers. Why then do governments
and ruling classes continue to accumulate them? A major
reason is that weapons are closely associated with the
way force is monopolized, hence state power appropriated.
Most items of military capital are too complex and expensive for revolutionaries--still less, ordinary citizens--
to acquire. Normally, only governments have the international contacts and the financial resources to acquire
armored cars, tanks, aircraft, and missile systems from
the international arms market and the facilities (maintenance installations, airfields, etc.) to make use of
them.
To be sure, there are advanced technologies, such
as antitank guided weapons, that revolutionary forces
have acquired and used to good effect, but usually only
after becoming well enough established to constitute an
alternative state and thus to secure their international
supply lines (like the Front for the Liberation of
Mozambique [FRELIMO] in the last stages of the war of
independence in Mozambique, the Eritrean People's
Liberation Front [EPLF] and the Eritrean Liberation
Front [ELF] in Eritrea, ZANLA or ZIPRA in Zimbabwe,
or the Polisario Front in the Western Sahara). Even so,
it has been the ability of such revolutionary movements
to create alternative ways of organizing military force
and of mobilizing political loyalties that has ultimately
determined their success or failure.

In contrast, however, governments invest in capital-intensive forms of force, organized and controlled through hierarchies of military command. Although the accumulation of weapons is almost invariably justified in terms of defense against external enemies, such weapons are often used for internal security or even outright repression. A substantial (and increasing) proportion of the trade in arms is in "counterinsurgency" weapons specifically adapted for this purpose. Yet one cannot make a hard and fast distinction between the technology of repression and conventional weapons. The latter are often used for internal security, like the Chieftain tanks that patrolled the streets during the shah's vain attempts to crush the Iranian revolution, the aircraft and missiles used to bombard villages in Eritrea and the Western Sahara, or the armored cars that until recently kept the roads open and the black population in terror in Zimbabwe.

The technology of repression is not necessarily used by the military alone (which often indeed keeps aloof from day-to-day policing), but also by the police and paramilitary forces. And its supply is sometimes tied into a broader cooperation between the military, security, and intelligence services of supplier and recipient, such as that which existed between SAVAK (the Iranian secret police) and the CIA; that which is maintained between the French security agencies and Francophone African governments; and that which (no doubt) the Soviet military, secret police (KGB), and the security apparatuses provide in countries such as Ethiopia or Democratic Yemen.

There are several countries in the two regions in which there has been little or no overt military repression; and many in which governments have care-fully avoided becoming incorporated in the security net-work of their arms suppliers. Nevertheless, all without exception are upheld by some kind of permanent organized force, based upon an imported technology of violence. At any one time in the 1970s almost half the self-governing African countries and one-third of their Middle Eastern neighbors were under military rule. Many others are or have been under regimes--some absolute monarchies, others one-party states, and others personal dictatorships--every bit as reliant on force as govern-ments formally controlled by the military. The most frequent instrument of political transition has been the coup, whether carried out to mediate between civilian factions, to install the military in power, or to redistribute power within the armed forces themselves. It is only in the Anglophone countries of West Africa (Nigeria and Sierra Leone--and Ghana, for only one and a half years) that the military has transferred power back to civilians; it is too early to judge whether the new civilian regimes will overcome the previous legacy of instability and violence. It would be seriously misleading, however, to analyze organized force purely as an aspect of the consolidation of military or, more broadly, bureaucratic-authoritarian regimes. For such force must be "produced" by employing a labor force of soldiers and by acquiring military capital goods. This in turn generates financial costs and backward linkages to the country's system of production or (insofar as it does not produce its own military goods) to the international division of labor.

The financial costs of the weapons supplied to Africa and the Middle East are difficult to determine because arms transfer statistics are based on estimates of the value of weapons transferred and not on what the importing country actually paid for them, which can vary greatly in accordance with the political and financial arrangements between supplier and recipient. The economic opportunity costs are still harder to measure. The value (and probably financial cost) of weapons transferred and the level of military spending are currently much greater relative to foreign trade, government spending, and the gross domestic product in the Middle East than in Africa. Yet it is clear that the opportunity costs of weapons in very poor countries, such as Upper Volta or Niger, where they are a relatively small fraction of imports, of total government spending, and of GNP, may in reality be much higher than in an oil-surplus country like Kuwait or the UAE, which spends a much higher percent of its foreign earnings, government revenues, and domestic product on its armory.

Statistical studies of the relationship between military spending and aggregate indicators of growth have not been conclusive. An early study by Benoit found that a positive relationship exists between levels of military spending and nonmilitary rates of economic growth in a sample of developing countries.[10]

More recent studies have failed to confirm this relationship, but neither do they provide conclusive support for the alternative hypothesis of a negative connection between military expenditure and growth. This lack of conclusiveness arises partly from the technical problems of statistical analysis. But it is also indicative of more fundamental theoretical limitations.

The major determinants of both military spending and nonmilitary accumulation in most developing countries are external. Hence, they are not adequately analyzed in studies comparing countries in isolation. Military expenditures are to a large extent influenced by the recycling of international earnings and of international power relations in the ways analyzed earlier in this chapter. Further, the accumulation of military goods can be sustained over the long run only by increasing

international earnings and thus tends to be associated
with strategies of development that seek to improve such
earnings and to reinforce class structures embedded within the existing international division of labor.

Also, in the absence of strong backward linkages
with the rest of the economy, military spending can
affect growth only to the extent that organized force
plays a role in the process of accumulation itself.
Many strategies of development make use of the coercive
power of the state: whether to break strikes and keep
wages low on behalf of capital, to hold down peasant
unrest resulting from low world commodity prices, or
(at the other end of the political spectrum) to expro-
priate existing propertied interests and carry out land
reform. Presumably, the burden of military expenditure
itself (if it is not met by reducing investments, hence
growth) must also fall on consumption and require
mechanisms for passing the cost on to the ordinary worker
or peasant. Thus the role of the military in development can scarcely be separated from the general role of
the state, military force being but one of the mechanisms
through which the state mobilizes resources and engineers
consent.

Finally, force--like all other modalities of state
intervention--cannot be class-neutral. It is used by
specific ruling classes or coalitions of classes to
impose the costs of development on other classes or
groups. Thus it is misleading to generalize about the
military and development without distinguishing between
societies with different histories, varying relationships
to the international economy, different production
structures, and contrasting configurations of class
conflict. In all modern societies, to be sure, there
is a general tendency to consolidate the repressive
power of the state, a tendency that can be observed even
after popular revolution. But what economic and social
functions state power and its weapons technology fulfill
cannot be analyzed without making much better qualitative
differentiations.

The following classification is only a first step,
based on two very crude distinctions. First, there are
the countries in which the surpluses earned from the
international economy have increased, and those in which
they have stagnated or decreased. This distinction
corresponds very approximately to the division between
OPEC and non-OPEC countries, despite considerable differences in foreign earnings and development constraints
within each of these two groups. In the latter, military
expenditure has higher opportunity costs relative to
foregone investment or consumption. Thus conflict
around the distribution of resources between classes,
regions, and ethnic groups tends to be all the more
acute.

Second, some broad distinctions can be made in

relation to the classes or class coalitions that have
effective control of a country's surplus-creating productive resources, including metropolitan capital,
coalitions between foreign capital and local bourgeoisies
or "auxiliary-bourgeoisies," coalitions between foreign
capital and local rentier classes, and finally, classes
that owe their control of productive resources directly
to the power of the state.

Such distinctions are static and somewhat arbitrary.
Nevertheless, they serve to establish a point, namely
that organized force can have a variety of very different
functions. It may be used to sustain a direct neocolonial relationship based on unequal exchange with a
former colonial power, as in some countries in former
French Africa; to cement alliances between local and
Western capital, as in Kenya, the Ivory Coast, or
Morocco; to support the use of petrofunds to create and
enrich a local bourgeoisie, as in Nigeria; to back crude
exploitation by military-based cliques, as in Amin's
Uganda or Bokassa's Central Africa; to guard a natural-
resource-based rentier class like that of Saudi Arabia
and protect its privileged relations with the industrial
countries that supply its arms and consume its raw
materials; to guarantee control by a state bourgeoisie
like that of Libya or Iraq over a process of accumulation
that nevertheless remains based on production for world
markets; to help garrison socialists (as in Ethiopia) or
revolutionary parties (as in South Yemen) to enforce
socialist transformation from above; or to assist in a
process of economic transformation that depends (as in
Mozambique) more on popular consent than on organized
coercion by the state.

These categories overlap in several areas. Zaire,
for instance, shares some of the features of both dependent and booty capitalism. The Ivory Coast has several
characteristics of dependent capitalism, but it has been
more successful in expanding its international earnings
than many other countries in the same category. The
ruling class of Iran before the revolution was clearly
more than simply a group of rentiers, although it
remains difficult to call it a bourgeoisie. The qualifi-
cations one could make are endless because the class
structures of the countries in question are far from
homogeneous and adequate analysis would require detailed
investigation of individual cases.

Moreover, there are certain characteristics that
most African and Middle Eastern states have in common,
and that should not be overlooked even when insisting on
qualitative distinctions between them. First, there is
the cardinal role played by the state in the allocation
of resources, even in countries where the state does not
directly own and control them. It is through the state
that members of local bourgeois or rentier classes
obtain access to the resources that they accumulate or

consume. And it is because of the pivotal role of the
organized force in determining who gains access to resources through the state and on what terms they do so
that the military has played such an important role in
politics in all the political systems with which we are
concerned. There are garrison socialists like the
current Ethiopian regime, as well as garrison capitalists;
military regimes in both oil-surplus and oil-deficit
countries; and some military establishments using state
power to transform the economy, others using it for
private appropriation or outright plunder.

Furthermore, the state has always played an important role in mediating relations with the international
economy, whether in a neocolonial framework or in one in
which local ruling classes claim a larger share in internationally earned surpluses. The extremely heterogeneous
Third World coalitions in the Group of 77 and in the Non-
Aligned Movement could be established because the ruling
classes concerned regarded their countries as system-
atically disadvantaged in the international division of
labor and hence could see the need for coordinated state
action at the international level. The almost equally
heterogeneous group contained within OPEC is held together by a similar perception that the rents that accrue
to them from oil can be safeguarded only by international
cooperation between member states.

The fact that state power helps determine who
appropriates surpluses within the international economy
and how they are appropriated is one major reason why
the ruling classes of OPEC (and of other African and
Middle Eastern countries) have accumulated military
capital, this being the mirror image of the industrial
North's attempts to recycle its control of world resources through the sale of arms, alliances with Third
World ruling classes, and military intervention. Conversely, military expansion has itself tended to
encourage militancy within OPEC in order to obtain the
surpluses with which further to expand the state and
its military machine--especially so in the countries
whose known reserves are small relative to their military
and industrial programs.

Yet the structural similarities that create the
basis for such broad alliances among Third World ruling
classes should not allow one to forget the differences--
differences (like that between the oil-surplus and oil-
deficit countries) that may affect the ability to
establish lasting agreement about how production, wealth,
and resources should be redistributed. Still more
important is to remember the differences that determine
how and by whom the benefits obtained from any compact or
bargain with the countries of the industrial North might
be shared--whether they are widely spread or appropriated
by dominant states, classes, and groups and whether this
distribution is achieved by development or under-

development as the consequence.

NOTES

1. Ali A. Mazrui, The Barrel of Oil and the Barrel of the Gun in the North-South Equation (New York: World Order Models Project Working Paper, 1979).

2. U.S., Congress, House of Representatives, Committee on International Relations, U.S. Arms Policies in the Persian Gulf and Red Sea Areas, Committee Print, 95th Congress, 1st Session, December 1977.

3. For a comprehensive exposition of the rationale behind the doctrine, see G. J. Pauker et al., "In Search of Self-Reliance: US Security Assistance to the Third World Under the Nixon Administration" (mimeo).

4. See Library of Congress, Congressional Research Service, Implications of President Carter's Conventional Arms Transfer Policy, 77-223F UA15 US, September 1977. There is a cogent analysis of the wide gap between promise and performance in Robert C. Johansen, Jimmy Carter's National Security Policy: A World Order Critique (New York: World Order Models Project Working Paper, 1980).

5. This chapter was sent to the editor before the war broke out. The damage to the international economy has been much less than it might have been had the war resulted in closing the Straits of Hormuz.

6. See P. Lellouche and D. Moisi, "French Policy in Africa: A Lonely Battle Against Destabilisation," International Security, Vol. 3, No. 4 (Spring 1979).

7. See U.S., Congress, House of Representatives, Committee on International Relations, The Soviet Union and the Third World: A Watershed in Great Power Policy? Committee Print, 95th Congress, 1st Session, 1977.

8. For a (somewhat dated) inventory of indigenous arms production by the developing countries and a discussion of some of its problems, see P. Lock and H. Wulf, "Register of Arms Production in Developing Countries" (mimeo), Hamburg Study Group on Armaments and Underdevelopment, 1977.

9. The peacekeeping force in Chad failed also because the confused political situation in Chad made it impossible to establish how and on behalf of whom such a force should intervene. Of the countries that agreed to participate in the force--Guinea, Benin, and the Congo Republic--only the latter sent troops, which it has now withdrawn. Algeria also provided logistical support for the force.

10. Emile Benoit, Defense and Economic Growth in Developing Countries (Lexington, Mass.: Lexington Books, 1973). One major attempt to reexamine these relationships is an ongoing study by R. Smith at Birkbeck College, University of London, for the United Nations.

Part 2

Natural Resources,
Oil Bills, and Patterns of Trade

4
Resources, Scarcity, and Development Priorities in Sub-Saharan Africa

Suleiman I. Kiggundu

A full picture of the resource base of sub-Saharan Africa would ideally require us to make an inventory of all natural and manmade resources. Natural resources would refer to "a concentration of naturally occurring solid, liquid, or gaseous material on the earth's crust."[1] If these command a positive price we refer to them as economic resources. But if they occur in abundance, like common water and air, and have a zero price, then they are grouped among the noneconomic resources. Generally, economic natural resources would include all land, forests, fisheries, animals, labor, water, and mineral resources. On the other hand, manmade resources are production inputs like capital equipment and raw materials, manmade forests and waters, labor skills, technology, and land improvements.

This second category of manmade resources is particularly difficult to inventory. Thus it is difficult to define the resource potential of any area of the world because technology and research and development can work miracles on natural resources. To avoid these problems this chapter will concentrate on analyzing the natural resource base of sub-Saharan Africa with only a few remarks suggesting the potential for its improvement. Within the limits of available data, the extent to which these natural resources have been exploited will be presented. Lack of manmade resources will be found in many cases to be the crucial bottleneck in the full utilization of natural resources. It would be useful to identify which of these resources constitute "economic reserves," that portion of the resource that can be economically and legally utilized under present economic, technological, and legal circumstances. The determination of reserves would require extensive studies on a national and a continental scale. Such studies should ideally follow a rough mapping of the type undertaken in this study and should be done on a country, sectoral, industrial, and project basis. Indeed, this will be the next phase when it comes to tightening African-Arab-OECD cooperation, when the partners in the game choose to act for economic or noneconomic imperatives. This chapter is divided into three main parts: First I present the natural resource base and discuss how and to what extent it has been utilized so far in the production process. Land resources are discussed in terms of how they are utilized in the production of food and nonfood crops and in livestock production. Then the forestry, fisheries, water, and mineral resource areas are discussed with respect to the wood industry's output, fishing, hydroelectric and other kinds of power production, and mineral exploitation. The focus is on existing and potential local and external markets. Next, I discuss the development priorities and identify the major constraints on the full utilization of the available resources. Finally, I suggest the possible areas and forms that African-Arab-OECD cooperation should aim at under the prevailing circumstances.

NATURAL RESOURCES

Land Resources

It is important to know the quantity and quality of the land resource base in order to judge the adequacy of its utilization and to determine its potential usefulness. Knowing the vegetation and the ecology of the land resources helps us understand the nature and potential of agricultural and livestock production. Soil texture and depth determine nutrient availability and water storage capacity of the land resource. Rainfall, humidity, and air movements are the primary factors of climate that influence vegetation, plant growth, and livestock production.
Africa's land area of about 3 billion hectares comprises arable land, permanent meadows and pastures, and forest and desert areas. Looking at the present performance and the future of agricultural activities in Africa south of the Sahara, as well as its forest production and industry potential, raises a number of questions. How much usable or arable land does Africa have as a percentage of such land in the world in general and in the developing world in particular? How much of it is already being utilized for crop production, livestock, and forestry? What should be the nature of the trade-off between these activities? What should be done to increase the utilization and productivity of this land area and how much capital investment is required for this purpose? What other constraints--including land tenure systems--impede better performance? Would it be better to use the already utilized areas more intensively than to adopt the extensive approach?[2]
It is estimated that only about 638 million hectares are potentially arable; 842 million hectares are permanent meadows and pastures; 800 million hectares are

forest areas; the rest is desert and semidesert.
Table 4.1 gives an estimate of the arable land for ninety
developing countries by region. Africa has about 30 percent and 20 percent of the total arable land in the
developing world and the whole world, respectively. On
the other hand, Table 4.2 gives total potential arable
land per capita for the different regions. Table 4.2
clearly shows that the land/man ratio for Africa is not
nearly as desperate as it is in the Near East and the Far
East; there is still a lot of room for commercial agriculture, both for increased domestic consumption and for
export. Given appropriate investments in food production,
Africa could be the granary of the desert Arab world,
supplying it with bananas, wheat, rice, barley, oats,
pineapples, beans, potatoes, onions, tomatoes, tea,
coffee, sugar, green vegetables such as cabbage, legumes,
eggplant, and other food crops. As Table 4.3 shows, at
present the Arab countries import about 90 percent of
their food requirements from Europe, Australia, New
Zealand, Indonesia, Latin America, and South Africa. The
extent of food dependence and the need for food security
arrangements is illuminated by the fact that today
eighteen Arab countries are food-deficit; Sudan and
Somalia are the only exceptions. Estimates of future
demand for food commodities in Arab countries show a big
import dependency. This is particularly true of oil-
exporting countries, such as UAE, Bahrain, Saudi Arabia,
Kuwait, Oman, Qatar, and Libya, that have very poor
agricultural resources.

Livestock Production

Turning to livestock production (which includes
cattle, camels, sheep, goats, pigs, and chickens), we
again find that Africa has substantial potential. This
potential transcends the meadows and pastures as an
ecological zone and includes other zones with varied
problems of use, including limited water in wet- and dry-
season grazing areas, fire and pests, soils, and en-
croachment of bush. In expanding grazing areas we
should worry not only about the required capital investment for economic development of water, elimination of
hazards of fire, overgrazing, and disease, and pest
control (such as of tsetse fly), but we should worry also
about the trade-off that exists between livestock production and other land uses that are important welfare
and revenue sources. These include food and cash crops,
wildlife--which gives rise to the vital tourist industry
and to game hunting--and the forestry industry, which can
be increased with manmade forests.
The determination of the extent to which livestock
land resources are utilized would require information on
livestock populations and production systems, as well as
a detailed description of the breeds of animals reared.

TABLE 4.1
LAND RESOURCE POTENTIAL IN DEVELOPING REGIONS (million hectares)

Region	Total mill. ha.	Good rainfall mill. ha.	%	Low rainfall mill. ha.	%	Problem areas mill. ha.	%	Naturally flooded areas mill. ha.	%	Desert[2] mill. ha.	%	Suitable for irrigation[3] mill. ha.
90 Developing countries	1774	580	33	219	12	646	36	300	17	29	1.7	394
Africa	638	244	38	61	10	288	45	44	7	1	0.2	115
Far East	354	82	23	82	23	101	29	74	21	15	4.3	181
Latin America	653	204	31	30	5	241	37	173	27	6	0.8	55
Near East	130	51	39	46	35	16	12	10	8	8	6.2	43
Low income countries	689	208	30	143	21	247	36	75	11	16	2.3	265

[1]The land and water classes are defined using suitability classes from the FAO Agro-Ecological Study. The four suitability classes--very suitable, suitable, marginally suitable and not suitable--are related to the anticipated yield as a percentage of the maximum attainable under optimum agro-climatic and soil conditions; thus yields on some marginally suitable lands may be as low as 10 percent of the optimum. They are as follows:

Good rainfall land: land with rainfall providing for 120-270 growing days, soil quality very suitable or suitable.

Low rainfall land: rainfall providing 75-120 growing days, soil quality very suitable, suitable or marginally suitable.

Problem areas: rainfall provides more than 270 days growing season; soils of all usable qualities in this zone, plus that part of the 120-270 growing day zone where soil rating is only marginally suitable.

Naturally flooded land: lands under water for part of the year and low land non-irrigated paddy-fields.

Irrigated, consisting of: Fully irrigated land--equipped with irrigation and suitable drainage and not suffering from water shortages. Partially irrigated land--equipped for irrigation but lacking drainage or reliable water supplies or with low quality and reliability of distribution.

[2]Desert lands under irrigation.

[3]Area already under irrigation (partially or fully equipped) plus area suitable for irrigation in the future. It is already included in the previous columns.

Source: Food and Agriculture Organization, Agriculture: Toward 2000 (Rome, 1979).

TABLE 4.2
TOTAL POTENTIAL ARABLE LAND PER CAPUT OF TOTAL POPULATION (hectares)

Region	Arable land used per caput			Potential arable land per caput		
	1980	1990	2000	1980	1990	2000
90 Developing countries	0.33	0.29	0.26	0.79	0.62	0.50
Africa	0.55	0.46	0.38	1.71	1.27	0.95
Far East	0.21	0.18	0.16	0.28	0.22	0.19
Latin America	0.52	0.50	0.48	1.79	1.38	1.09
Near East	0.39	0.31	0.25	0.60	0.45	0.36
Low income countries	0.29	0.25	0.22	0.61	0.49	0.40

Source: Food and Agriculture Organization, Agriculture: Toward 2000 (Rome, 1979).

Such information would tell us to what extent the area's carrying capacity is being utilized and to what extent the introduction of exotic breeds for herd improvement is possible within the limits of the adequacy of nutritional, health, and farm management standards.   This information is, however, difficult to come by on a country level, let alone a continental level, because of poor statistical records and inadequate studies.   In the absence of this information a good proxy for land utilization is live-stock output, which includes meat, milk, skins, and wool. Some of these, especially meat and milk, are not captured in reported statistics as they often do not enter the monetary market economy in many parts of Africa.   This is particularly truer for goats and sheep than for cattle.
     Table 4.4 gives the gross value of Africa's live-stock production and compares it with that of other developing regions.   Table 4.5 gives Africa's production structure in the livestock industry and its share in the total output of ninety developing countries studied by the Food and Agriculture Organization (FAO).
     Most livestock production, but especially of sheep and goats, takes place under traditional systems (small ruminant production).   Under this system, the animals are in poor condition; their product output is low be-cause they have to adapt and survive in hostile environ-ments.   Obviously such improvements as the introduction of exotic breeds and the development of ranches (private, group, cooperative, and parastatal) in the ecological zones should improve productivity of indigenous animals a great deal.   Improved quality of the products and the dependability of the supply source are two factors vital to export trade.   This export potential is particularly promising in sheep and goat meat production.   Already

TABLE 4.3
OPEC MEMBERS: STRUCTURE OF IMPORTS--PERCENTAGE SHARES BY ORIGIN AND BY MAJOR COMMODITY GROUPS, 1973

Origin/commodity groups	World	Developed market economy countries[a]	Developing countries and territories			Socialist countries of E. Europe		Socialist countries of Asia	Developing countries and territories by major region				
			Total	OPEC	Other	Total	USSR		America		AFRICA	Asia	
									Total	LAFTA		West Asia	South & S.E. Asia
						Values (in $ Million)							
All products	20,150	16,260	2,640	245	2,395	1,100	520	155	520	480	320	610	1,170
						Percentage shares by origin							
All products	100.0	80.7	13.1	1.2	11.9	5.5	2.6	0.8	2.6	2.4	1.6	3.0	5.8
All food items (SITC 0+1+22+4)	100.0	65.2	30.1	1.0	29.1	3.6	0.5	1.1	9.6	8.7	6.9	4.7	8.8
Agricultural raw materials (SITC 2-22-27-28)	100.0	63.4	22.1	4.3	17.8	11.2	6.4	1.9	4.1	3.9	6.2	3.9	8.1
Ores and metals (SITC 27+28+67+68)	100.0	84.7	10.5	0.2	10.3	4.8	2.1	0.4	1.0	0.9	0.8	1.5	5.8
Fuels (SITC 3)	100.0	48.2	44.5	15.0	29.6	7.9	1.4	--	26.4	24.3	1.1	12.5	3.9
Manufactured goods (SITC 5 to 8 less 67+68)	100.0	84.5	9.6	1.1	8.5	5.2	2.3	0.8	1.0	1.0	0.6	2.8	5.4
						Percentage shares by major commodity groups							
All food items (SITC 0+1+22+4)	13.4	10.8	30.7	11.4	32.7	8.7	2.7	18.7	50.0	49.0	58.4	20.8	20.3
Agricultural raw materials (SITC 2-22-27-28)	2.4	1.9	4.1	8.6	3.6	4.9	6.0	5.8	3.8	4.0	9.4	3.1	3.3

80

	U.S.	Canada	Japan	Total	Total	EEC	New EEC	Old EFTA	EFTA	U.K.	Other	Australia and New Zealand	South Africa
Ores and metals (SITC 27+28+67+68)	10.2	10.7	8.1	1.6	8.8	9.0	8.3	5.8	3.8	3.8	5.0	4.9	10.1
Fuels (SITC 3)	1.4	0.8	4.7	17.1	3.5	2.0	0.8	--	14.2	14.2	0.9	5.7	0.9
Manufactured goods (SITC 5 to 9 less 67+68)	69.9	73.2	51.0	60.4	50.1	66.0	62.7	68.4	27.1	29.0	25.3	63.9	65.1

a Developed market-economy countries by major area

Western Europe / Industrial countries

	U.S.	Canada	Japan	Total	Total	EEC	New EEC	Old EFTA	EFTA	U.K.	Other	Australia and New Zealand	South Africa
(values in $ million)	3600	270	2720	9300	8840	8030	6300	820	2540	1610	460	290	37
Percentage shares by origin													
	17.9	1.3	13.5	46.2	43.9	39.9	31.3	4.1	12.6	8.0	2.3	1.4	0.2
	26.2	2.2	2.6	29.5	26.9	25.9	19.8	1.3	7.1	4.2	2.6	4.1	--
	19.6	2.9	9.9	25.8	22.5	12.6	10.5	9.9	12.0	1.7	3.3	5.0	--
	8.1	1.4	31.5	41.7	39.5	38.3	34.1	1.2	5.4	4.2	2.2	1.5	--
	6.8	--	3.2	37.5	36.1	35.4	27.1	0.7	8.9	8.2	1.4	0.4	--
	16.4	1.2	13.8	52.0	49.8	45.0	34.6	4.8	15.1	9.8	2.2	0.8	--
Percentage shares by major commodity groups													
	19.6	21.9	2.6	8.6	8.2	8.7	8.5	4.1	7.6	7.1	15.2	37.9	--
	2.6	5.2	1.8	1.3	1.2	0.8	0.8	5.9	2.3	0.5	3.5	8.3	--
	4.6	10.7	23.7	9.2	9.1	9.8	11.1	3.0	4.4	5.3	10.0	10.7	--
	0.5	--	0.3	1.1	1.1	1.2	1.2	0.2	1.0	1.4	0.9	0.3	--
	64.0	60.4	71.2	78.7	79.3	78.9	77.4	82.3	83.9	85.5	67.6	40.7	--

Source: United Nations Conference on Trade and Development, Handbook of International Trade and Development Statistics (Geneva, 1976).

TABLE 4.4
GROSS VALUE OF LIVESTOCK PRODUCTION ('000 MILLION $)

Regions	1963	1975	1980	1990	2000
90 Developing countries	37.5	52.4	60.0	95.3	151
Africa	4.6	5.9	6.6	10.6	18.1
Far East	11.2	15.3	17.3	26.7	44.1
Latin America	17.3	25.0	28.8	45.8	68.5
Near East	4.4	6.2	7.2	12.1	19.9
Low income countries	11.6	14.6	16.5	23.9	37.9

Source: Food and Agriculture Organization, Agriculture: Toward 2000 (Rome, 1979).

Africa contains more than one-quarter of the world's goats and one-tenth of its sheep; Africa's breeds have high fertility as a result of their year-round breeding season. In this connection the countries of the Sahel, Somalia, Sudan, and Ethiopia, among others, should be given particular attention.[3]

Forestry Resources

As already indicated, the forests in Africa cover about 800 million hectares, which is about 20 percent of the total forest area of the world. Forests are a source of roundwood on which a number of wood industries depend, including sawmilling, pulp and paper, charcoal, fuel wood, industrial roundwood (saw logs and veneer logs, poles, pit props, and pulp wood), sawn wood, and wood-based panels. A number of secondary industries depend on wood products, including joinery and furniture workshops, boat making, fencing, and electricity and telephone services. Depending on demand availability for wood and wood products, the forest area of Africa can be extended by developing manmade forests including the most desired species like tropical hardwoods. The wood-rich areas are mainly in West and Central Africa--in Liberia, Ivory Coast, Ghana, Nigeria, Cameroon, Gabon, Congo, the Central African Republic, Zaire, and Angola--and a bit of Eastern Africa, including Uganda, Tanzania, Zimbabwe, and Swaziland, with potential in the Kenya highlands. Identification of markets, normalization of supply, and solution to the transport problem are factors that have to be carefully explored when designing production for export markets to complement local demand, which is still very low.

TABLE 4.5
LIVESTOCK PRODUCTION IN AFRICA AND IN NINETY DEVELOPING
COUNTRIES FOR 1980

	Numbers in the herds	Production
Cattle and buffalo meat		
Africa	132[a]	1,732[b]
90 developing countries	852[a]	12,583[b]
Cattle and buffalo milk		
Africa	18.2[c]	6.0[d]
90 developing countries	132.4[c]	84.4[d]
Sheep and goat meat		
Africa	222.8[e]	747[b]
90 developing countries	791.5[e]	3,037[b]
Pig meat		
Africa	6.3[f]	235[b]
90 developing countries	138.1[f]	4,232[b]
Poultry meat		
Africa	489[g]	600[b]
90 developing countries	2,416[g]	4,480[b]
Eggs		
Africa	241[h]	582[b]
90 developing countries	918[h]	4,900[b]

[a] '000 of million animals   [e] '000 of animals
[b] '000 tons   [f] Million animals
[c] Millions of animals milked   [g] Million birds
[d] Million tons   [h] Million laying hens

Source: Compiled from Food and Agriculture Organization,
Agriculture: Toward 2000 (Rome, 1979).

Fishery Resources

No comprehensive stock assessment, to my knowledge,
has yet been undertaken on the level of harvestable
fisheries resources of Africa. Fisheries resources include oceans and inland lakes and rivers. [4] A study on
fish and fish products in the Economic Community of West

African States (ECOWAS) subregion estimates that fishery
resources of the region are producing 4.5 million metric
tons per year: 3.5 million metric tons from the marine
resources alone and 1 to 1.5 million metric tons from the
inland waters. The types of fish available include,
among others, tilapia, Nile perch, demersal species such
as grouper and sea bream, pelagic species such as sar-
dines, horse market, tuna, and shrimps. This figure is
an underestimate because apparently about 2 million tonnes
of fish are taken out of the region by foreign vessels,
and a substantial amount either does not go through the
market or is not reported for a variety of reasons.[5]
    Given modern fishing capabilities, which are
currently lacking in the region, a much higher catch
could be realized--especially with better storage
facilities, surveillance and monitoring of the activities
of foreign vessels acting under license, and better credit
facilities for the fishing industry. If we add to the
above estimate the fishery resources from East, Central,
and Southern Africa, Africa south of the Sahara seems to
have a good potential for fish and fish products for
internal consumption and export. The export market
would require developing facilities for tinned fish,
frozen fish, smoked or dried fish, and stockfish that
could be exported in substantial quantities.

Water and Other Energy Resources

    Although the availability of water in Africa per unit
area is the lowest in the world, because of the Sahara
Desert, the Kalahari Desert, and the arid and semiarid
areas in almost all parts of the continent, Africa south
of the Sahara has a great wealth and abundance of water
resources. The Nile is the longest river in the world;
the Congo River is the second largest in the world after
the Amazon; Lake Victoria is the second largest fresh-
water lake in the world (after Lake Superior); Lake
Tanganyika is the second deepest lake in the world (after
Lake Baikal in the USSR). There are also the lake
systems in the Rift Valley and several inland lake basins
like those of Lake Chad, Lake Rudolf, and many others in
Africa south of the Sahara. A complete inventory of all
rivers and lakes of the region indicates that the total
surface water of Africa is about 2,481 billion cubic
meters. It is not possible, with present knowledge,
to estimate quantitatively Africa's groundwater resources. It is, however, generally known that groundwater resources exist in almost all parts of the region.
    Measures for the full utilization and development
of water resources--for agriculture, industry, hydropower generation, community water supplies, wastewater
disposal, and inland water transport--are still needed,
as the present levels of utilization are far from
exhausting the potential.

Apart from water, there are other energy resources that play a vital role in industrial transportation and general economic development. These include renewable and nonrenewable resources. Among the nonrenewable resources (NRER) are coal and lignite, oil shales, tar sands, crude oil, natural gas, uranium, and thorium. The new and renewable energy resources include hydropower, geothermal power, solar energy, wind power, biomass, and ocean energy resources. Africa possesses these in reasonable quantities. Table 4.6 gives the resource and production levels of some of the nonrenewable energy resources of Africa.

African coal constitutes about 3 percent of the world total and is widely distributed in Africa. African production of crude oil from the ten producing countries of Algeria, Angola, Congo, Egypt, Gabon, Libya, Morocco, Nigeria, Tunisia, and Zaire was 700,000 metric tons per day on the average in 1975, which was about 10 percent of the world daily production. New producers include Benin, Cameroon, and Ghana, and there are good prospects in Chad, Ivory Coast, Ethiopia, Niger, Senegal, and Sudan. Proven reserves of oil in Africa were 11.9 billion metric tons in 1978, which was then about 7 percent of total world reserves. The African share of reserves of natural gas, uranium, and thorium is approximately 6 percent, 33 percent and 6 percent, respectively, of the world total. Natural gas reserves were estimated at 5,919 billion cubic meters in 1978--from Algeria, Libya, Egypt, Tunisia, Nigeria, Angola, Congo, Zaire, Mozambique,

TABLE 4.6
RESOURCES AND PRODUCTION LEVELS OF SOME NRER OF AFRICA

Resource	Resource level	Production level
1. Coal, lignite and brown coal (million metric tons)	--	93.8 (1978)
2. Crude oil (million metric tons)	9,232 (1976)	285.6 (1978)
3. Natural gas (billion cubic meters)	5,919 (1978)	15 (1977)
4. Uranium (thousand metric tons)	523.8 (1978)	8.305 (1977)
5. Thorium (metric tons)	306,000 (1977)	--

Source: Compiled from United Nations Economic Commission for Africa Energy Resource Unit, "Traditional and Renewable Sources of Energy in Africa," 1979.

Tanzania, Ethiopia, and Sudan. Uranium, on the other
hand, exists with reasonable abundance in Niger, Gabon,
Somalia, Algeria, Namibia, Central African Republic,
South Africa, and Zaire, and thorium resources in Africa
are to be found in Egypt, Liberia, and South Africa.
The other nonrenewable resources of Africa are tar
sands and oil shales. Tar sands are sands impregnated
with a heavy viscous oil, from which oil can be produced
economically, given the present technology and the current
prices of petroleum and its products. Tar sands are
already known to exist in Gabon, Ghana, Ivory Coast,
Madagascar, and Nigeria. Oil shales--sedimentary lami-
nated rock containing kerogen--are used primarily as raw
material for producing liquid fuels. These oil shales
are found in Zaire, South Africa, Madagascar, Egypt,
Gabon, Mali, Morocco, Niger, Somalia, Tanzania, Tunisia,
Uganda, and Zambia. More concrete estimates are yet to
be made, although present knowledge indicates that Zaire
has 15 billion tonnes of reserves, South Africa 19
million tonnes, and Madagascar 4 million tonnes. Since
oil shale extraction is now generally economic given the
prices of crude oil, more discoveries and concrete
estimates are necessary.

New and Renewable Energy Resources

Hydropower. Africa's hydropower potential is
enormous, of the order of 200 million megawatts--about
35 percent of the hydroelectric capacity yet to be
harnessed in the world. This potential is concentrated
in the equatorial zone in large waterways such as the
Senegal, Niger, Konkouré, Cavally, Comoe, and Volta
rivers in West Africa; the Senage, Ayong, Dgeone,
Cuanza, Cunene, and Zaire rivers and tributaries in
Central Africa; the Zambezi, Pangani, Shire, and Ruzizi
rivers in Eastern Africa; the Limpopo and Orange rivers
in Southern Africa; and finally the Nile River in the
center of Northeastern Africa. The share of African
countries in this potential is Zaire, 530 billion kwh per
year; Angola, 230; Madagascar, 144; Cameroon, 100;
Tanzania, 75; Kenya, 30; Sudan, 50; Gabon, 48;
Mozambique, 45; and Ethiopia, 45. Installed capacity
represents only about 6 percent of the potential hydropower projects. The principal producers of hydroenergy
in Africa are Egypt, Zambia, Zimbabwe, Ghana, Zaire,
Nigeria, Cameroon, and Morocco, which together account
for about 70 percent of total output.

Geothermal. Geothermal power derives from the heat
stored in the earth by volcanoes and hot water and hot
streams filling the natural underground reservoirs. No
estimates of Africa's geothermal potential are available,
but exploration work is under way in Ethiopia, Kenya,
Djibouti, Tanzania, and Uganda. Potential is known to

exist also in Algeria, Cameroon, Central African
Republic, Chad, Malawi, Somalia, and Zaire.

Solar, wind, and biomass energy resources. These
are other sources of energy that could be developed with
adequate research and technology. Solar energy derives
from solar radiation that reaches the earth's surface.
It could be used directly as heat, and in some regions of
the world it is already used competitively as an alternative source to other fuels and electricity. Wind,
especially in the windy areas on the oceans, coasts,
plains, and mountainsides, can also be used as a source
of energy for water pumping, irrigation, and low-power
windmills. Biomass residues and wastes, on the other
hand, can be used to produce electricity, steam, liquid
fuels for transportation, low and intermediate gas,
synthetic natural gas, and other energy-intensive
materials such as petrochemical substitutes and fertilizers. Biomass residues include agricultural manures and
crop and forest residues. Wastes include garbage,
sewage, and manufacturing by-products. These are available in different parts of Africa; with adequate conversion technology and systems they could be a significant source of energy.

Fuelwood, charcoal, and ocean energy resources.
Fuelwood and charcoal are the major sources of energy for
more than 90 percent of the African population residing
in the rural areas. This energy resource can be inferred from the section treating Africa's forestry
resources, although undesirable effects of deforestation
on the soil, water table, and general climate characteristics make it inadvisable to depend too heavily on this
resource in the future. Besides, other vital uses for
forest products must be considered.
    Among other energy resources yet to be determined
for Africa are ocean thermal gradient conversion, wave
energy, and tidal energy.

Mineral Resources

    The determination of mineral resource availability
is a very expensive operation in terms of capital, manpower, and technology. Hitherto the picture we have had
of Africa's mineral resource endowments has been based
largely on the exploration efforts of multinational
corporations. However, systematic exploration has not
been undertaken, as multinational exploration ventures
have been only in response to world mineral demand. Much
of Africa's mineral potential may therefore have been
ignored, overlooked, or not reported because the present
world demand is either low or easily satisfied by other
than African sources. It is thus not surprising to find
that literature on African mineral exploration by foreign

concerns frequently describes resources as indications, prospects, or occurrences to be further explored in the future, "when the foreign investor so desires."

A full picture of Africa's mineral resource base, therefore, awaits exploration by African governments and institutions with an entirely different exploration objective. Even on the basis of existing information Africa has a substantial resource base. Mineral resources can be divided into six major groups based on their use and their physical and chemical features. These are (1) energy minerals, including coal, petroleum, natural gas, and uranium; (2) ferrometals, which are used mainly in the iron and steel industries; (3) base metals; (4) industrial minerals and rocks (sand, gravel, salt, clay, limestone, etc.); (5) precious metals; and (6) chemical minerals. Tables 4.7 through 4.11 give the world mineral resource and production by region. (Energy minerals are not shown.) From these tables we can see that Africa has 96 percent of total world chromite, 80 percent of phosphates, 58 percent of gold, 50 percent of manganese, 40 percent of vermiculite, and 32 percent of cobalt. However, this should not lead to an inflated estimate of Africa's mineral resource wealth, because Africa is not very rich in those energy minerals that have the most economic importance. Table 4.12 shows the relative importance of the various raw materials in the mineral world.

It is important to note that both exploration and exploitation expenditures for most mineral commodities run into tens of millions of dollars. Exploration alone is a very risky capital investment, as the probability of discovering viable mineral deposits is small. Indeed the international corporations are able to venture exploration because they have the necessary capital, skills, and technological resources and are in a position to spread their risks, given their worldwide operations. But even so, as mentioned before, large areas of the earth's crust, and particularly of Africa, remain unexplored.

Production levels fall below the resource availability for a number of reasons. First, the state of world demand may not permit exploitation. Unfortunately for Africa, local demand for its minerals is very low; it has to depend mainly on the demand and supply conditions of the developed countries. Second, after the size, grade, and amenability to recovery of a mineral deposit have been determined, various aspects of economic viability have to be assessed before it can be produced. The state of the world market and the financing situation must be studied, and it must be determined whether the necessary infrastructure for production can be obtained, including power and water supply; railroad and port facilities for incoming supplies and the outgoing product; availability of exporting ships; and the development of

TABLE 4.7
AFRICA'S FERROMETAL RESOURCES AND PRODUCTION AS A PERCENTAGE OF THE WORLD TOTAL

	Mineral/Source							
	Manganese (1975)[a]	Nickel (1975)[b]	Iron (1977)[c]	Titanium (1977)[a]	Tungsten (1977)[d]	Molybdenum (1977)[d]	Cobalt [e]	Chromite (1976)[f]
Total Africa resource	1,807,100	9,000	8,000	11[c]	53[g]	100[g]	1,534,700	1,124,860[h]
Total Africa production	4,250	53	38.2	--	1,690	--	--	1,491.5
Total Europe production	3,480	216	204.8	402	24,600	21,400	--	1,758.5
Total North America production	150	287	79.6	569	10,100	158,673	--	--
Total South America production	894	--	81.5	5	10,800	25,271	--	10
Total Asia production	1,157	36	72.8	132	37,200	562	--	440.7
Total Oceania production	879	229	66.1	400	4,265	25	--	--
Total World production	10,810	898	543.0	1,508	88,700	205,931	--	3,700
Africa as a percentage of world production	39.3%	5.9%	6.0%	6.1%	1.9%	--	--	40.3%
Total Africa as a percentage of world resources	50.2%	5.1%	3.7%		0.4%	0.23%	32.3%	95.6%

[a] Thousand tons.
[b] Thousand tons.
[c] Million short tons.
[d] Thousand pounds.
[e] Tonnes.
[f] Thousand tonnes.
[g] Million pounds.
[h] High chromium thousand metric tons.

Source: U.S. Bureau of Mines, Mineral Facts and Problems, Bulletin No. 667.

TABLE 4.8
AFRICA'S BASE METAL RESOURCES AND PRODUCTION AS A PERCENTAGE
OF THE WORLD TOTAL

	Copper (mine) 1976 (thousand short tons)	Lead (mine) 1976	Zinc (mine) 1977	Tin 1977 (thousand metric tons)
Total Africa production	1,820	155	280	--
Total Europe production	280	1,296	2,200	--
Total North America production	3,120	1,135	2,090	--
Total South America production	1,380	400	680	--
Total Asia production	590	397	840	--
Total Oceania production	480	439	530	--
Total world production	9,140*	3,704	6,620	--
Africa as a percentage of world production	20%	4.2%	4.2%	--
Total Africa resource	190 (million short tons)	24 (million short tons)	24 (million short tons)	3,700 (thousand metric tons)
Total Africa as a percentage of world resources	7.7%	7.9%	7.5%	10%

*Includes production of centrally planned economies, which is 1,700
thousand short tons.

Source: U.S. Bureau of Mines, Mineral Facts and Problems,
Bulletin No. 667.

townships with housing, schools, and shops to meet the
economic and social needs of the workers. The infrastructural development itself, like the exploration
stage, may take up to a decade. International companies
may not be ready yet to sink large investments just for
the sake of deposits that may not be big enough to
justify such an investment. They may thus deliberately
wait for the country itself to lay down most of that
infrastructure. The Kilembe copper mine in Uganda, which
called for the initial construction of the railroad line

TABLE 4.9
AFRICA'S INDUSTRIAL MINERAL RESOURCES AND PRODUCTION AS A
PERCENTAGE OF THE WORLD TOTAL

	Silicon 1977	Asbestos 1975 (thousand	Cement 1977 short tons)	Vermiculite 1977
Total Africa production	120	384	26.8	250
Total Europe production	1,241	2,293	428.0	--
Total North America production	635	1,239	111.6	--
Total South America production	64	73	41.4	--
Total Asia production	424	251	229.8	--
Total Oceania production	12	40	6.7	--
Total world production	2,496	4,280	844.3	629
Africa as a percentage of world production	5%	9%	3.2%	40%
Total Africa resource	--	36 (million short tons)	--	Large
Total Africa as a percentage of world resources	--	13.8%	--	--

Source: U.S. Bureau of Mines, Mineral Facts and Problems,
Bulletin No. 667.

and the construction of the Jinja Dam, and the infrastructural requirements for the exploitation of Swazi
iron ore and bauxite in Cameroon, prove the point.
     The level of mineral processing and fabrication is
virtually nil in Africa, and yet this is the stage that
is most profitable and creates the most jobs. This low
level is due partly to lack of skills, capital, and
technology, but more important, local demand for the
minerals for industrial use and final consumption is
depressingly low. Yet our society is dependent on
minerals, and meaningful economic development relies
heavily on them. For example, building materials include sand, gravel, stone, clay, steel, aluminum,
asphalt, and glass; plumbing and wiring materials include iron and steel, copper, brass, lead, cement,
asbestos, glass, tile, and plastic; insulating materials

TABLE 4.10
AFRICA'S PRECIOUS METAL RESOURCES AND PRODUCTION AS A
PERCENTAGE OF THE WORLD TOTAL

	Gold 1977 (thousand Troy ounces)	Silver (mine) 1977
Total Africa production	23,717	13
Total Europe production	8,494	78
Total North America production	3,461	135
Total South America production	712	55
Total Asia production	1,169	17
Total Oceania production	1,413	27
Total World production	38,966	325
Africa as a percentage of world production	60.6%	4%
Total Africa resource	1,100 (million Troy ounces)	200
Total Africa as a percentage of world resources	57.8%	0.9%

Source: U.S. Bureau of Mines, Mineral Facts and Problems,
Bulletin No. 667.

include rock wool, fiberglass, and gypsum (plaster and
wall board); wallpaper materials include mineral pigments,
such as iron, zinc, titanium, talc, and asbestos; plastic
floor tiles and other plastics include talc, asbestos,
pigments, and petroleum products; appliances include
iron, copper, and many rare metals; clothing includes
natural fiber grown with mineral fertilizers. Food, too,
is grown with mineral fertilizers and processed and
packaged by machines made of metals; furniture requires
synthetic fibers and steel bearings; drugs and cosmetics
require mineral chemicals; other items, such as windows,
screens, light bulbs, porcelain fixtures, china, utensils,
and jewelry, are all made from mineral products. It is
easy to go on listing the various uses of minerals. The
point I wish to emphasize is that Africa, alone or in

TABLE 4.11
AFRICA'S CHEMICAL MINERAL RESOURCES AND PRODUCTION AS A
PERCENTAGE OF THE WORLD TOTAL

	Phosphates 1973 (thousand short tons)	Sulphur 1973 (thousand long tons)	Sodium Soda Ash 1973 (thousand short tons)	Potash 1973 (thousand short tons)
Total Africa production	30,259	600	274	350
Total Europe production	23,542	18,650	12,758	15,848
Total North America production	42,316	20,450	7,888	7,035
Total South America production	364	300	176	28
Total Asia production	8,192	5,700	2,202	912
Total Oceania production	3,387	300	--	--
Total World production	108,060	46,000	23,298	24,173
Africa as a percentage of world production	27%	1.3%	1.2%	1.5%
Total Africa resource	66,800 (million short tons)	20 (million long tons)	168 (million short tons)	115 (million short tons)
Total Africa as a percentage of world resources	79.6%	1%	0.4%	0.18%

Source: U.S. Bureau of Mines, Mineral Facts and Problems, Bulletin No. 667.

cooperation with the oil-rich countries, must aim at increased mineral processing and fabrication to meet local
industrial product needs, for which local industries must
be created. The processing industries may have formed
linkages for such industries or such industries may have
backward linkages for mineral processing.

DEVELOPMENT PRIORITIES AND MAJOR CONSTRAINTS

As I showed in the previous section, Africa south of
the Sahara is not poor in minerals and arable land,
forestry and fishery resources, and animal and energy
resources. Yet the level of poverty and underdevelopment

TABLE 4.12
RELATIVE ECONOMIC IMPORTANCE OF VARIOUS RAW MATERIALS BY VALUE
OF PRODUCTION AS PART OF TOTAL WORLD MINERAL PRODUCTION (1976)

Energy minerals	86.7 percent
Oil	56.7
Natural gas and condensate	10.8
Brown coal	18.3
Lignite	1.6
Uranium	0.3
Metallic minerals	9.8 percent
Iron ore	3.3
Copper ore	2.3
Gold	1.2
Nickel ore	0.6
Zinc ore	0.6
Tin ore	0.4
Lead ore	0.3
Platinum	0.2
Bauxite	0.2
Other metallic ores (Manganese, Chrome, Ferroalloys, etc.)	0.7
Industrial minerals	3.5 percent
Phosphate	0.7
Potash	0.5
Sulphur	0.5
Salt	0.5
Asbestos	0.4
Diamonds	0.3
Other nonmetallic ores (including building materials)	0.8

Source: France, Ministry of Industries, "Les chiffres des oles
matières penceres minerals--1979."

in Africa is still very depressing. By any development
indicator, ranging from income per capita, literacy rate,
human skills, health standards, nutritional standards,
housing, to infrastructural development, Africa remains
very poor. The average per capita income (generally a
good proxy for development) for Africa (excluding oil-
exporting countries) was $166 in 1978; twenty of the
world's thirty-one least developed countries are in
Africa. These figures indicate that Africa occupies the
worst position in the worldwide struggle against underdevelopment.

A good summary of Africa's development objectives
is contained in the Monrovia Strategy and Declaration of
Commitment on the guidelines and measures for national
and collective self-reliance in social and economic

development for the establishment of the New International Economic Order (NIEO), adopted by the OAU in July 1979.[6] The aim of the guidelines is to improve the standards of living of the mass of the people by providing for basic human needs and reducing mass unemployment. The principal feature of the plan to achieve these goals is contained in "The Plan for Action," recommended by the conference of ministers of economic development in April 1980 and summarized here.

The plan recognizes that Africa must pay equal attention to the two leading production sectors--agriculture and industry--because of their interdependence. In essence it recommends the "balanced approach" to development. The industrial structure should be designed to supply inputs for agricultural production, processing, storage, and transportation apart from final consumption output. These inputs include agricultural chemicals, implements and tools, building materials, food processing and storage equipment, and transport equipment. The food and agriculture program should provide inputs into processing industries as well as markets for the industrial outputs. The industrial program should go further to produce building materials, metal and engineering products, and chemicals for transport and communications, mining, energy, and the other sectors. The target is to lessen dependence on imports, achieve self-sufficiency, and create surpluses in food, animal products, industrial products, forest products, and energy through fuller utilization of Africa's natural resources. The plan recommends that particular attention be paid to strategic mineral resources that are essential for establishing basic industries that make intermediate products such as iron and steel, aluminum, base metals, petrochemical products, fertilizers, and cement.

It will not be enough to expand and improve agriculture through irrigation, extended and intensified rainfed agriculture, increased use of fertilizers, and appropriate mechanical power on farms if adequate agricultural output handling, marketing, and storage arrangements and transport facilities are not increased pari passu. Currently it is reported that although Africa is still experiencing large deficits in food trade, about 40 to 50 percent of the food produced in African countries is wasted because they lack these facilities.

Major Constraints on African Development

The major constraints on the development and full utilization of natural resources as specified in "The Plan for Action" for Africa and confirmed by national plans and policy pronouncements of African governments can be inferred from a general development framework. They include the following variables: capital stock, including plant and machinery, manmade raw material

inputs and financial capital; labor stock, including un-
skilled and skilled labor, managerial labor, and
entrepreneurship; natural resources; technology; social
and institutional parameters, including government
stability and management, land tenure systems, infrastructural development, private and public corporations,
and financial institutions; and the nature of external
contact, that is, how the country relates to the rest of
the world in trade, capital, technology skilled manpower,
and other resource flows.

It can be shown that Africa is not well endowed
with most of the above development variables, and it is
lack of these that constrains full utilization of its
natural resource potential. For example, The Regional
Food Plan for Africa states that "among the reasons for
the slow growth of production of most food commodities
have been insufficient expansion of cultivated area,
slow growth of yields and inadequate spread of improved
technology, recurring droughts, parasite problems, lack
of infrastructural facilities, and social and political
constraints."[7] Studies in livestock production indicate
that this subsector needs to undergo even more radical
changes than crop production. These would include
changes in the composition of livestock, the methods of
production, livestock production's links to crop production, and the technology used. Although production
will continue to be based primarily on grasslands, feeds
in the form of roughages, concentrates, feed grains, and
crop by-products have to be increased substantially.
And in addition to increasing productivity of grazing
lands by changes in technology and through fertilization
and reseeding with more productive species, there is a
need for better animal husbandry through expansion of
veterinary services and medicines.[8] With respect to
fuller utilization of fishery resources, it has already
been pointed out that it will require better fishing
technology, better storage facilities, better marketing
information, increased local processing activities, and
improved transport and communication facilities. The
same goes for the forestry and wood industries, for
which domestic processing of wood before export, better
marketing institutions, and transport facilities are
recommended. Planting new and less common wood species
to meet market demand with normalized supply is also
recommended. Development of secondary wood industries
and complementary industries is also crucial.

From the above it is clear that for better performance in the above sectors, a lot of capital investment, professional and management skills and technology,
and changes in institutional structures will be
necessary. When we introduce the requirements for
fuller utilization of mineral resources and the development of the industrial structure envisaged in the
development target, the need for these resources

(capital, labor, technology, infrastructure, external
relations) becomes even more critical. As I have already pointed out, mineral resource exploration and
development is a multimillion dollar exercise, with very
heavy risks and a long gestation period--possibly running
into more than a decade before returns can be realized.
The plant and machinery requirements, the financial
capital, and the skilled manpower and technology required
for mineral and industrial development and marketing of
the products are needs that Africa just cannot afford to
meet at present by mobilizing domestic resources alone.
It has to look elsewhere for financial aid and investment,
real resource aid and investment, and technical assistance. I will discuss this subject in the following
section.

SUGGESTIONS AND CONCLUSION

The foregoing analysis clearly indicates that
Africa badly needs outside cooperation in order to
develop its vast resources and to implement its development strategy in the 1980s and beyond. Its present
domestic financial resources, skills, manpower development, and technological capacity can hardly suffice.
Although no estimates and specifications are given in
this study of the capital investment requirements, the
management and technical skills, and the type of
technology that would be required, nobody doubts that
sub-Saharan Africa is short of all of these. Beyond the
above constraints, which outsiders can help to alleviate,
there are a variety of institutional bottlenecks that
African countries must resolve on their own. These include the instability of governments in Africa, the
insecurity of business property due to unnecessary
government intervention, and the lack of land reform,
respect for law and order, and international codes.
The traditional outside sources of funds for
African economic development are the Western countries,
private Western investors, and international agencies.
The increasing financial power of the oil-rich Arab
countries, which began to challenge the Western world
in the 1970s, creates another viable source of financing
that Africans must look to. These countries now have
huge financial reserves in Western financial institutions
(private and official) as well as their own national and
multilateral financial institutions engaged in aiding
and lending for economic and social development. Sub-
Saharan Africa must redirect itself and turn away from
hammering the old argument that its underdevelopment is
a direct consequence of many centuries of colonialism
and domination under which both its population and raw
materials were ruthlessly exploited.
Realistically, in this and in coming decades, Africa

must expect the cooperation of others only if it is
mutually beneficial. The proposed Afro-Arab-OECD cooperation is based on the expectation that all three parties
stand to gain from it.

Direct Rechanneling of Investment Capital

From the point of view of investment capital, both
Africa and the Arab countries stand to gain, other things
being equal, from a direct rechanneling of large financial reserves rather than going through Western financial
intermediaries. The Arab countries would get higher
rates of return, both pecuniary and nonpecuniary, and
could invest in ventures in which they gain some ownership rights. Africa, on the other hand, could borrow at
lower or no interest rates, as in the case of the Islamic
Development Bank. The repayment periods allowed on Arab
loans extend to seventeen years and more. In addition,
Arab loans are neither tied to procurement nor given in
a package deal including equipment, technology, and
management personnel, as is the case with most official
and private loans from the Western countries. Such requirements raise the cost of borrowing very considerably.
Africa would then have the option of purchasing equipment, technology, and management from the cheapest and
most appropriate sources.

Cooperation in Industry and Mineral Development

In this connection, too, Africa would be in a
position to get funds for certain industries, like the
iron and steel industry, that Western sources may be
reluctant to finance. For example, it is reported that
Western sources fear that steel production in the
least developed countries (LDCs) threatens the captains
of industry in the West and Japan because of overcapacity
in the industry. Development of such industries in LDCs
would take place on the basis of modern and more
efficient technology; not only would it encroach on
Western markets, where the industry is established, but
it could also eat into other markets that could have
been supplied by Western sources through export. For
this reason, steel companies and unions in the United
States are pressuring Congress to stop financing this
overcapitalized industry. For a number of industries,
the Arab countries could import African mineral resources
or finance processing activities in Africa as a way of
establishing alternative inputs for their industry.
Through careful studies, complementary industrial development between Africa and the OAPEC could be achieved.
Even if the former course is adopted, Africa would at
least gain through diversifying export markets. The
latter would mean greater leverage by OAPEC countries
on growth and employment in Africa, but greater initial

political and economic stability in Africa would be
necessary before the OAPEC could have trust and confidence to invest heavy sums of money on a long-range basis.

Cooperation in Food and Livestock Products

Cooperation between Africa and the oil-rich Arab
countries has more potential in the field of food and
livestock production. The Arab countries import most of
their food and livestock products from the developed
countries. Given sufficient investment in agriculture,
Africa could meet its own food requirements as well as
become the granary of the Arab world and supply it with
livestock and livestock products. This cooperation might
be in the form of joint ventures, direct Arab investments,
or trade agreements. These arrangements might call for
prior cooperation in establishment of transport and
communication links, import-export financing arrangements, bilateral and multilateral payments, and clearing
arrangements between the two groups of countries.

The Importance of OECD Countries in the Cooperation

What Africa and the Arab countries lack most is
managerial and technical skills and technology. Even if
they want labor-intensive (appropriate) technology to
produce certain commodities, they still have to look to
OECD countries for the necessary research and development. Hence the case for including OECD countries in the
cooperation. It would be simplistic to imagine that if
given money, OECD countries would be prepared to develop
and sell all kinds of technology, unless they were part
and parcel of the venture in one way or another. The
product cycle theory of international trade tells us that
at certain stages of product development, companies are
more willing to operate as international monopolies
supplying all markets than to sell their technological
and managerial know-how to someone else. Thus it is
necessary to identify the types of industries for which
OECD countries, for a price, are willing to supply
technology and managerial skills.

NOTES

1. Economic Commission for Africa (ECA), "Mineral Resources
Perspectives," Geological Survey Professional Paper 940, Addis
Ababa, 1975.
2. Frank D. Abercombe, Range Development and Management in
Africa (Washington, D.C.: United States Agency for International
Development, 1974).
3. International Livestock Center for Africa, Bulletin
(Nairobi), March 1980.
4. There are estimates of ocean fish resources. Because these
involve common waters, it is difficult to know how much of these

stocks should be assigned to which continent. Estimates for total catch of marine fish for 1977 are 23.5 million tons, 28.9 million tons, 3.8 million tons and 1.1 million tons for the Atlantic Ocean, the Pacific Ocean, the Indian Ocean, and the Mediterranean Sea, respectively. As for inland fisheries, there are only isolated studies, which do not give a complete picture.

    5. Joint Economic Commission for Africa/Food and Agriculture Organization Division, Cooperation and Trade in Fish and Fish Products in ECOWAS Sub-Region (Addis Ababa: Economic Commission for Africa, 1976).

    6. Economic Commission for Africa, Plan of Action for the Implementation of the Monrovian Strategy for the Economic Development of Africa (Addis Ababa, 1979).

    7. Food and Agriculture Organization, Regional Food Plan for Africa (Rome, ARC/78/5, July 1978).

    8. Food and Agriculture Organization, Agriculture: Toward 2000 (Rome, C/79/24, July 1979).

BIBLIOGRAPHY

Economic Commission for Africa, Problems of Water Resource Development in Africa, Addis Ababa, E/CN. 14/NRD/WR/1 Rev. 1, 21 October 1976.
___, Survey of Economic Conditions for Africa, Addis Ababa, 1979.
Economic Commission for Africa/Food and Agriculture Organization, Forest Industries Advisory Group for Africa, Trends and Potential of Wood-Based Panel Industries in Africa, Addis Ababa, January 1975.
Economic Commission for Africa/Food and Agriculture Organization, Agricultural Division, Cooperation and Trade in Forestry and Forest Products in the ECOWAS Sub-Region, Addis Ababa, November 1979.
International Livestock Centre for Africa (ILCA), Bulletin (Nairobi), September and December 1978, March, June, September, and December 1979.
___, "Livestock Development Projects in Africa South of the Sahara," Nairobi, draft paper, 1979.
Mining Journal, Annual Review of Mining, London, 1979.
United Nations Conference on Trade and Development, Handbook of International Trade and Development Statistics, Geneva, 1976.
U.S. Bureau of Mines Bulletins, Mineral Facts and Problems, Washington, D.C., 1978-1979.
Vharf, E., "The Wood Charcoal Industry in Africa," Memorandum for the Food and Agriculture Organization, Rome, AFC/76/10, January 1976.

5
Africa, the Energy Crisis, and the Triangular Relationship

Ernest J. Wilson III

RESOURCES FOR THE FUTURE

The original source of our contemporary concern with African-Arab-OECD relations is the sudden oil shock of 1973, which radically changed the old international regime of oil production, pricing, and distribution, and which transferred enormous sums of liquid assets from oil-importer to oil-exporter nations. The international context in which this event occurred was that of a cyclical downturn in the world capitalist economy. It may be instructive to reexamine this original source of our interest as we look ahead to consider African-Arab-OECD relations for the decade of the 1980s.

The critical period between 1973 and 1975 has proved to be a key moment in the post-World War II era for some reasons that were important and clear at the time, and for other reasons that, with the benefit of hindsight, became clear later. From the beginning of the oil shock in late 1973 it was obvious that it would be necessary to make a rapid short-term adjustment to the sharply higher prices. Less certain at the time was the degree to which other structural adaptations involving medium-term responses of new capital/labor mixes, interfuel substitutions, import reductions, sectoral adjustments, desperate attempts to expand exports, and slower economic growth were also in the cards for many of the world's poor countries. Also less clear at the time, but certainly more and more visible every day, was the pressing need to analyze the energy impacts in terms of the underdeveloped and dependent character of African political economies as a whole. For whatever may be the impact of oil on African countries, the fact of the matter is that had the OPEC-sparked oil price rises not occurred, Africa would still be underdeveloped and dependent. Perhaps one of the most painful lessons of this period is that the much touted but barely heeded notion of "self-reliance" is even more imperative today than in the past, but it is one that is further from realization than even the most pessimistic forecasters envisioned only a decade ago. The period of 1973-1975 made this abundantly clear.

Today's African-Arab-OECD relations with respect to energy and other issues must be traced back to this topsy-turvy period, and these relations in turn must be set within the broader context of the contemporary crisis of international capitalism. Here we again must be careful, because the rhetorical uses of "energy" have been as inflammatory and widespread as they have been based on misinformation and half-truths. The critical starting point for discussion must be to situate the "energy crisis" of 1973-1975 within the broader issues of development and underdevelopment. We are led therefore to pose the following questions: What were the impacts of the initial 1973-1975 oil shock on Africa? How was the energy crisis related to the current crisis of the world capitalist system? Can we separate the effects of the two crises? What short-term and medium-term strategies did African countries actually follow and which ones could they have followed that would have both strengthened the autonomy of African nations and increased the welfare of the masses of the African population?

In dealing with these questions we assume that the ultimate goal of African political action is to reduce and eliminate African underdevelopment.[1] For Africa, the conditions of underdevelopment demand strategies that break the dominant exploitative international relationships while building the political and productive capacity of the masses domestically.[2]

I have elsewhere[3] analyzed the causes of the so-called energy crisis--really an oil crisis, as other fuels were not directly affected--as a crisis primarily of pricing rather than supply, the result of a period of compression in which a threefold increase in price took place in only four months. Of the thirty-three countries selected by the United Nations as most seriously affected by the energy crisis, twenty-one are in Africa.

The degree to which a single African country is affected by the energy crisis depends upon several critical factors, the principal ones being the structure of its national political economy and the sources of its energy supply. When discussing the importance of the structure of the political economy we are referring to the relative weights of the agricultural, mining, commercial, industrial, and transportation sectors of the economy, and the political and economic interests that are generated around each. These relations of production in turn help determine the kinds of political institutions that are employed to command the accumulation of economic surplus. We can say therefore that the political economy ultimately determines the energy demand patterns. It is the association of these particular demand patterns with available energy supply--coal, hydro, oil, etc.--that gives each country its own

peculiar configuration of energy supply and demand.
Whether or not these supplies are available domestically
or must be imported is another key variable in considering energy policy. It is this combination of sectoral
structure of the political economy and control over the
sources of supply that generates conflict among social
classes and strata as they struggle to articulate and
implement a national energy policy that will serve their
own particular interests.

Before turning to the consequences of the crisis
and a discussion of long-range strategies to meet it we
will first briefly examine the impact the crisis has had
on the neo-colonial political economies.

ENERGY USE IN THE NEOCOLONIAL POLITICAL ECONOMY

In most African countries, the transition from
colonialism to independence was accomplished with little
change in the economic structures characteristic of
colonialism, which involved external economic dependence
and distorted, irrational, and poverty-generating
internal policies. [4] In focusing on the discontinuities
of the oil crisis we must not become blind to the even
greater historical continuities of continental exploitation within which it occurred.

Agricultural Sector

The base of African political economy is a huge
rural agricultural sector with a few appended cities and
industries. Eighty percent of Africa's people are engaged in agriculture, the vast majority at a near-
subsistence level on small, usually communally owned
plots, a mode of production characteristic of Africa
over centuries. We must start here, rather than with
industry as most analyses have done, to understand the
effect of the crisis and to project strategies. The
agricultural sector's contribution to the gross domestic
product (GDP) in 1971 was greater than 40 percent in
nineteen of the forty-one independent developing African
countries, and greater than 50 percent in nine countries.
Only nineteen countries had manufacturing sectors that
made up 10 percent or more of their GDP. [5] Although
manufacturing and other sectors are expanding more
rapidly than agriculture, this expansion is still far
from significantly altering the primacy of agriculture.

Although in traditional agriculture animal power has
been and is used in some areas, the main nonhuman energy
resource has been fuel wood and its derivative, charcoal. Both are essentially noncommercial fuels, as
supplies are obtained outside the cash economy. Recently this source has been supplemented by the use of
waste materials from various agricultural processing
plants. [6]

The most important commercial form of energy in
Africa is petroleum. Liquid fuels accounted for 62.5 percent of total commercial energy distribution in 1970,
followed by hydroelectric power (22 percent), solid
fuels (10.6 percent) and natural gas (4.4 percent).[7]
In the rural areas, light distillates--mainly
kerosene--are used for heating and cooking. Other grades
run small grist mills or electric motors for refriger-
ation and lighting in small commercial enterprises. In
short, rural Africans rely heavily on rudimentary energy
forms. The FAO has estimated that African agriculture
has the world's lowest energy consumption. Whereas
Europe has available 0.93 horsepower per hectare for its
farms, and the United States, Latin America, and Asia
have 1.03, 0.27, and 0.19, respectively, Africa uses
only 0.05 horsepower per hectare for its agricultural
production.[8]
Despite agriculture's major contribution to African
GDPs, the direct effect of the oil price increase on
agricultural output is limited. Human labor, rather
than mechanical energy, is the basic input into tilling,
sowing, and harvesting both staple consumer crops and
most export commodities. The daily life of the farmer
has changed little since the independence of most
African countries in the early 1960s.
However, a major indirect impact stems from the
simultaneous rise in price and decline in supply of
fertilizer. Africa, which produces only two-thirds of
its own fertilizer needs, is required to compete on a
world market where a 95-million-ton demand was estimated
to exceed output by 4 million tons in 1974,[9] with a
similar gap anticipated for 1975.
Because of the short supply and the ability of
producing firms in the developed countries to set prices,
increased costs for fertilizer can be traced only in part
to the 300 percent rise in the pricing of petroleum, the
base for many commercial fertilizers. For example, the
price of urea, the main fertilizer in underdeveloped
countries, rose 560 percent in twenty-one months, from
$50 in June 1972 to $280 in March 1974.[10] Clearly,
expanding producer profits are a factor. According to
one aid organization, Dutch firms, "the export leaders in
fertilizers (in 1973) [,] produced the product at about $30
a ton and sold it at $300 a ton. A U.S. company, W. R.
Grace, one of the world's largest producers of nitrogen
fertilizer, increased its profits of its agricultural
products division from $7.6 million in 1971 to $24.4
million in 1973."[11]
Unfortunately, the promise of the Green Revolution
has begun to turn brown under the double impact of Western capitalist curtailment of the production of its
mainstay, fertilizer, and the spiraling price of fertilizer's principal input, petroleum.

Industrial and Commercial Sector

In Africa, industry and commerce are much less significant economically than agriculture. Commerce tends to be more important to GDP than is industry, "contributing possibly ten percent or more to GDP regardless of the stage of development."[12] It also employs more people. In 1970 industrial input into African GDPs ranged from 1 percent in Malawi to 28 percent in South Africa. Only in nine countries did it exceed 17 percent.[13] Overall, manufacturing's share of Africa's GDP rose only from 11 percent to 12 percent between 1960 and 1970. But manufacturing, so much beloved by foreign advisers and investors, has political strength far beyond its size. Owners usually have easy access to government policy-makers at all levels, especially to gain loans, special credits, and other economic guarantees.[14]

In contrast to agriculture, production units in the industrial sector rely heavily on commercial power, consuming a high proportion of the available electricity, coal, and gas. The industries forming the base of economic development--cement, textiles, paper, and steel--are the most energy-intensive. They are often promoted in underdeveloped countries, as they are easily assembled, require little trained manpower, and through import substitution conserve scarce foreign exchange. An analysis of the ratio of input of energy in British thermal units (Btus) to each dollar of final output shows that items like electrical appliances, usually not made in developing countries, require only 0.08 Btus per dollar, while asphalt and paving mixtures require 0.45 Btus, hydraulic cement, 0.42, primary aluminum, 0.38, and industrial chemicals, 0.32.[15]

Mining Sector

With the exception of Algeria, Libya, Liberia, Nigeria, Gabon, Zaire, and Zambia, mining has not made a significant contribution to GDP on the continent. Whereas in 1970 agriculture contributed a total of 32 percent for the continent as a whole, mining contributed 10.5 percent (up from 4 percent in 1960, for a decade's growth rate of 12 percent per annum).[16] Unlike other kinds of economic activities, mining generates few economic linkages with the rest of the economy. Thus its impact upon the lives of the majority of the African population is minimal. Although central government receipts from mining are theoretically available for nationwide social services, graft and corruption in neocolonial African states minimize the share that "trickles down" to the bottom 80 percent of the population. As Scott Pearson has shown for oil, and Pearson and Cownie for other export commodities, African workers have little

opportunity to benefit directly from national export
earnings from mining.[17] And as with other export
products, mining is oriented not toward domestic consumption, but rather toward the world commodity markets.
   Mining, like industry, is a heavy user of commercial
energy. In the 1980s we can expect to see even more
energy committed to this sector as governments attempt to
add to the value of their exports by increasing industrial processing (smelting, refining, etc.), all requiring
enormous amounts of energy. The value of a ton of
aluminum is estimated to be twenty to thirty times higher
than that of a ton of raw or semiprocessed bauxite ore.
But processing requires about 20,000 kilowatt-hours per
ton; copper requires about 3,000 kilowatt-hours per
ton.[18] It remains to be seen whether such commitment of
energy in an effort to increase value added is a qualita-
tively different policy or, as other sectors are likely
to be ignored as a result, merely the logical extension
of a neocolonial policy.
   Although mining is energy-intensive, oil tends not
to be its main fuel. Because thousands of kilowatt-hours
are needed to transform copper, bauxite, or iron ores
into commercially usable metal, mining operations try
whenever possible to develop hydroelectric power nearby
rather than rely on more expensive thermal plants. Here
as in agriculture the oil price increase has had only a
marginal impact, as 65 percent of electrical supply in
Africa comes from hydroelectric power.

Transport Sector
_____

   Transportation, the fourth key sector of the
economic structure, is a critical consideration in
determining the effect of the energy crisis on African
political economies. To examine a map of the transportation grid in Africa is to see neocolonialism at work.
The transport network (especially railroads) was con-
structed to evacuate to the sea primary products mined
and produced in the interior for export to Europe and
America. Because the neocolonial governments have defined their own interests as coincident with the existing
structures and interests, there has been little change in
the organization and distribution of the transport
system. The railroad in Africa still relies mainly on
coal and, for diesel engines, oil. Only in a few areas,
e.g., southern Zaire, is there a movement toward electric-
powered trains. The use of trucks is especially important in Africa for commercial goods and foodstuffs.
Tinned meat and fish, portable radios, and shoes are
carried into all areas of the country by merchants
employing trucks. Changes in oil prices will hit the
African consumer through higher internal transport costs.
   The principal consumers of oil products in Africa
are commercial road vehicles and diesel trains; the former

rose in number from 612,000 in 1965 to 913,000 in 1970, an increase of about 50 percent.[19] For the masses of the population, the direct impact of price changes is much greater in the transport sector than in other sectors. As fuel costs are passed on from OPEC to the major oil companies, to the government wholesaler and refiner, to the individual retailer at the service station, to the car or truck owner, and finally to the African consumer, the energy crisis will begin to bite into the already meager income of the African wage earner and farmer. This will be especially burdensome for rural people carrying their surplus agricultural products to markets in small towns and cities. The merchant and commercial classes will charge higher prices for all goods and passengers carried by buses, trucks, or diesel-powered trains.

More seriously affected than the farmer are the urban wage worker and urban unemployed who must pay for subsistence items brought from the countryside by bus and truck, as well as for manufactured goods and social services--which in rural areas are free or at least not assigned monetary value. Higher transport costs will also have an indirect impact on industrial and commercial activities.

THE IMPACT OF THE OIL CRISIS ON AFRICA

The oil crisis brings into sharp focus the critical question for African nations: What is to be done with an economic structure imposed during the colonial period? That structure does not serve the needs of Africa. African growth rates, at 4.6 percent per annum, have failed to meet even the modest 6 percent target of the Second U.N. Development Decade. In agriculture, food production on a per capita basis tumbled by 7 percent between 1970 and 1973. The African population, increasing at roughly 2.7 million annually, is expected to double to 800 million by the year 2000.[20]

Another result of this structure can be seen in per capita income figures, which (for forty underdeveloped countries for which data are available) show 20 percent of the population appropriating 55 percent of the national income, with the lowest 20 percent receiving only 5 percent.[21] Distribution of public services, health care, education, water, and energy is also distorted, resulting in disparities between urban and rural life, and within the urban areas, between the new political and administrative bourgeoisie and the working (and nonworking) classes. The last group is rapidly expanding as agricultural stagnation and the paucity of rural public services drive more young people from the village to the city, creating a new subproletariat of unemployed and underemployed.

In the area of social overhead capital or

infrastructure, including energy, the pattern of state
policy serving neocolonial interests has remained the
same. Little if any infrastructure has been built to
serve the interests of rural workers.[22] Railroad lines,
roads, and electric power were all introduced to serve
European commercial interests. Where power has been
made available, it has been used to transform agricultural goods or minerals to facilitate their transport to
Europe. Examples include the mining complexes in Liberia
and Ghana and agricultural processing plants in Lever-
ville in Zaire. Any benefit that energy distribution
may have brought to the African population has been
purely ancillary to the primary purposes of economic
exploitation.

These economic characteristics are reproduced in the
political institutions of neocolonial Africa. Just as
the formal end of European domination did little to alter
economic relations, so it did little to change political
relations. In most instances the "transfer of power"
simply replaced white faces with black ones; there have
been few if any substantive structural changes in the
institutions of the state.[23] Where change has occurred,
it has usually been in the direction of reducing the
modicum of mass political participation that did exist in
the terminal years of colonialism. The franchise has
been suppressed, and mass political initiative stifled.
The multinational corporations, the foreign embassies,
and the foundations are too often the "silent partners"
of African politics. It is precisely these kinds of
relationships within the neocolonial political economy
that must be broken if genuine development is to occur.

A European colonial oligarchy, acting on European
economic and political interests, created the kind of
economic structure that has made Africa especially
susceptible to an energy crisis. This not inconsiderable
feat was achieved by orienting the colonial (and in turn
neocolonial) political economy toward a nearly total
reliance on Europe for everything from cloth to copper
wire. Policies to suppress self-sustaining enterprises
ensured that the slightest break with Europe would bring
hardship, especially for those in the cash economy.[24]

It is against this background that we turn to an
analysis of the consequences of the crisis, both direct
and indirect, that place severe pressures on Africa's
foreign exchange holdings and foreign debt.

Direct Impact

In order to gauge accurately the direct effect the
crisis has had on Africa we must separate countries that
are self-sufficient in oil from those that must import.
Although Africa is a major source of petroleum, in 1970
Africans consumed less than 14 percent of the continental
output.[25] In the early 1970s Nigeria, Black Africa's

largest oil exporter, still imported more than 10 percent
of its refined products because its refinery capacity
was inadequate. For the thirty-six importing nations a
near balance of trade in 1973 was transformed, after the
price increase in that year, into a trade deficit of
$2.4 million, despite a $2.4 billion increase in the
value of exports.

Beyond this broad dichotomy of the "haves" and
"have nots," we may further distinguish between importer
countries with oil refineries and those without. The
significance of this distinction lies in two areas:
economics and security. It is easier to obtain crude
than to obtain refined petroleum, and a nation's
security is lessened when its energy supply is at the
mercy of another. As one Indian economist put it:
"From the point of view of the oil importing countries
like India, the establishment of a domestic refining
industry ensures regularity of oil supply, makes it less
dependent on the powerful international oil companies,
makes a significant contribution to the industrial
development of the country, and also saves a substantial
amount of foreign exchange."[26] Refineries are important
economically precisely because they can save foreign
exchange. There is a price differential in the costs of
crude oil a nation imports and refines itself and
imported oil that is already refined. Those eleven
countries[27] with refineries have benefited from this
differential, saving thousands of dollars per day in
precious foreign exchange. The problem is exacerbated
for the nine nonrefining countries with no direct access
to the sea. For them transport costs (made even more
expensive by fuel costs) must be added to the coastal
delivery price.

Indirect Impact and the Cyclical International Recession

The indirect effect of the energy crisis on Africa
results from changes due to its impact on the developed
countries. It is very difficult to separate this
effect from a multitude of other factors that have also
contributed to the economic downturn in the industrialized countries. However, it is generally conceded
now—although not at the time—that energy was a contributing factor, but not the primary factor, that led
to the recession. For example, during this period it
probably contributed only about one-third of the
inflation rate.

It is imperative that we understand the magnitude
of the exchanges between Africa and the OECD countries,
as only a small fraction of all African trade is with
other African countries. A far larger percentage of both
its imports and exports has been with Europe and the
United States. Thus an African country's fragile

political economy can be more easily affected by events
in Europe than by those elsewhere. As the OECD countries,
especially in Europe, slackened their demand for imported
raw materials in the face of the world recession, this
was transmitted to Africa as fewer exports and hence less
foreign exchange to pay for imports. Not only did demand
fall, but the terms of trade also went against African
exporters. World commodity prices declined. Using the
1970 price as a base of 100, industrial raw materials
prices declined from 192 in February of 1974 to 133 in
October, and within this category fibers and metals, both
important African export commodities, declined in the
same period from 237 to 172 and 170 to 109, respectively.[28]
     This decline in world commodity prices was simply
one result of what the OECD (the world's twenty-four most
industrialized capitalist countries) has called "the
after-effects of the excessive demand that (the OECD
governments) allowed to build up in 1973, and from the
external shock of the sudden and sharp rise of oil
prices."[29] Total growth of GNP for the developed countries fell from 6.3 percent in 1973 to 0.25 percent in
1974 and (estimated) 0.50 percent in 1975. At the same
time consumer prices have skyrocketed. Consumer prices
in the seven major OECD countries rose at an annual
rate of only 3.3 percent between 1959-1960 and 1971-1972
and 13.75 percent between 1973 and 1974. And for one of
the seven major countries (Italy) the rate was as high
as 25 percent.[30]
     Despite the decline in raw material prices, manu-
factured products from the developed nations--which
Africa must import--have risen in price. In part, at
least, this must be attributed to the increase in oil
prices. Arthur D. Little has analyzed the rise in the
portion of the cost of selected manufactured products
for which petroleum is responsible. The percentage
figure for steel products rose from 1972 to 1974 from
1.1 to 4.0, for construction materials from 1.6 to 6.0,
for autos from 0.8 to 3.0, and for textiles from 1.3 to
4.6.[31] Although even the 1974 overall figures are not
large, the effect, combined with other factors in the
capitalist economies, has been to noticeably increase
the prices of manufactured products.
     Thus, the indirect impact of the crisis, in lowered
prices for the products African nations have to sell
and higher prices for those they must buy, has been
significant. Tables 5.1 and 5.2 present a clear statement of the relative importance of different kinds of
goods imported into Africa. Note that although fuel
imports almost doubled between 1973 and 1974 as a share
of total imports, even after the jump they represented
the smallest single category of imports. This indicates
that the direct and the indirect impact of fuel price
hikes was more modest than was often claimed at the
time.

TABLE 5.1
STRUCTURE OF AFRICAN IMPORTS (PERCENTAGE)

	Food	Raw materials	Fuels	Capital goods	Manufactured goods
1970	13.2	4.6	5.4	38.5	28.4
1972	13.1	4.3	4.5	42.9	26.0
1973	14.4	4.3	4.6	43.3	24.5
1974	15.3	4.9	8.8	36.8	25.3
1975	13.8	3.7	7.5	41.7	24.9
1976	12.3	3.4	7.4	45.7	23.2
1977	12.6	3.8	6.6	44.6	24.0

Source: United Nations, Trade Statistics (New York, 1978).

TABLE 5.2
AVERAGE ANNUAL RATE OF GROWTH OF AFRICAN IMPORTS
BY COMMODITY (PERCENTAGE)

	Food	Fuels	Capital goods	Manufactured goods
1970-1977	23.0	27.4	26.3	20.8
1970-1973	22.8	13.2	24.3	13.8
1973-1977	22.8	39.6	27.7	25.7

Source: United Nations, Trade Statistics (New York, 1978).

ENERGY STRATEGIES AND NEOCOLONIALISM

It is clear from this analysis that both the rapid
petroleum price rise and, more importantly, the international impact of Western stagflation were responsible
for the 1973-1975 crisis in the underdeveloped countries.
Effective development strategies must take into account
both factors, for both internal domestic and international political reasons. In our normative perspective
the central goals of these strategies should be directed
toward eliminating African poverty, which focuses the
discussion on the four out of five Africans who are
poor and live on the land.

To move in that direction requires increasing both
the people's welfare and productivity and the national
autonomy of African countries vis-à-vis foreign capitalist countries and their institutions. These two goals
may appear to be contradictory, especially in specific

time frames. Breaking disadvantageous trade relations to increase national autonomy may, in the short term, reduce popular welfare by decreasing the amount of goods, especially food, available to the masses. Conversely, increasing popular welfare through increased imports may decrease national independence. Strategies must therefore be devised and evaluated for their ability, over the medium and long term, to meet both goals simultaneously.[32]

A simple quantitative reduction of imports, whether of capital, technology, foodstuffs, or oil, is an insufficient strategy of self-reliance. Retreat is no substitute for positive strategy. A positive strategy may in fact mean expanding international contacts, but only with careful control over the distribution of benefits and costs to all classes. Autonomy and self-reliance mean increased control over external relations rather than their absence.[33]

Ultimately this is a question of political power. If the people at the top, as in many countries in the 1970s, seek to use nationalization of foreign corporations and "indigenization" as a means to increase elite control and their own class autonomy, then the benefit to the masses will be slight. However, in certain countries, the 1970s have also demonstrated that genuine anti-underdevelopment programs are possible where the masses or those who act in their interests control the state apparatus. This has been the case in Algeria, China, Cuba, Guinea-Bissau, and to a degree in Tanzania and Guinea.[34] The same of course holds true for energy strategies: Will they be solely and reflexively urban-oriented or more concerned with promoting a balanced energy strategy that considers rural and agricultural needs as well?

Short-Term Strategies

The immediate short-term dilemma faced by African governments during the energy crisis was to find ways to close the foreign exchange shortfall caused by sharply higher prices for imported oil in a period when neither the volume nor the unit price of African exports was rising as rapidly. Governments have generally relied on five short-term (0-2 years) strategies to try to meet this problem: special pricing arrangements with oil exporters; importing less oil; improving domestic energy efficiency; importing more or the same amounts of oil, but less of something else; and continuing to import oil and other goods and services by borrowing the foreign exchange necessary to cover the shortfall. It should be noted that after the huge jump in 1973-1974, the real price of oil adjusted for inflation remained flat until 1978-1979, which partially eased the transition problem. However, for some of the more fragile economies, that was small comfort when they were faced with an oil bill that increased 40 percent in nominal terms in one year.

Multitiered pricing. This kind of pricing system operates when exporters charge different rates to different customers, usually based on the ability to pay or on other criteria such as common culture and religion or geographic proximity. Although a few short-lived ad hoc arrangements were made during the crisis, exporters have held a number of objections to the plan proposed by African and other importers for cut-rate oil. Objections have centered on the problem of resale to a third party at a higher price. Given the energy-hungry state of most LDCs, this may be a spurious challenge. For example, a two-rung approach was employed on a limited basis, with strings attached, between Iran and India. This is something of a special case, because Iran was buying both Indian technicians and Indian political quiescence in the bargain. Despite Arab reservations about this tiered strategy, African states continued to press their claims. A close reading of the African press during the early stages of the energy embargo reveals that the initial assumption was that a quid pro quo for the breaking of diplomatic relations with Israel would be cut-rate oil.[35]

Serious discussion of a two-tiered system was held as late as February 1975, at the Ministerial Council of the U.N. Economic Commission for Africa. The Nigerian representative made an apparent offer of concessionary rates to African states with refineries, but the Nigerian commissioner for mines and power later denied this offer, confirming the OPEC position that any such concessions must be made by the organization rather than by individual members. The first major and sustained effort at what becomes, de facto, a two-tiered system is the current program by Mexico and Venezuela to lessen the oil-payments burden on nine Latin American neighbors through loans, grants, and subsidies. Nothing of the sort has emerged in Africa. It remains to be seen if African importers will benefit from such regional programs; if so, clearly Nigeria will be the key.

Importing less oil and improving domestic energy efficiency. This is a very difficult short-term strategy to implement because countries at the early stages of economic development have tremendous energy requirements that push the annual rate of energy growth very high, usually higher than the rate of increase in GNP. A unilateral oil import restriction would be likely to disrupt key sectors of the economy, especially transportation and, to a lesser extent, industry. An option taken by the world's rich countries, and a cornerstone of Project Independence in the United States, this strategy consists of government action to flatten out demand curves for energy in selected areas of the economy by using the price mechanism and/or by government

administrative order. Closely related are efforts to
improve the efficiency of the energy plants and conversion units. But as most African economies are operating
at low levels of output and productivity, and as energy
is already directed to the key sectors of the industrial
economy, these strategies have extremely limited usefulness for them. Reduction in the energy available for
consumers would have little net effect on aggregate consumption levels, as the consumption of the few household
consumers and private automobiles in African countries
is small relative to that of the mining, public transport, and industrial sectors. Over the short term, then,
imports did not decline in the aggregate. There are
indications that energy efficiency has increased slightly
in industry, but to gain the reductions seen in industrialized countries would require not only more technical skills than are currently available, but also a more
industrialized economy. Politically, of course, such
price pass-throughs are difficult, and most governments
during the energy crisis tried to protect the consumer
from the full blast of international prices by con-
trolling domestic prices for products like kerosene
(used especially by low-income people).

Reducing nonenergy imports. The logic of this short-
term strategy is that it would free foreign exchange
from nonoil purchases so that it could be spent on critical oil imports. In the period under review, however,
this strategy was not followed, in part because of the
same reasons that it proved difficult to cut back oil
imports. Reducing food and equipment imports may slow
economic growth and quicken political conflict, something most governments want to avoid. (This strategy
was followed more frequently over the middle term.) The
value and volumes of capital goods imported increased
over this period. While the value may vary from country
to country, the aggregate data show that African imports
from OECD countries went up from $16.314 billion in 1973
to $32.460 in 1975. Imports from OPEC countries went up
from $536 million to $1.622 billion in those same years,
according to 1978 U.N. trade statistics.

International borrowing. Without the widespread use
of international borrowing, the economic development
strategies that most countries followed during the
crisis--in essence, more of the same--could not have
worked. Nor, for that matter, could their energy
strategies, such as they were, have worked as well as
they did. African countries were able to get through the
first difficult years of the crisis without taking
serious domestic actions (i.e., import reductions) that
would have led to economic or political dislocation because they were able to get loans from abroad, mostly
from private banks.

Traditionally, the sources of most loans to African
countries have been the International Bank for Reconstruction and Development (IBRD) and its sister agency,
the International Development Association (IDA), which
together make up the World Bank; European development
funds come from individual countries or from the
European Economic Community as a unit. Private capital
markets played a smaller role. This has changed since
1973-1974. However, the private bank loans usually offer
the worst terms for poor borrowers. In fact, even before the 1973 oil price compression, "bankers were already warning each other to cut back on credits to some
developing countries that were going heavily into
debt."[36]

It is difficult to assess the full impact of the
energy crisis on official government bilateral and multilateral aid from the industrialized countries, because
aid has also been affected by the recession. The combination, whatever the proportions, appears to have frozen
and, in some cases, reduced official development assistance.

The role of the World Bank as the main facility for
loans to underdeveloped countries in Africa and elsewhere
has been questioned by some potential donors. The Arabs
have tended to see weighted votes in the World Bank as
making it a U.S.-dominated institution able to block
their efforts to determine the criteria and recipients of
petroloans. OPEC as a whole has made more than $1.8
billion available to the World Bank and $3.4 billion to
the IMF, but it has not placed all its aid funds there,
having established regional and other kinds of new lending institutions over which it has more control.
Naturally, the United States (and Europe to a lesser
extent) would prefer that funds be distributed through
one of the "traditional" institutions dominated by the
industrialized countries.

The communist countries, which were second to the
West in total aid funds, have dropped to number three as
development assistance from OPEC countries has risen.

The oil-exporting countries are therefore now
emerging as an important source of development assistance for Africa and other developing areas. Initially,
Arab members of OPEC pledged $200 million to African
countries, through the OAU, to offset the price of oil.
A Committee of Seven, then a Committee of Twelve[37]
(Committee of Afro-Arab Cooperation) was established to
handle the money. Through 1975, however, the actual
transfer of funds was disappointing. Funds dribbled in
slowly and were directed not to the African Development
Bank, but to the Arab League in Cairo. By the first
quarter of 1975, loans totaling $125.55 million had been
disbursed to thirty-one African countries. In terms of
total OPEC aid, bilateral assistance to Africa accounted
for about 6 percent of all funds disbursed. The largest

amount of aid went to Muslim countries, which received approximately 80 percent of total OPEC assistance.

Of the $9.6 billion formally committed by the Arab countries to various loan agencies and other recipients, $2.6 billion was actually transferred; first, non-oil-producing states in the Middle East, and then nearby Muslim countries, were given priority. A similar pattern has been followed by Venezuela, whose aid proposals are limited to Latin America.

For the sub-Saharan African countries, similar sources of regional loan assistance are limited. Nigeria, the most likely donor, has huge internal demands on its oil revenues. Whereas Qatar has a mere 143,000 citizens to ask for goods and services from the central government, Nigeria has nearly 80 million. Gabon, a second possibility, has a tiny population but a much lower oil production. Angola, through its contested Cabinda territory, is also a significant producer--but all its oil revenues, if they prove to be available, must go toward reconstruction and development.

Thus, with the developed countries themselves competing for oil loans from the private capital markets and the IMF; with the Arab nations uncommitted to a global, rather than regional, loan strategy; and with limited possibilities for loans from sub-Saharan exporters, prospects for the poorer African states to finance even their then current levels of oil consumption were not bright. Africa's import bill went over $1 billion. Unfortunately, their slim recourse to expensive loans only exacerbated an already dangerous situation, as most African countries were already deeply in debt. Even in 1970, Africa's aggregate debt was $10.69 billion.

In summary, African countries that import oil are severely constrained in their short-term strategies by their external dependence on Europe and the United States and their internal reliance on distorted neo-colonial economic structures. Four key constraints indicate some of the problems they face:

1. Additional capital required for investment in the rural areas will come in part from external sources, thereby increasing dependency in the short run.

2. Although there is room for more rational allocative efficiency, oil is to a considerable degree consumed in key areas such as truck transport and import substitution industries and cannot be cut back without some damage to economic growth.

3. Energy sources are underdeveloped and insufficiently flexible to be changed overnight to favor rural development. To do so in the short run may mean diverting investment funds from other social services into, for example, research and development of solar energy.

4. There is not at the moment a strong, progressive political vanguard to agitate for a radical

elimination of neocolonial institutions and neocolonial "development" policies and to replace them with instruments to serve the needs of the African masses.

Medium-Term Strategies

Medium-term strategies were developed as African governments more fully assessed the threat that higher oil prices in a recessionary world posed to their national economies. Again, their dilemma was that their foreign exchange earnings did not keep pace with their oil bills. Something had to give. Once the initial shock was over, governments had to choose, whether consciously or by default, which policies they would follow to adjust their foreign spending patterns to the new revenue conditions. This in turn required domestic adjustments and hence raised serious political questions. To what extent would domestic energy industries have to be restructured, and who would be made to bear the burden of change during the transition to higher-priced and less secure oil?

These medium-term strategies (again, like short-term strategies) could be defined as narrow energy strategies as such or as macroeconomic or sectoral adjustments. Specific energy strategies include exploring for and producing oil domestically, diversifying the domestic mix of total energy supply to rely more heavily on local hydro and coal resources, and trying to cut overall domestic oil consumption. Most countries considered all possibilities. The number of hydroelectric projects included in African development plans grew during this period, as in Kenya and Ivory Coast. Ghana and Tanzania pushed ahead with oil exploration, and Cameroon accelerated its own oil program, which was already under way. The number of exploratory wells dug in non-OPEC Africa increased steadily after the 1973-1974 crisis from 157 in 1973 to 208 in 1978, after fluctuating in the early 1970s. Interestingly enough, however, the percentage of wells completed in Africa as a fraction of the wells completed worldwide declined between 1970 and 1978. Some countries, such as Nigeria, undertook studies to modernize and expand coal production, although the push toward coal has had only marginal success for managerial and infrastructural reasons.

African governments during the middle 1970s also tried to diversify their foreign sources of oil. This meant scrambling about, seeking what they hoped were more secure deals with more exporter governments. This was the period (1974-1979) when the OPEC governments themselves were squeezing the major international oil corporations out of the control of the business. The corporations, faced with reduced crude supplies, in turn cut back third-party sales drastically. Many of these sales had been to Third World countries. This new strategy in most cases led to direct oil deals with the

OPEC governments. These new international changes meant that African governments could no longer leave the supply of oil to the private companies. The state had to get involved, and this placed additional pressures on the already fragile machinery of the African energy ministries and state-owned oil companies.

It is important to keep in mind that the development of these medium-term strategies was additive; they were not either/or choices. They represented a range of strategies and policy instruments to be combined in a "basket" of national energy policies. In addition, short-term strategies such as external borrowing and special pricing arrangements continued as the other medium-term programs were phased into operation.

African governments also employed macroeconomic policies, as well as more targeted economic efforts, to affect energy use. One strategy available to all importers was to deflate the economy, as a sluggish economy uses less oil. This did occur in many African countries but probably as a result more of the world recession than of conscious government policies. The central overall macroeconomic strategies are to export more and import less. We have seen that the volume of African exports rose in the 1970s. However, lacking the strength and flexibility of the economies of Korea or Taiwan, which did follow massive export strategies, African LDCs were still not able to cover their increased oil costs. Stagflation reduced the value of their exports. The other part of this policy--importing less--was followed by many African countries in the medium term. Some imposed import restrictions; others were responding to the slack world economy. For example, the rate of growth of imports fell in most countries, and five East and South African countries reduced their absolute volume of imports as a result of balance of payments problems.[38] The problem here, of course, is that such reductions, once the "fat" of luxury goods is cut out, begin to chop into capital and intermediate goods (especially spare parts) needed to maintain industrial production (and hence employment). The other response is to cut back on social services. However, this was not followed in many countries as a serious medium-range adjustment issue, because it entailed great economic and political costs. In the 1980s this will be an explosive issue as the World Bank, and private bankers as well, seek to impose "conditionality" for any new large loans.

In the medium term, the problem of trying to meet high oil prices recedes and there is a range of potential energy strategies that may be seen as extending along a continuum, with an industrial strategy at one end and an agricultural one at the other. As one observer put it: "In assessing the need for energy the LDCs will have to make a hard choice between energy for industry and energy

for farming."[39] Although it may perhaps be expressed too
dichotomously, the statement nonetheless captures the
essence of what is required if African governments are to
win the struggle to defeat underdevelopment. A conscious
political decision must be made to redress the current
imbalance of goods and services made available to the
agricultural sector of the economy.

Rural electrification. The arguments for promoting
agricultural and rural development have been made elsewhere on grounds of both morality and efficiency and will
not be elaborated upon here.[40] It will be assumed that
it is immoral to continue to deprive the vast majority
of the population of energy and other resources and that
economic development (as distinct from mere quantitative
economic growth) simply cannot take place unless the
productive capacity of the rural masses is multiplied
many times over. Political, economic, and educational
mobilization of the African masses will be needed before
progressive structural changes in the political economy
can take place.

Making energy resources available to the rural
population is a part of any political and economic
strategy that aims toward self-reliance. In addition to
providing more energy to rural farmers, it can create the
conditions for energy distribution to rural-based industries.

Increased inputs of commercial energy into rural
communities may considerably contribute to rural development as part of a coordinated program aimed at reducing
rural poverty and raising rural productivity. There
are numerous historical examples of clear-cut advances
in agriculture, industries, and public administration and
public services made with the addition of energy resources. Light industry oriented toward the rural sector
can prosper and ably serve rural (and urban) demands for
processed foodstuffs and agricultural products such as
palm oil, flour, nuts, and so on. This includes dehy-
drating or canning locally produced foods and reducing
fish to fish meal for both rural and urban consumption.
Export crops, such as lumber, cotton, and sisal, can be
processed close to the point of actual production.

The most striking advantage of additional energy
resources, with considerable spillover effects, could
come through the provision of electricity to schools,
hospitals, and local government offices. It is impossible to calculate the effects numerically, but the
addition of such services as part of a coordinated
development program could do much to slow the rush of
rural villagers to the large cities. In government
service, the provision of electricity could help attract
a higher caliber of people willing to serve in the rural
areas and hence can provide development skills where
they are most needed.

Rural or village electrification through the use of
multipurpose hydroelectric dams can control flooding,
permit new irrigation, and power electric pumps to get at
deep subterranean water tables, as well as dramatically
increase agricultural productivity. Clearly, it is not
the mere provision of power that achieves such results,
but rather power as an integral part of a rural development strategy. On the other hand, the availability of
power can often determine whether a given project will
succeed or fail, and here much depends upon the technological modifications that are made to suit local conditions.

There is a tendency when speaking or writing of
things technological, including energy and power, to
endow them with a fictive life of their own.[41] We are
told that "energy" can transform societies or that the
lack of energy dooms nations to permanent poverty.
Energy, we are told, is all-important, or not important
at all. When referring to development, we are sometimes
told that "energy" can transform a nation, or a region,
as if energy or power could act independently of people.

This tendency to confuse technology and humanity
often appears when we are told what "energy" can or cannot do. Some commentators begin with a list of what
energy is supposed to be capable of transforming and
under what conditions; strategies are worked out from the
energy on down, rather than beginning with the people's
needs and working up from that base. To begin with
human needs and then move to an inventory of available
resources sometimes leads to ingenious solutions of what
previously would have been technologically impossible.

This technological bias is found among many who insist that energy distribution should be oriented toward
industry and urban areas because of the economies of
scale. Although such economies are important, they
should not be the sole determining factor. Economies
of scale refers to situations in which the need can
support large investment. In most of Africa, such
situations are not common. Villages are scattered
throughout the countryside; urbanization is relatively
low.[42] By the standard analyses looking for economies of
scale, the provision of electricity is expensive,
especially when capital is scarce. And precisely because
of the international energy crisis, with its higher oil
costs, the smallest local development scheme is going to
have to more carefully consider how much must be spent
to supply it with light and power.

Perhaps China provides the most dramatic example of
the ways in which power can serve the needs of the people.
China has made an impressive commitment to rural development, with the provision of cheap energy as one of the
cornerstones--a commitment that Africa would do well to
imitate.

The Chinese put their resources into small-scale,

decentralized generators that could rely on local inputs.
They achieved enormous progress by relying on multipurpose hydrostations that not only generate power, but also
help control flooding and promote irrigation and have the
advantage of using "free" fuel--naturally flowing water.
Under this program, fully 16 percent of China's total
hydropower is captured by 35,000 small-scale generators.
Between 1958 and 1964, the horsepower available for
China's farms grew four times; most of this growth was
oriented toward pumps for irrigation and drainage.

Yet few countries have experienced a revolutionary
upheaval that powerfully reorients the political and
productive processes of the nation toward increasing
popular welfare and reducing international dependence.
What can we anticipate from the majority of African
countries whose leaders reached a peaceful settlement
with colonialism? Unfortunately, few countries have made
rural development or rural electrification a part of
national development policy or even a formal goal.
Energy resources, like other resources, are reserved
for the urban elite. Should the extension of electric
and other power facilities to broader segments of the
population occur, it will be done as a result of militant
actions by rural masses who want to improve their general
welfare. Today's extension usually occurs through the
more conventional pressures brought by African elites
with interests outside the city. In Nigeria the central
power authority, unable to meet rising demands for power
and increasingly criticized by local businessmen outside
Lagos, finally delegated authority to develop rural
electrification to the twelve state governments.

The criteria used for rural electrification are
important. The Federal Military Government of Nigeria
approved a plan to allocate electricity according to an
area's population, industrial development, and political
and administrative importance. The potential for industrial development was to be measured by the presence or
absence of such things as railheads, waterworks, and
schools. The presence or absence of divisional headquarters, prisons, emirates, and so on determines the
political and administrative factor. More specifically,
the 136 towns chosen for electrification were selected
on the following basis:[43]

1. Population of 5,000 or more and firm potential
   for industrial growth
2. Population of 10,000 or more and a divisional
   headquarters, plus a large number of social
   services such as waterworks, hospitals, or
   schools
3. Population of 20,000 or more, a large number
   of social services, but no other apparent
   justification

4. Population of 25,000 or more, even if no other justification exists

New energy technology. There are a range of energy strategies available that can, if adopted, move Africa toward a more self-reliant position. Both popular welfare and international autonomy can be improved through low-cost, labor-intensive technologies for prospecting, generating, and distributing power--whether from water, coal, or petroleum. Africa is rich in water and oil; it must become richer in the tools and knowledge necessary to tap these resources. Africa must look beyond merely coping with the crisis. It must find ways to turn disadvantage to advantage. For example, some African countries may, in the medium term, benefit from increased oil prices. Some could gain a comparative advantage if they are able to offer potential investors low-cost hydroelectric power. We may see a steady flow of energy-intensive industries seeking cheap power into these areas of Africa.

Another energy source to be developed is as plentiful as the technology to harness it commercially on a large scale is scarce. That is solar energy. The raw material--sunlight--is plentiful in Africa. However, just as oil in the ground requires the application of technology to extract and process it, so solar and other renewables require technology if they are to be "processed" into more usable forms. During the crisis, only very limited work was being done on solar energy, precisely because oil was relatively cheap and convenient. The resolution of the problem of how to harness and use this "free" energy in socially useful forms is a political and technical-financial problem. The developed countries must promote R&D more seriously with government backing. African governments also must be more committed than they have been to exploring the use of solar to improve rural life (this, too, requires state backing). Solar is still an expensive way to generate electricity, but it does have immediate passive heating, cooling, and drying possibilities that some countries were exploring during the energy crisis.

In Bamako, Mali, in Dakar, and at the Office de l'Energie Solaire du Niger (Onersol), solar devices are being tested that can cook food and raise water from wells. The devices tested thus far have been designed as small, self-contained units in which the power is locally consumed and not transmitted over long distances. Such solar devices would be appropriate to the needs of the rural population--improving the conditions of daily life as well as expanding local productivity by providing water for crops and herds. In the Sahel, small pumps are already operating on 1 kilowatt of solar energy, and with minimal attention and care, they may automatically pump from 50 to 80 cubic meters per day, depending upon the depth of the water table. It is for these kinds of reasons that the director of Onersol has said that solar energy has a real role to play in the energy policies of the countries of the Sahel, "where conditions for solar energy are the best in the world."[44]

Regional Strategies

An important economic imperative involves reorienting energy production and distribution schemes for petroleum, coal, and hydroelectricity from the national to the regional level. A major disadvantage of energy purchasing, production, and distribution in African countries today is that, due to their small market size, they are unable to take advantage of the economies of scale associated with the operation of larger facilities. This is easily seen in the case of petroleum.

Petroleum. To gain such advantages, regional buying groups could be formed to purchase oil in bulk at an improved rate. Even assuming the worst--that the price would not be lowered for bulk buying--the regional petroleum importers (RPIs) would be in an improved commercial bargaining position. During the months of the 1973 oil boycott, the press reported that oil companies were rerouting supplies from Africa at will. Individually, African countries lacked the power to back up their complaints; if they had been organized as RPIs, their bargaining position would have been stronger.

Directly associated with regional imports is the possibility of building larger refineries to serve regional markets. Whereas the world average size of a refinery (outside North America) is about 78,000 barrels per day, in Africa the figure averages 31,000 barrels per day. Although the demand for smaller refineries to fit smaller market needs has resulted in less technologically complex refinery designs, the fact remains that regional buying and refining schemes would be more economic. An added advantage would be the more efficient distribution and utilization of surplus products. Most LDCs with refineries actually export certain grades of oil. This anomaly results from a national demand that is skewed toward the lighter distillates, such as kerosene and automobile fuel, and away from the heavier fuel oils that are used in industrial plants. A regional refinery could, via pipelines, redirect this surplus to those countries and areas with a demand for heavy fuel oils. Under current conditions, the surplus must be shipped at high cost to distant consumers.

Another advantage of a regional petroleum scheme would be the possibility of developing closer direct relationships with the oil-exporting countries, with benefits beyond the efficiencies of transportation and refining costs. The Arab exporters have shown a certain impatience in dealing with the myriad demands now placed on them by dozens of individual African states. Consolidated policies would improve the African bargaining position, as well as make it easier for the Arab exporters to meet these demands. OPEC or OAPEC would no doubt rather deal with four or five regional associations than with forty individual applicants.

Coal. Regional sharing of coal reserves presents greater problems, because of coal's greater scarcity in Africa and the high cost of transporting it. The high costs of mining and transporting coal helped to shift Zaire's energy demand for its Shaba mines away from coal toward hydro, and similar "incentives were even stronger to the construction of the Kariba Dam to dispense with the dependence by the Zambian Copper Belt upon coal from the Rhodesian colleries at Wankie, and the long haul from the latter to the former."[45] In other areas of Africa, however, there has rarely been any realistic choice between these two forms (Nigeria being one of the exceptions, South Africa the other) precisely because coal is rare and remote. For these reasons, regional energy policies based upon coal are not an important goal today for most of Africa.

Electricity. Beyond primary energy sources like coal or petroleum, economy-of-scale gains obtain as well in the case of electricity, a secondary form of energy. Regional electricity production, transportation, and distribution networks would greatly reduce costs to consumers and are economically superior to national grids in small countries. Several such schemes already exist on a limited basis--notably in East Africa, where power is generated from Owen Falls in Uganda and distributed within Uganda and to Kenya. This holds true also for several countries in West Africa, where negotiations have been undertaken to link the Akosombo Dam on the Volta River in Ghana to the national electric grid in Nigeria and in the process provide improved electrical supply for the two intervening countries--Togo and Benin. Such projects offer greater economic potential for the development of industrial complexes in Togo and Benin.

The toughest and thorniest problems involved in regional energy sharing will be questions of siting. Where, for example, will refineries be located? Where will major electric installations be located, and where will the transmission lines pass? Some of these issues will be settled by establishing economic criteria such as port facilities and availability of fuel, but many others will require political criteria that are bound to rankle one or the other partner in a regional agreement. Such differences can be resolved by the various national administrative elites only on the basis of what they perceive to be in their own, and perhaps their countries', best interests.

Development priority should clearly be assigned to hydroelectric projects, where resources are available, particularly in the face of the oil crisis. Africa is the richest continent in the world in hydroelectric resources. If oil prices remain high, African countries may well adopt strategies that rely on hydrogenerated electricity for a wider range of uses than is now the case, reserving oil for uses for which alternatives are not available. Thus long-distance transportation systems may be electrified if it is found that the cost in foreign exchange is high for oil (even though the total costs for an electrified train system may be higher, they might be less expensive in terms of foreign exchange). In fact, East African Railways is considering electrifying parts of its system and replacing the diesel engines it now uses with electric trains.

AFRICAN-ARAB RELATIONS: 1973-1975

Prior to October 1973 there was little in the way of direct African-Arab contact beyond the customary exchange of cultural and diplomatic missions and some limited trade, plus the involvement of Arab states in Africa in the OAU. The October 1973 war resulted in the OAU declaration against Israeli aggression into African (Egyptian) territory and the almost complete rupture of African diplomatic relations with Israel. So began Africa's ambiguous but politically charged minuet with the Arab world.

The Arab response to African support against Israel first emerged clearly at the Arab summit of 1973 held in Algiers. The document adopted by the meeting called for the following:

- the accelerated development of diplomatic relations between Arab states and African states;
- increased aid for countries suffering from the drought;
- the development of economic, financial, and cultural cooperation between the Arab world and Africa, both at the level of bilateral relations and at the level of institutions for regional cooperation; and
- the creation of an Arab fund specializing in the economic and social development of Africa, to include the necessary technical assistance.

Also included, it should be noted carefully, was a commitment to cut off oil supplies for South Africa, Rhodesia, and Portugal.

Considerable political contention has emerged around this question: What was the quid pro quo for

African support of the Arab cause against Israel?
African governments evidently assumed that it would be
Arab guarantees of cheap oil. The Arab countries seem to
have defined it as breaking off their oil sales to the
colonial powers of Southern Africa. African states broke
diplomatic relations with Israel; Arab states broke
commercial relations with South Africa, Rhodesia, and
Portugal.

The sub-Saharan African governments have been somewhat dissatisfied with the institutional arrangements
established to channel Arab foreign aid. The initial
formal arrangement was the creation of a special committee within the OAU to handle African-Arab affairs. However, according to most reports, this committee has not
played a large part in the disbursement of funds. The
initial, and most important, financial instrument to date
has been the Special Arab Fund for Loans to African
Countries, to which $200 million was promised. There had
been some hope that the money would flow through the
African Development Bank based in Abidjan, thereby per-
mitting more African input into the allotment of monies.
The Arab Fund, however, took the lead, with only limited
African participation. Other institutions were established on paper but were not operational by 1975. One,
the Arab Bank for Economic Development in Africa, is
based in Khartoum and set an initial goal of $230
million. In addition there is the Arab Fund for Technical Assistance in Africa, which had a formal commitment of
$25 million. The latter's governing body then comprised
representatives of the United Arab Emirates, Algeria,
Saudi Arabia, Iraq, Egypt, Libya, and the Palestine
Liberation Organization (PLO).[46]

Aside from the organizational forms, there was some
dissatisfaction in Africa over the amounts of money involved. Whereas Africa's oil bill rose over $1 billion,
the original amount of aid had been $200 million, and
only a portion of that was actually distributed. In
addition, all of these monies were in the form of re-
payable loans, not grants.

It is critical when discussing these figures to keep
in mind that they do not represent the major burden upon
African development. Oil imports at the time represented
only between 8 percent and 15 percent of the total import
bill of the underdeveloped countries. The principal
contradiction lies between all the underdeveloped countries on the one hand and the developed countries on the
other. Nonetheless, the political problems growing out
of differences of perception of the "oil crisis" on the
part of Africans and Arabs can have a definite impact on
the future evolution of relations between the two areas.
After the soft prices of 1975-1978, the 1979 increases
renewed frictions between African importers and OPEC.

One of the best statements of the African-Arab situation was made in 1974 in an article in the influential

weekly review Jeune Afrique. Although the magazine is
written with an eye toward an Africa-wide audience, the
editorial staff and orientation are nonetheless North
African and Arab. The article sheds quite a bit of light
on the question at hand.[47] Written by staff writer Paul
Bernetel, the article highlights the differences in
expectations on the part of Africans and Arabs, each
group with its own historically given attitudes toward
the other. It also stresses that the Arab world, like
the African world, is not homogeneous. There are two
broad groups of Arabs. There are those of North Africa,
more oriented toward Europe and the rest of Africa and,
due to their own political histories, more politically
progressive. These states include Algeria, Morocco,
Tunisia, Libya, Mauritania, and Egypt. The eastern Arabs,
with smaller and less politically and economically
mobilized populations, are led by more conservative
elements. As Bernetel characterized the differences, "The
(former) pose the problem of solidarity in political
terms, the (latter) giving priority to the commercial
and economic aspects."[48]
    The differences between the two sets of Arab states
are more than geographically inspired, and it is here
that Bernetel's analysis falls short of the mark. The
critical difference is the fact of differential imperialist penetration and exploitation of feudal Arab societies. It is no accident that the most radical states--
Algeria and Libya--were among the most effectively
colonized by European capitalist expansion. Saudi
Arabia, Kuwait, and the other conservative regimes never
suffered to the same degree under colonialism. Hence
their relative lack of appreciation for the fraternity
of the "damnés de la terre." There is less genuine
sense of Third World solidarity where there has been no
capitalist exploitation and its dialectical opposite,
antiimperialist struggle.
    As African-Arab strategies related to commodity
control represent a spillover from the issue area of
energy, there is another extremely important issue that
arises from energy strategies: the expansion of Arab
private investments into African economies.
    Mega-billions of dollars are at present pouring
into the Arab states at such a rate and in amounts so huge
that their economies cannot possibly absorb them. This
structural incapacity to absorb new wealth has led Arab
money managers to look for sources of investment abroad.
For the most part a coherent pan-Arab strategy of investments has not been worked out. Most of this money will
find its way into investment projects in the United
States and Europe, where the returns are, on the average,
greater and where there is more selection as to the type
of investment that can be made than there is in the LDCs.
Some investments, however, will find their way into
African countries, particularly as income and savings

in the European countries decline in the face of higher
oil prices.

The question for Africa will be how to channel and
monitor this capital inflow so that, intentionally or
not, African countries are not recolonized by massive
doses of Arab capital. This may seem to be an unlikely
event now, but it could occur if the capital inflow is
not carefully monitored.[49]

OECD COUNTERSTRATEGIES: 1973-1975

We now turn briefly to the counterstrategies with
which African states have had to contend in the world
capitalist arena. In this context, the United States
has taken the most rigid and conservative of positions,
France the most progressive, and the rest of Europe and
Japan positions lying somewhere between. The counterstrategies have centered on three fundamental issues:
(1) Who should talk to whom? (2) About what? (3) With
what result? The first two issues, while highly
charged politically, are in essence procedural; the
third is more substantive. However, as the resolution
of the first two issues will largely determine the third,
they are critically important to worldwide energy
policies. These positions are still contested today.

The conservative end of the energy-policy spectrum,
occupied by the United States, has argued that, first
and foremost, the rich oil-importing nations (those be-
longing to OECD) should meet and reach a consensus on
international energy policy. All other nations would be
excluded from this initial meeting. Subsequently the
OECD countries would meet with the OPEC countries.
Finally, toward the end, the underdeveloped oil-importing
countries (i.e., most of Africa, Asia, and South America)
would be allowed to participate. Second, the conserva-
tives want to restrict the discussions to oil only--
pricing, security of supply, and so on--omitting consideration of any other economic issues. Third, the con-
servatives argue that the result of such discussions
should be the maintenance of the U.S.-dominated status
quo in the world political economy.

The Nixon-Kissinger-Ford-Rockefeller strategy on the
energy crisis was that of a fireman trying to contain a
dangerous Molotov cocktail blaze to one room of an old
wooden mansion. The fireman tries desperately to prevent the blaze from spreading; however, spontaneous
combustion threatens to ignite issues in other rooms--
issues like food, aid, and monetary policies. The United
States hoped that by maintaining a stubborn stand on
energy, where it felt its dominance slipping, it could
prevent its worldwide hegemony from being eroded
in other policy areas. The basic contradiction of U.S.
foreign policy has lain in this fact. The Third World
nations have tried to follow the example of OPEC by

tossing Molotovs into every room in the wooden, rickety
structure of international capitalism, uniting the struggle over raw materials with their dissatisfaction over a
myriad of related policy areas: aid, Special Drawing
Rights (SDRs), access to developed countries' markets,
food supplies, and worldwide inflation. In other words,
they are demanding a restructuring of the world political
economy, of which energy is only a single component.
     The right wing of U.S. foreign economic policy
traditionally has had its major spokesman in the U.S.
Treasury Department. It is the Treasury Department that
pushed the isolation of energy from all other policy
areas as the bulwark of the U.S. international position.
In November 1974, the conservative wing presided over the
formulation of Project Independence, a manifesto of
energy isolation that boldly declared the United States's
intention to become totally self-sufficient in energy.
When this work of fiction became increasingly difficult
to defend, to both the developed and the underdeveloped
countries, in the face of events in the real world, it
was eased aside. Yet on other fronts the United States
continued to uphold this utopian vision. Just as the
conservative wing balked at realistically linking
domestic and international energy issues in Project
Independence, so they adamantly refused to consider
energy-nonenergy linkages. This refusal of the right
wing of U.S. foreign policy to consider "bundling" issues
together was an expression of that faction's desire to
shore up its "structure of peace" (a thinly disguised
euphemism for containment of the Third World).
     The left wing of America's foreign policy establish-
ment has been represented by people like C. Fred
Bergsten, then at Brookings and now a senior Treasury
official. It also has proponents in the Department of
State. This faction came closer to reading the hand-
writing on the wall and called for U.S. participation in
multilateral negotiations with producer and consumer
nations on a wide range of international issues, from oil
to the use of the ocean. This "head-'em-off-at-the-
pass" faction is more realistic in its assessment of
rising Third World militance and has recognized that
continued U.S. intransigence will simply harden the lines
of conflict. In 1973-1975, the conservative wing was
dominant.
     U.S. policy on the energy question in the 1970s
has been to establish new agencies under its control
(first the International Energy Group, then the International Energy Agency) in which to argue its energy-
isolationism position or to use existing institutions
under its control (IBRD, IMF) to do the same. It is for
this reason that it resisted the first U.N. Special
Session on Raw Materials, as well as the demands by the
French and others that the Paris energy conference of
April 1975 be given a broader mandate. The United States

initially rejected these demands. The U.S. delegation
to the meeting found itself unable to impose its view
upon either the European "allies" or the representatives
of the underdeveloped countries.[50] Henry Kissinger later
declared, in a speech before the Ministerial Council for
the OECD in May: "Confrontation and cooperation cannot
be carried on simultaneously. International meetings
that exhaust themselves in self-indulgent rhetoric or
self-righteous propaganda help no one and no cause. We
do not consider it constructive to participate in such
exercises; we have a clear interest in resisting bloc
pressure tactics or attempts to impose solutions through
hostility."[51]

However, faced with an open alliance of progressive
and antiimperialist Third World countries, the conservative elements of U.S. foreign policy had to back off
from their earlier position and articulate a new raw
materials tactic. By so doing Kissinger et al. gave the
appearance of moving closer to the less conservative
wing of the establishment and more in line with the
repeatedly stated European policy of increased consulta-
tion and cooperation between rich and poor nations.[52]
However, this "new" position was still a long way from
meeting Africa and the rest of the raw materials-export-
ing countries even halfway. The most fundamental reforms proposed by the underdeveloped countries--re-
structuring international aid and monetary relations,
and indexing goods to minimize the effect of inflation--
were rejected.

The French position on the three issues--who should
meet with whom, about what, and with what results--was
at odds with the U.S. position and more nearly attuned
to that of the underdeveloped countries. With its long
history of colonial rule and its greater dependence on
imported raw materials, the French leadership took a
characteristically independent stand. Procedurally,
the French favored the inclusion of rich and poor
importers, as well as the exporters, in a single international conference that would not be restricted to discussions of energy. Substantively they hoped to increase
their own power, at the expense of the United States if
necessary, by concentrating on direct deals with the oil-
exporting countries, at the same time negotiating in
multilateral forums.

Like France, and unlike the United States, the rest
of Western Europe relies almost entirely on imported oil
and other raw materials. Thus such countries can afford
less than the United States to antagonize the underdeveloped countries on which they rely so heavily.
The United States was then two-thirds self-sufficient in
oil and is rich in other commodities. It is therefore
not surprising that U.S. and European policies diverge.
Thus, the policies of West Germany, Italy, Britain,
Japan, and other industrialized countries tend to

fluctuate between the reactionary policies of the United
States and the slightly more progressive policies of
France, although they are usually closer to the latter.

RECAPITULATION

Robbed of its spectacular hocus-pocus, the energy
crisis is merely one brief moment in the changing relations between the world's rich and the world's poor.
As such, it has created new problems and new opportunities for the African masses.
The major issues raised in this chapter have been
the following:
1. The vast majority of the African population relies on energy sources other than the infamous oil: wood,
charcoal, and so on. The average African unit of pro-
duction--the family farm--is a low user of nonhuman
energy.
2. The highest energy users are those productive
units owned by non-Africans.
3. Rather than changing this trend, African governments continue to channel energy supplies not to the
farms owned and worked by the 80 percent of the population in the countryside, but firms that are urban-based
and essentially controlled by expatriate bourgeois
interests in cooperation with elements of the small
national bourgeoisie.
4. The energy crisis has revealed the distortion of
development at both the local and the national levels,
which extends beyond energy supplies to credit, social
services, and infrastructure.
5. Finally, to change these relations within Africa
requires major changes in the balance of political power
in African societies. Mass political movements must
struggle against the domination of the urban-based local
and international bourgeoisies.
The energy crisis has been made to seem notorious
not because of its intrinsic significance but because it
occurred simultaneously with a deep cyclical recession
in the capitalist world economies. It is the confluence
of these two distinct but interrelated occurrences that
led to the worldwide notoriety of oil. Because all
definitions are contextual, the energy crisis can only be
understood within this larger setting.
Many important issues remain to be investigated:
questions of trade agreements, raw materials producer
associations, and the like. For Africa, they can be
summed up under the proposition that the African masses,
while struggling for a more modern political economy
capable of absorbing and distributing the fruits of
advanced technology, must capture and maintain a measure
of autonomy and self-reliance. This will require
patterns of production and consumption oriented not
mainly toward the needs of the international capitalist

economy, but toward building the domestic political and economic capacity of the masses of the African people.

NOTES

1. W. Rodney, How Europe Underdeveloped Africa (London: Bogle L'Ouverture, 1972). Rodney's position is that the phenomenon we call underdevelopment has three essential features. The first is that it is a relationship between two political economies or areas, and hence underdevelopment is a comparative relationship. Second, it is a condition of exploitation. Third, there is the element of lost initiative; priorities and policies are set not by the initiative or participation of the masses, but by men in the capitalist countries to serve their own interests. Development, the obverse term, would then require mass political initiative to end exploitation within the country and between that country and others. C. Furtado, in his Diagnosis of the Brazilian Crisis (Berkeley: University of California Press, 1965), described the internal process of development as "a process of social change by which a growing number of human needs--either those already in existence or those created by the change itself--are satisfied by means of differentiation in the productive system resulting from the introduction of technical innovations" (p. 17).

2. See Furtado, Diagnosis of the Brazilian Crisis, p. 17. To the definition of development provided in note 1 should be added the caveat that this process of social change is usually self-sustaining over time. It is not the result of windfall profits resulting from changes in the price level of, for example, raw materials. The change is qualitative and must be based upon the increased productivity of the national labor force. Increased productivity can be brought about only by providing the working population with the necessary capital goods and infrastructure. This includes the more equitable and efficient distribution of energy resources.

3. E. Wilson, "The Great Energy Gap: 1970-1990," Black Scholar, March 1974.

4. By external aspects of underdevelopment we mean the position of unequal exchange between underdeveloped countries and the world's capitalist powers. This asymmetry leads to Underdeveloped Country (UDC) exploitation in commercial, military, cultural, and monetary relations. By the internal aspects we mean a special configuration of indigenous class relations and institutions. These internal dynamics are the product of past conflict and accommodations between local and foreign social systems. The two aspects--internal and external--are complementary when the African elite aligns its material interests with the external capitalist system irrespective of indigenous mass development needs.

5. First Biennial Review of African Performance, Second United Nations Development Decade (New York: United Nations, 1973), p. 4.

6. Situations, Trends and Prospects of Electric Power Supply in Africa (New York: United Nations, 1965).

7. Survey of Economic Conditions in Africa (New York: United Nations, 1971).

8. *Provisional Indicative World Plan for Agriculture Production* (Rome: Food and Agricultural Organization, 1970).

9. *African Development*, December 1974, p. 26.

10. *Petroleum, Raw Materials and Development.* Memorandum submitted by Algeria on the occasion of the special session of the United Nations General Assembly, 1974 (New York: United Nations, 1974).

11. *African Development*, December 1974, p. 26.

12. *African Economic Indicators: 1970* (Addis Ababa, 1972), p. 11.

13. Ibid.

14. C. Leys, *Underdevelopment in Kenya* (Berkeley: University of California Press, 1974).

15. *New York Times*, 9 December 1973.

16. *African Economic Indicators: 1970*, p. 14.

17. S. Pearson, *Petroleum and the Nigerian Economy* (Palo Alto, Calif.: Stanford University Press, 1970); Scott R. Pearson and John Cownie, *Commodity Exports and African Economic Development* (Lexington, Mass.: D. C. Heath, 1974).

18. *New York Times*, 9 December 1973.

19. *African Economic Indicators: 1970*, p. 33.

20. Economic Commission for Africa, 1974.

21. Address to the Board of Governors, by Robert S. McNamara, president, World Bank Group, Nairobi, 24 September 1973, p. 10.

22. I. Adelman and C. Morris, *Economic Growth and Social Equity in Developing Countries* (Palo Alto, Calif.: Stanford University Press, 1973).

23. F. Fanon, *The Wretched of the Earth* (New York: Grove Press, 1966).

24. R. Green, *Unity or Poverty* (Baltimore: Penguin, 1967), p. 14.

25. *African Economic Indicators*, p. 29. For an analysis of production and consumption, see Table 2, Emembolu and Pannu, p. 42.

26. Quoted in Zuhayr Mikdashi, "Economic Considerations in Refinery Development," paper presented at the U.N. Interregional Seminar on Petroleum Refining in Developing Countries, New Delhi, 1973, p. 15.

27. Ethiopia, Ghana, Ivory Coast, Kenya, Liberia, Malagasy Republic, Senegal, Sierra Leone, Tanzania, Zaire, Zambia.

28. *OECD Observer*, No. 73, January-February 1975, p. 34.

29. Ibid., p. 27.

30. Ibid., p. 34.

31. *Petroleum, Raw Materials and Development*, p. 140.

32. For an insight into this dilemma see Green, "National Independence and the National Economy: An Essay on the Political Economy of Decolonization," in *African Perspectives*, edited by Christopher Allan and R. W. Johnson (Cambridge: Cambridge University Press, 1970).

33. *Fortune*, August 1975, p. 158.

34. I. G. Shivji, *The Silent Class Struggle* (Dar es Salaam: Tanzanian Publishing House, 1973). See especially the article by Walter Rodney.

35. See especially the Kenyan press, e.g., *Daily Nation*, or the *Ghanian Daily Graphic* or *Times*, during the period between

January 1974 and January 1975.
36. Business Week, 2 October 1974, p. 113.
37. Algeria, Botswana, Burundi, Cameroon, Ghana, Egypt, Mali, Senegal, Sierra Leone, Sudan, Tanzania, Zaire.
38. Ravei Gulhati, Eastern and Southern Africa: Past Trends and Future Prospects, World Bank Staff Working Paper No. 413 (Washington, D.C.: World Bank, August 1980), pp. 5-6.
39. L. Hewes, "Rural Progress and the Role of Energy Among Less Developed Countries," Dialogue discussion paper, Center for the Study of Democratic Institutions, p. 14.
40. See the World Bank study, Rural Development: Sector Policy Paper, Washington, D.C., 1975. For a fascinating account of agricultural needs during the current drought in Africa, see C. Meillassoux, "Sahel Famine," Review of African Political Economy, No. 1, 1974.
41. H. Nau, National Politics and International Technology: Nuclear Research Development in Western Europe (Baltimore: Johns Hopkins University Press, 1974), p. 205.
42. Hewes, "Rural Progress": "The problem is not to electrify the aggregate . . . rural landscape or energies of Asian or African agriculture in vast plantations, but rather to distribute energy in a usable form to small populations, villages of a few hundred or a few thousand people with a local agricultural land base that may not exceed one or two thousand acres divided into very small farms" (p. 7).
43. M. Tanzer, The Political Economy of International Oil and the Underdeveloped Countries (Boston: Beacon Press, 1968), pp. 277-288.
44. Jeune Afrique, No. 706, 20 July 1974, p. 54. See also A. Moumouni, "Solar Energy in African Countries," Présence Africaine, Vol. 22, No. 50, 1964, p. 8.
45. W. Warren and N. Rubin, eds., Dams in Africa (London: Frank Cass, 1968).
46. Middle East, No. 9, June 1975, p. 29.
47. Jeune Afrique, No. 682, 2 February 1974, p. 14.
48. Ibid., p. 15.
49. Another unlikely possibility would be an alliance of Arab capital with South African technology and industry. Such an "unholy alliance" would wreak havoc with Black African strategies for independence. Although such an alliance is unlikely, its effect would be so disastrous that we should allow ourselves to think the unthinkable. This scenario would be based upon the complementarity of the economies of the two regions. The Middle East and North Africa have oil and money and need technological know-how and finished manufactured goods. Southern Africa needs oil and capital and has technological know-how and finished manufactured goods. Their combined weight would tend to dominate the entire continent. Aside from the economic weight, Black Africa would then find itself sandwiched between two hostile groups. This underscores Black Africa's need to develop and maintain institutional relations with the Arab world. It also heightens again the absolute need of Africa to rid itself of the malignancy of the white cancer in Southern Africa. Thus the fact that African pressure was successfully brought to bear on the Arabs to extend the boycott of oil to

Portugal and Southern Africa becomes even more significant in the long run.

50. A central pillar of Kissinger's international energy policy was an ill-conceived floor price on imported oil, below which the price of oil would not fall. Its goal was to prevent OPEC from undercutting alternative energy sources that would be below the current price of oil.

51. U.S., State Department, press release, May 1975.

52. Compare, for example, European cooperation with the African, Caribbean, and Pacific (ACP) nations at the Lomé negotiations. The EEC has also agreed to establish a $450 million fund to help stabilize commodity export earnings of the APC nations. Actually, U.S.-African trade and aid relations are secondary compared to European-African relations: only about 7 percent of total African trade is with the United States.

6
Patterns of Trade and Prospects for Growth in a Triregional System: Arab Oil Exporters, Sub-Saharan Developing Africa, and the OECD

Frank A. Ocwieja

Although the value and importance of international trade between the developing countries of sub-Saharan Africa[1] and Arab oil-exporting countries[2] grew rapidly during the 1970s, its scope remains very narrow. Trade between the two regions and the industrialized market economies (members of OECD) has also expanded greatly. But, in contrast, the character of this trade is broad.

The trade interaction of these three groupings of economies still reflects the legacy of colonial history. Its underlying structure was formalized in the agreements on trade and payments made at Havana and Bretton Woods following World War II. However, by the 1960s the foundations of this system had already begun to shift. The political emergence of the newly independent developing countries brought with it an economic nationalism that challenged the dominance of the industrialized countries by restricting the freedom of the multinational companies to conduct their business as usual. Soon the rapid growth and maturation of many industrial economies strained the international monetary system, forcing the abandonment of fixed exchange rates. Finally, the OPEC oil price increases of 1973-1974, made possible by the dependence of the industrial economies on imported energy, created a drastic redistribution of monetary wealth in the world. That event was the coup de grace to the old economic order. However, no coherent framework like that of Bretton Woods has yet emerged for the new system.

One of the potential opportunities that the shift in wealth seems to offer is the devotion of a part of it to financing the establishment of a New International Economic Order (NIEO). The new order would, it is claimed, be based on an equitable division between the supplying and the consuming countries of the benefits of international trade and investment. The definition of this equity is a controversial subject that I choose to leave open in this chapter. Nevertheless, one of those benefits is supposed to be the economic development that is generated by the expansion of trade.

137

138

The purpose of this chapter is to describe the current patterns of trade among the three groups of countries described above in light of the major changes sustained by the international economic system. The practical measures that have been and can be taken to expand that trade can be examined using actual data. My particular interest will be in how the economic power of the Arab oil-exporting nations may be used to generate new export opportunities for the states of sub-Saharan Africa.

INTERREGIONAL TRADE PATTERNS

The gross value of trade among the developing countries of sub-Saharan Africa, Arab oil-exporting countries, and the OECD, shown in Table 6.1, increased by 254 percent from 1973 through 1978--from $43.7 billion to $154.9 billion. The gain in the value of exports from the Arab oil exporters (299 percent) was nearly matched by the OECD increase in export value (288 percent). By far the largest gain in the value of imports (exports from the other regions) was posted by the Arab oil exporters (477 percent). Sub-Saharan Africa's trade with the other two regions increased by only a relatively modest amount (exports 123 percent, imports 163 percent). During the same period, total trade of the three regions grew by 223 percent, and thus the share of world trade[3] represented by transactions among these three regions increased from 9.9 percent to 16.2 percent. The overwhelming majority of this trade is between

TABLE 6.1
OECD, SUB-SAHARAN AFRICA, ARAB OIL EXPORTERS, INTERREGIONAL EXPORT 1973 AND 1978 ($ BILLIONS)

	Exports to							
	OECD		Sub-Saharan Africa		Arab oil exporters		Total interregional	
Exports from	1973	1978	1973	1978	1973	1978	1973	1978
OECD	--	--	9.2	24.0	7.1	39.2	16.3	63.2
Sub-Saharan Africa	9.9	22.1	--	--	0.1	0.2	10.0	22.3
Arab oil exporters	17.2	68.7	0.2	0.7	--	--	17.4	69.4
Total interregional	27.1	90.8	9.4	24.7	7.2	39.4	43.7	154.9

Source: IMF, Direction of Trade Statistics (Washington, D.C., 1980).

TABLE 6.2
OECD, SUB-SAHARAN AFRICA, ARAB OIL EXPORTERS, SHARE OF INTER-
REGIONAL TRADE IN TOTAL TRADE (TRADE WITH PARTNER REGION AS
PERCENTAGE OF REFERENCE REGION'S TOTAL WORLD TRADE)

			Partner region			
	OECD		Sub-Saharan Africa		Arab oil exporters	
Reference region	1973	1978	1973	1978	1973	1978
OECD	--	--	2.3%	2.6%	3.0%	6.2%
Sub-Saharan Africa	77.6%	76.6%	--	--	1.2%	1.5%
Arab oil exporters	78.9%	78.9%	1.0%	0.7%	--	--

Source: IMF, Direction of Trade Statistics (Washington, D.C.: 1980).

the OECD on one hand and either the African or Arab group
on the other hand. In fact, trade with OECD countries
represents more than three-fourths of the imports and
exports of both regions, as shown in Table 6.2.
    In contrast, trade between sub-Saharan Africa and
the Arab oil exporters is small, constituting 1.5 percent or less of the total trade of either region. Moreover, this trade has not grown as fast as the total world
trade of the two regions during the period and thus has
decreased its share of their overall trade activity.

Composition of Trade Involving OECD

    It is important to analyze the commodity breakdown
of the trade among the three regions, not only to
realistically assess its significance, but also to
identify those areas that hold opportunity for expansion.
    In 1977, the latest year for which complete figures
are available, OECD transactions with the other two
regions were characterized by the importation of primary
and semimanufactured products and the exportation of manufactured goods of all kinds, as shown in Table 6.3. In
particular,

● 95.6 percent of OECD imports from sub-Saharan
  Africa were in Standard International Trade
  Classification (SITC) categories 0, 1, 2, 3,
  and 6--i.e., primary products and semimanufactures;
● 99.2 percent of OECD imports from the Arab oil
  exporters were crude oil and refined petroleum
  products;
● 88.2 percent of OECD exports to the African countries were in categories 5, 6, 7, and 8--i.e.,

TABLE 6.3
OECD INTERNATIONAL TRADE BY PARTNER COUNTRIES, 1973 AND 1977 ($ BILLIONS)

SITC Category	Sub-Saharan Africa				Arab oil exporters				OECD				Total non-OECD				World			
	Imports (c.i.f.)		Exports (f.o.b.)		Imports (c.i.f.)		Exports (f.o.b.)		Imports (c.i.f.)		Exports (f.o.b.)		Imports (c.i.f.)		Exports (f.o.b.)		Imports (c.i.f.)		Exports (f.o.b.)	
	1973	1977	1973	1977	1973	1977	1973	1977	1973	1977	1973	1977	1973	1977	1973	1977	1973	1977	1973	1977
0-Food & live animals	2.9	7.5	0.9	1.8	0.1	0.1	0.6	2.3	32.4	48.0	28.0	46.1	19.2	36.0	11.3	17.6	51.6	84.0	39.3	63.7
1-Beverages & tobacco	0.1	0.1	0.1	0.4	0.1	--	0.1	0.3	4.6	6.4	4.6	6.5	0.9	1.4	1.0	2.2	5.5	7.8	5.6	8.7
2-Crude materials except fuels	2.9	3.5	0.1	0.2	0.1	0.1	0.1	0.3	28.8	40.1	23.3	36.3	16.9	23.8	4.4	9.1	45.7	63.9	27.7	45.4
3-Mineral fuels	2.5	10.8	0.1	0.5	18.4	74.0	0.1	0.3	12.3	32.4	12.0	30.7	36.1	137.4	1.7	5.0	48.4	169.8	13.7	35.7
4-Oils & fats	0.2	0.3	--	0.2	--	--	0.1	0.1	1.4	2.2	1.4	2.2	1.1	2.0	0.7	1.8	2.5	4.2	2.1	4.0
5-Chemicals	0.1	0.2	0.8	1.8	--	--	0.4	1.4	25.0	48.7	24.4	46.5	1.9	4.2	10.4	21.8	26.9	52.9	34.8	68.3
6-Mfd. goods by material	2.2	2.2	1.7	3.9	0.1	0.1	1.7	7.3	62.5	101.1	63.3	99.1	15.8	22.3	21.3	44.6	78.3	123.4	84.6	143.7
7-Machinery & transport equipment	0.1	0.1	5.5	13.5	--	--	3.1	17.9	97.1	173.2	100.1	171.2	4.7	10.4	40.1	101.0	101.8	183.6	140.1	272.2
8-Misc. mfrs.	--	0.1	0.5	1.2	--	--	0.5	2.9	29.6	51.8	28.9	50.2	7.6	18.3	5.5	13.0	37.2	70.1	34.4	63.2
9-Non-classified	--	0.2	0.1	0.2	--	0.1	0.1	0.7	3.4	5.9	2.3	5.1	0.9	1.8	2.4	5.1	4.3	7.7	4.7	10.2
TOTAL*	11.0	24.9	9.9	23.7	18.8	74.5	6.7	33.5	297.1	509.8	288.4	493.8	105.2	257.2	98.7	221.1	402.3	767.5	387.1	714.9

*May not add due to rounding.

Source: OECD, Statistics of Foreign Trade, Series C (Paris, 1979).

manufactured goods;
* 87.8 percent of OECD exports to the Arab group were in the same categories.

The importance of these transactions to the OECD countries in 1977 may best be measured in terms of their share of OECD trade with non-OECD countries:

* OECD imports from sub-Saharan Africa of SITC categories 0, 1, 2, 3, and 6 constituted 10.9 percent of all such imports originating outside OECD;
* OECD imports from the Arab oil exporters of fuels constituted 53.9 percent of all such imports from outside OECD;
* Exports from the OECD of categories 5, 6, 7, and 8 to the African and Arab countries constituted 11.3 percent and 16.3 percent respectively of all such exports to destinations outside the OECD.

The only drastic change in those shares in the years between 1973 and 1977 was, as expected, the more than doubling of the Arab oil exporters' importance as a market for OECD manufactures, from 7.4 percent of the total in 1973.

There are four obvious features that distinguish the OECD trade with sub-Saharan Africa from that with the Arab oil exporters.

Fuels. Virtually the whole of OECD imports from the Arab group of countries is crude oil, making this trade much more critical to the OECD economies than its gross value might indicate. The same fact underlines the importance of Arab exports to sub-Saharan Africa. However, while the increase in the price of oil had the effect of more than doubling the share of OECD trade accounted for by the Arab countries, it did not have as large an impact on the regional balance of African trade, for three reasons:

* African economies are much less energy-intensive than those of the OECD;
* Africa is a net energy exporter, and a larger share of its crude oil needs than those of the OECD is supplied from within the region;
* Africa still imports approximately one-fourth of its energy needs in the form of refined products from the OECD and other crude oil-importing countries.

Food. The African countries enjoy a net surplus in their trade with the OECD in the category of food and live animals. This is largely due to the well-developed tropical cash-crop industries, particularly coffee, cocoa, tea, and spices. Together, these products accounted for $6.2 billion in exports to the OECD in 1977, or 83 percent of all African food shipments. Of OECD exports in this category to the other two regions the largest component was grains (38.1 percent of exports to Africa and 47.7 percent of exports to the Arab countries in 1977).

Crude Materials. Africa is a major source of non-fuel raw materials for a wide variety of OECD industries. The largest exports of these in 1977 were metalliferous ores, wood, textile fiber, and rubber. The Arab oil exporters, except for Algeria, have yet to develop important alternative primary industries for export to the OECD.

Semimanufactures. Finally, sub-Saharan Africa exported $2.2 billion worth of semimanufactured items to the OECD in 1977 (SITC category 6). The largest component of this category was nonferrous metals (77 percent), which are refined before export.

Composition of Arab-African Trade

Trade between the developing countries of sub-Saharan Africa and Arab oil-exporting countries is generally very narrow in scope with regard to both the number of partners and the variety of commodities traded. The geographical concentration is illustrated by the following facts:

● Only eight African countries, shown on Table 6.4, accounted for 53.2 percent of the total amount of trade between the two regions in 1978.
● These eight countries, moreover, originated 81.5 percent of total exports from the African group to the Arab oil exporters.
● Of the eight countries, six (Ethiopia, Djibouti, Somalia, Sudan, Kenya, and Tanzania) are located on the East African littoral and trade mainly with the countries of the Arabian peninsula.

As indicated earlier in Table 6.2, trade with sub-Saharan Africa equals less than 1 percent of the worldwide trade of the Arab oil exporters. Table 6.5 shows the imports of the five countries in the Arab group for which statistics are available. It confirms the relative insignificance of their imports from sub-Saharan Africa and the narrowness of that trade:

● Less than 1 percent of the worldwide imports of the Arab oil exporters come from sub-Saharan Africa.
● Three-quarters of those imports from Africa were in the category of food and live animals.
● Those imports of food and live animals from Africa, however, constituted less than 5 percent of the Arab countries' total imports in that category.

TABLE 6.4
TRADE WITH ARAB OIL EXPORTERS: LARGEST SUB-SAHARAN AFRICAN
PARTNERS, 1978 ($ MILLIONS)

Country	Exports to Arabs	Imports from Arabs
Djibouti	11	3
Ethiopia	17	39
Ivory Coast	6	42
Kenya	14	44
Somalia	42	24
Sudan	37	126
Tanzania	5	40
Uganda	13	--
Total	145	318

Source: IMF, Directory of Trade Statistics (Washington, D.C., 1980).

DEVELOPMENTAL ROOTS FOR TRADE PATTERNS

The differing patterns of trade among the three
groups of countries under study are rooted in certain
historical developments that have not yet been overtaken
by the effects of the redistribution of global wealth in
the mid-1970s. Broadly speaking, three factors can be
isolated:

- the existence of an economic subregion surrounding the Red Sea and Indian Ocean characterized
  by commercial contacts and population movements
- the fundamental role of large, primarily European-
  based trading companies in developing the international commerce of the African countries with a
  colonial history
- the relatively restricted transfer of industrial
  technologies from the OECD nations to the other
  two regions that accompanied the growth in their
  trade with each other

Red Sea-Indian Ocean Subregion

The rapid economic growth of the oil-exporting
countries on the Arabian Peninsula seems only to have
reinforced their traditional patterns of commerce with
sub-Saharan Africa. In addition to the predominance of
East African partners in Arab oil exporters' trade with

TABLE 6.5
ARAB OIL-EXPORTING COUNTRIES, COMMODITY COMPOSITION OF IMPORTS (C.I.F.) ($ MILLIONS)

SITC Category	Algeria 1977 Total	From Africa	Iraq 1975* Total	From Africa	Kuwait 1977 Total	From Africa	Libya 1977 Total	From Africa	Saudi Arabia 1977 Total	From Africa
0-Food & live animals	1,042	80	650	7	516	5	642	17	1,283	95
1-Beverages & tobacco	20	1	8	3	49	--	19	--	162	--
2-Crude materials excluding fuels	268	15	133	6	75	13	100	1	250	5
3-Mineral fuels	97	--	12	--	35	--	21	--	81	--
4-Oils & fats	127	--	77	--	9	--	44	--	59	--
5-Chemicals	388	--	247	--	146	--	135	--	578	1
6-Mfd. goods	1,688	1	1,255	1	1,047	1	826	7	4,248	4
7-Mach. & trans. equipment	3,230	--	1,724	--	2,205	--	1,414	--	5,851	2
8-Misc. mfrs.	242	--	95	--	726	--	571	3	1,711	2
9-Non-classified	1	--	--	--	37	--	--	--	125	--
TOTAL**	7,102	97	4,201	17	4,845	19	3,773	29	14,289	109

*Most recent year available.
**May not add due to rounding.

Source: United Nations Statistical Office, Trade Statistics Microfiche (New York, 1980).

Africa, the immigration of African nationals into the
Arab countries has also been largely from the eastern
part of the continent, especially Sudan. This is illustrated by Table 6.6, which shows the numbers of pilgrims
and others, presumably workers, from sub-Saharan Africa
who entered Saudi Arabia or received residence permits in
1977. The major exception to that phenomenon is Nigeria,
which has sent 100,000 pilgrims to the hajj in each of
the last few years. However, it is the exception that
proves the rule, for trade between Nigeria and the Arab
oil-exporting countries was virtually nil throughout the
1973-1978 period. Thus, the increased personal contact
between Arabs and Africans caused by the economic boom in
the oil-exporting countries has not in itself been
sufficient to generate a higher level of trade between
the two regions.

On the contrary, the apparent correlation between
personal contacts and trade between the Eastern African
countries and Saudi Arabia is probably a vestige of
traditional commerce between them. The need for foreign
laborers in the Saudi economy has been more easily filled
from Eastern Africa than from other non-Arab parts of the
continent not only because of proximity, but also because
of the history of commerce between the regions. The
growth in personal contacts since 1973 mirrors increased
trade transactions between the regions but cannot be said
to have caused them to increase.

European Trading Companies

The role of major trading houses--most of them
connected with large multinational corporations--in
fostering the growth of exports of primary commodities
from sub-Saharan Africa has been amply documented (see,
for example, the considerable amount of research on the
subject done by UNCTAD). An important element of the
role the trading houses have played and continue to play
is assuring dedicated markets for those commodities, as
many of the houses are in some way related to the end-
user of the product. It is estimated that 50 percent of
all less developed country trade consists of transactions
between branches or affiliates of single multinational
companies based in the OECD countries,[4] a figure that
we assume applies at least as well to Africa.

The benefits of the trading relationships created by
these companies are hotly debated. On one hand, it is
clear that they have successfully generated a large and
important volume of commerce in both directions between
the OECD and sub-Saharan Africa. This has increased the
per capita incomes of all the economies involved. On
the other hand, the balance of these benefits, particularly in the case of commodity exports, has generally
favored the partner that has undertaken the financing
and marketing functions (i.e., the OECD countries) over

146

TABLE 6.6
SAUDI ARABIA, POPULATION MOVEMENTS: 1973-1977

Country of origin	Pilgrims 1977	Foreigners entering 1973	Foreigners entering 1977	Residence permits granted 1973	Residence permits granted 1977
Ethiopia	1,121	1,208	3,308	623	2,159
Kenya	590	n.a.	n.a.	16	52
Somalia	4,786	843	n.a.	228	3,381
Sudan	32,352	20,011	57,756	2,127	15,892
Tanzania	1,086	n.a.	n.a.	12	31
Uganda	4,621	n.a.	n.a.	7	19
Nigeria	104,577	1,312	14,915	40	53
Others	24,415	1,892	13,482	210	664
TOTAL (Sub-Saharan Africa)	173,548	25,266	89,461	3,263	22,251

Source: Kingdom of Saudi Arabia, Central Department of Statistics, Statistical Yearbook (Riyadh, 1978).

the producers of the commodities.

Nevertheless, the two trading partners do have common interests, as illustrated by the agreements negotiated between them in the 1960s and 1970s to stabilize the prices of important commodities such as coffee, cocoa, tin, and sugar. Similarly, the development and distribution of Arab oil resources is still dominated by OECD-based multinational corporations. Except in the case of Algeria, little attention has been paid to exporting other commodities, although mineral and agricultural potential has been proven to exist in the Arabian Peninsula and elsewhere.

Selective Transfer of Technology

Certain technologies have been transferred to both the sub-Saharan Africa countries and the Arab oil exporters by the OECD nations in the course of their trade. However, the importance and variety of these transfers have been limited, as evidenced by the amount of the former's exports to the OECD of semimanufactured and manufactured products. Although processing and manufacturing industries have been established to serve domestic and intraregional markets, few are sufficiently competitive to find significant markets back in the OECD. This is illustrated by two characteristics of inter-regional trade:

- More than 80 percent of the exports from Arab oil exporters of nonfood semimanufactures and manu-factures to the OECD in 1977 were refined petroleum products.
- More than 75 percent of 1977 exports of the same categories of products to the OECD from African countries were refined metals and minerals, and animal and vegetable oils.

Table 6.7 shows sub-Saharan Africa's exports of crude materials to the OECD in 1977, as well as trade with the OECD in the corresponding semimanufactures. Outside the area of oilseeds and minerals and metals, this comparison demonstrates that Africa's crude materi-als are often processed outside the country of origin. The exceptions can be explained by the relatively simple technology involved in extracting oils, on the one hand, and the costliness of transporting metal and mineral ores, on the other hand.

PROSPECTS FOR INCREASED TRADE

The patterns of trade among the developing coun-tries of sub-Saharan Africa, the Arab oil-exporting countries, and the OECD have changed but little since the oil price actions taken by OPEC in 1973-1974. Africa is still a minor element in the Arab trade picture, and trade with Africa has even diminished slightly in its relative importance to the OECD. Moreover, the commodity balance of that trade, in which the OECD is the center of industrial activity purchasing raw materials from and selling finished goods to the other two regions, has not measurably changed. There are, in fact, two separate and asymmetrical international trading systems among these three regions:

- Direct trade between them. The most important of these channels is trade between OECD nations on one side and either of the other two regions on the other. Direct trade between the African and Arab groups of countries has barely progressed in recent years beyond its traditional scope and relative size.
- Intermediated trade in which the OECD acts as a consumer of energy and processor of materials from the other two regions in order to supply them both with manufactured goods.

While these patterns have not changed, the volume of trade, measured by the value of interregional exports,

TABLE 6.7
OECD TRADE WITH SUB-SAHARAN AFRICA, 1977 ($ MILLIONS)

SITC Number and description	Imports from Sub-Saharan Africa	SITC Number and description	Imports from Sub-Saharan Africa	Exports to Sub-Saharan Africa
21-Hides and skins	117	61-Leather mfrs.	39	43
22-Oilseeds	356	4-Oils	329	151
23-Crude rubber	137	62-Rubber mfrs.	1	258
24-Wood, lumber, cork	902	63-Wood, etc., mfrs.	72	48
25-Pulp and paper	12	64-Paper mfrs.	--	326
26-Textile fibres	476	65-Textile yarn, fibres	61	759
27-Crude fertilizers and minerals	227	56-Mfd. fertilizers 66-Mineral mfrs.	308	496
28-Metal ores and scrap	1,164	67-Iron and steel 68-Non-ferrous metals 69-Metal mfrs.	1,753	2,092

Source: OECD, Statistics of Foreign Trade, Series C (Paris, 1979).

has grown greatly (see Table 6.1). However, the sub-Saharan countries have not experienced as large a gain in either interregional or overall exports as the OECD or the Arab oil exporters. In fact, if Nigeria, a major oil exporter, is left out of the calculation, sub-Saharan Africa's total exports during 1973-1978 grew by only 96 percent, much slower than those of all non-oil-exporting countries, whose combined exports during that period grew by 117 percent.

The question posed at the outset of this chapter was how the high levels of national spending in the Arab oil-exporting countries, and the surplus investment capital in some of them, can be used to increase trade among the three regions, particularly exports from sub-Saharan Africa. Of course, in at least two ways this is already being done:

- The massive rise in imports by the Arab countries, although supplied primarily from the OECD, has fostered greater demand for raw materials exports from sub-Saharan Africa as well. This is the trickle-down effect.
- Large investments by the Arab countries of their "surplus" capital, through bilateral economic assistance and grants and loans from the Arab oil funds and the World Bank, have been directed into infrastructure and other projects in African countries that are related to their export industries.

However, the mechanisms of the trickle-down effect and foreign aid are notoriously inefficient and slow. The record indicates that they have not yet proven successful.

This analysis of the actual trade patterns among the three regions suggests that there may be more promising ways in which the new spending power and financial clout of the Arab oil-exporting countries can be used to increase exports from sub-Saharan Africa. These possibilities can be divided according to three alternative immediate objectives they would seek to achieve:

- expanding direct trade between developing countries in general and, in the context of this chapter, between the sub-Saharan countries and the Arab oil exporters
- disintermediating interregional trade by circumventing the middle role of the OECD
- expanding intermediated trade, making it more efficient as a mechanism of economic growth

Each of these alternatives deserves a brief discussion.

Expansion of Direct Trade

There are some obvious complementarities between the
economies of sub-Saharan Africa and the Arab oil-exporting
states that could be exploited through increased trade.
Three possibilities are often singled out:

- export of food from Africa to the Arab countries,
  particularly to those on the Arabian Peninsula
- export of certain crude minerals to oil-exporting
  countries for energy-intensive processing near a
  cheap energy source like gas
- export of relatively simple manufactured goods to
  labor-short Arab markets

One way of gauging the potential for trade in these
areas is to compare current Arab oil exporters' imports
of these products with current African exports. As
shown in Table 6.8, the Arab imports of these product
categories are significant when compared with the amounts
African countries are already exporting to the OECD.
However, specific opportunities for export sales within
those gross numbers can be identified only by actual
marketing efforts. Principally through the workings of
UNCTAD, many solutions have been offered to the problem
of encouraging increased trade among developing countries.
These have included a global system of trade preferences,
export credit guarantee schemes, cooperation among state
trading corporations, the strengthening of interregional
economic cooperation, multilateral clearing and payments
arrangements, and other measures of cooperation. Although they all have definite merit and could contribute
to an atmosphere more conducive to trade, there can be
no substitute for personal contact and the negotiation of
specific deals when it comes to increasing export sales.
    Indeed, state trading corporations are able to
conclude agreements that may create new trade between
highly centralized economies in the two regions. For
example, Angola and Algeria signed a commercial agreement
in 1980 that provides for an $80 million exchange of
textiles, shoes, canned foods, gas, and wine from Algeria
for coffee, wood, hides, and skins from Angola.[5] A
similar agreement between Mozambique and Iraq has also
been recently reported.[6]
    In most cases, however, one or both of the economies
on either end of the trade will be market economies.
In such a case, persistent marketing by private companies
is likely to be the only productive mechanism for generating new business ties. Both official approaches and
private initiatives have been tried in Kenya. Although
the establishment of a joint trading company has been
agreed to by the Saudi and Kenyan governments, concrete
results have been more easily achieved through govern-
ment-supported trade missions in the Middle East.[7] Kenya

TABLE 6.8
ARAB-AFRICAN TRADE IN SELECTED COMMODITIES, 1977 ($ BILLIONS)

SITC number and description	Imports by OECD from Sub-Saharan Africa	Total imports by five Arab countries
0-Food & live animals	7.5	4.1
2-Crude materials	3.5	0.8
6-Manufactured goods	2.2	9.1

Source: United Nations Statistical Office, Trade Statistics Microfiche (New York, 1980).

has begun to export a variety of foods, manufactures and clothing to the Arab oil-exporting countries, mainly as a result of the efforts of individual businessmen.

Other methods for fostering increased direct trade between the regions are more grandiose and promise long-term benefits. The celebrated case of the Kenana Sugar Project in Sudan illustrates the kind of initiating role an Arab financial institution (in this case, the Kuwait Foreign Trading, Contracting and Investment Company) can play in building a project to export food products from Africa to the Middle East. It also serves warning that many difficulties must be overcome, including lack of infrastructure, competing interests of technical and equity partners, and the need to finance cost escalations that are the more intractable the larger the project is.

Several other projects involving Arab capital have been proposed that would seek to satisfy Middle Eastern markets for food with African products. The fact they must all eventually face is that only in a few particular cases in which a dedicated market can be defined and served are large export-oriented projects really a wise investment. Thus, export-oriented projects should start from the base of a good sales organization in the target markets. Otherwise, the surer way to foster increased trade between sub-Saharan Africa and the Arab oil exporters is the segmentation and dogged pursuit in both regions of markets for each other's goods produced by industries that already have a base in their domestic economies or in other traditional markets.

Another direction that Arab-African cooperation could take would be to finance the expansion of intra-African trade. For an industry to successfully exploit new international markets, it should be able to count on strong domestic demand to ensure an economic base level of production. Continuing efforts to promote regional economic integration in Africa, such as ECOWAS, the Customs Union of West African States (UDEAO), the Mano River Union, and others, aim at strengthening the base

market for African exports. Established intra-African
export industries will be reliable sources of supply for
Arab markets, and Arab investment in their development
should be a key element in any strategy for cooperation.

Disintermediation of Interregional Trade

Another way to generate increased trade between the
African and Arab groups is to short-circuit indirect
trade that now passes through the OECD or elsewhere on
its way between them. In certain cases, this diversion
of trade is justified by external economies. For example,
to save transportation costs, small refineries have been
established in many African countries, making them
independent of outside sources of refined oil products
and allowing them to export certain products, such as
heavy distillates, to OECD countries. The availability
of relatively cheap gas in the Middle East is making it
attractive to start energy-intensive metallurgical
industries there, such as the steel mill in Qatar that
now makes that Arab oil-exporting country a market for
iron ore.
The potential for disintermediating a large share
of Africa's current trade through the OECD, however, is
limited by the size of the Arab markets for consumer
goods and the availability of the labor and industrial
base necessary to process Africa's traditional exports
there. An alternative approach would involve the
establishment of more processing industries in the
African countries with Arab capital. These industries
could then serve both OECD and Arab markets. Such a
strategy falls in well with the objectives of the
proponents of the New International Economic Order,
who seek to make the suppliers of primary products less
dependent on multinational corporations for their
markets. However, as in the case of direct trade, the
key ingredient for the success of this kind of project
would be the involvement of an effective sales organization to ensure a market for the product.

Expansion of Intermediated Trade

Finally, Arab capital can also be used to improve
the efficiency with which present trading patterns bring
benefits to the supplying countries in sub-Saharan
Africa.
Producers in these countries could develop either
new markets in the OECD countries or alternative
channels of distribution, if they had the necessary
financial backing. This backing could include joint
trade-financing schemes, support for stabilization funds
for internationally traded commodities, and capital to
strengthen the marketing and distribution capabilities
of African exporters. One of the options UNCTAD is

studying is the creation of multinational trading
enterprises to pool the information, promotional, and
supply resources of several developing countries to sell
common products in nontraditional markets. This goal is
apparently being successfully achieved by COMUNBANA, a
joint marketing company formed by five Latin American
countries. COMUNBANA is complementing the traditional
sales channels for bananas provided by multinational
companies with additional direct sales in OECD markets.[8]
Providing the financing necessary to mobilize such an
effort might be an attractive venture for Arab capital
and one that could have a relatively short-term payout.

CONCLUSIONS

    Although trade among the OECD nations, the develop-
ing countries of sub-Saharan Africa, and the Arab oil-
exporting states has grown by a large percentage since
1973, the structure of that trade has not changed. The
OECD is still the keystone of interregional trade,
acting as the major consumer of raw materials and
supplier of manufactured goods. In particular, trade
between the African and Arab groups remains very small
and restricted to mainly traditional partners and
commodities.
    The increased wealth and spending power of the Arab
oil exporters offers African countries an opportunity
to generate economic development through higher levels
of exports, taking advantage of Arab markets and private
and public sources of capital. Businessmen and governments in Africa may find specific trading possibilities
that will involve any of the following:

● creation of additional sales of food and manufactured goods to expanding Arab markets
● diversion of current raw materials exports away
  from the OECD processors to economically better
  located processors established in the Arab
  countries or in Africa, with Arab financing
● enterprises and efforts to expand and broaden
  African exports to the OECD, financed with Arab
  capital

    The key ingredient for success in any of these
efforts is the ability to identify, define, and secure
markets for the products to be exported. These activities must be undertaken at the initiative of the African
exporters themselves, whether state corporations or
private businessmen. Continuous personal contact is
required to gain the confidence of potential business
partners in the Arab world (an important lesson for OECD
exporters as well). No amount of government-to-govern-
ment cooperative agreements, tariff preferences, tax
incentives, or concessionary financing will ever be an

154

adequate substitute.

NOTES

1. All countries on the African continent and surrounding islands except Egypt, Libya, Tunisia, Algeria, Morocco, and South Africa.
2. Algeria, Iraq, Kuwait, Libya, Oman, Qatar, Saudi Arabia, and UAE.
3. Unfortunately, the IMF direction of trade statistics on which this part of the analysis is based do not fully account for trade with nonmarket economies (China, the Soviet Union, and Eastern Europe) that are not members of the IMF.
4. UNCTAD Document No. TD/BC2/197, May 1979, p. 24.
5. Afrique-Asie, 21 January 1980, p. 40.
6. African Business, March 1980, p. 28.
7. African Business, March 1980, p. 59.
8. UNCTAD Document No. TD 229 Supp. 3, May 1979, p. 22.

Part 3

Petrofunds and the Legal Framework for Triangular Cooperation

7
Financial Flows from the Arab Middle East and the OECD Nations to Sub-Saharan Africa: An Assessment and Prospects

Kamal Hossain

INTRODUCTION

The first part of this chapter analyzes financial flows and commitments from 1973 to 1979 from the Arab Middle East to sub-Saharan Africa. The Arab Middle East is defined as the twenty-one countries that are members of the Arab League, but the sources of identified financial flows and commitment are mainly confined to the seven Arab members of OPEC and OPEC/Arab international financial institutions. Sub-Saharan Africa is defined as the forty African countries to which the Arab Bank for Economic Development in Africa (BADEA) has made loan commitments, excluding the four sub-Saharan Arab countries (Djibouti, Mauritania, Somalia, and Sudan), Namibia, Zimbabwe, South Africa, and certain British and French overseas possessions (St. Helena, Mayotte, and Réunion). The forty countries are divided into the seven Sahel countries, twelve other least developed countries (LDCs), eleven other low-income countries (LICs), and ten other countries, which include two members of OPEC (Gabon and Nigeria).[1] Financial flows are confined to capital account transactions (defined as including official transfers), and those identified include concessional and nonconcessional transfers from the seven original Arab members of OPEC (bilateral) and OPEC/Arab international financial institutions (multilateral). The financial flows and commitments from the Arab Middle East that reach sub-Saharan Africa via other international financial institutions (e.g., the IMF, World Bank group, African Development Bank) have not been identified and are therefore excluded (with the exception of the Arab share of commitment by the IMF oil facility). However, such flows and commitments up to 1976 have been identified for OPEC as a whole by Klaus Netter of UNCTAD and increase the total flows from and commitments by OPEC by up to 50 percent (the difference being mainly nonconcessional flows and commitments).
Sub-Saharan Africa may be viewed as a region of

157

paradoxical extremes: Generously endowed with mineral and land resources and considerable human potential, its record of economic development in the postwar period is characterized by poor growth performance and continued widespread hunger and poverty. In spite of attractive investment possibilities, this region has not succeeded in attracting adequate resource flows from commercial sources. Failure to attract commercial investment has been due to a number of factors: political instability of some countries of the region and the lack of legal safeguards for investment; inadequacy of existing infrastructure, particularly in transportation and communications; paucity of skilled manpower; and finally, perhaps ignorance on the part of potential foreign investors about investment possibilities in the region. Not all of these problems are insurmountable and the prospects for dealing with them will be examined below, with special reference to the institutional mechanisms set up by the OPEC states.

The oil price increase of 1973 and the consequent accumulation of surpluses by the OPEC states engendered hopes among developing African states that, although hard hit by the price increases, felt they might become major recipients of the total financial flows from the OPEC states. There was seen to be a complementarity of interests--Africa required large flows of capital to develop its untapped resources, while the OPEC states sought profitable investment opportunities for the funds that their economies could not immediately absorb in productive activities. Total Arab aid commitments to sub-Saharan Africa from 1973-1978 have been estimated to be on the order of $3,874 million.[2] There is, however, scope for a much larger commitment. An examination of the cumulative OPEC surplus from 1974-1978 indicates that only one-quarter went to LDCs and multilateral institutions, although the share going to LDCs had risen to about one-third in 1978.[3]

The level of financial flows to sub-Saharan Africa has declined in nominal as well as real terms since the peak of $991.4 million in 1975.[4] This is not surprising in view of the erosion of the surplus between 1975 and 1978; the 1979 increases in oil prices will partially restore the level of OPEC surpluses and raise expectations of increased resource flows to LDCs. To keep the level of Arab aid in perspective, it is useful to note that in terms of the ratio of donor aid to GNP, total commitment of the Arab OPEC countries to Africa represents no less than 0.5 percent of their combined GNP.[5] This is an impressive contribution relative to those of the Development Assistance Committee (DAC) countries, particularly if it is kept in mind that these represent contributions from sales of nonrenewable resources on the part of the OPEC donors, i.e., contributions made from stocks rather than flows.

Identified net Arab flows to sub-Saharan Africa
(1973-1978) totalled $1,078 million. Of this, $824
million (76 percent) was concessional ($455 million, or
42 percent, bilateral; $368 million, or 34 percent, multi-
lateral); and $255 million (24 percent) bilateral non-
concessional. By country group, the LDCs, including
Senegal ("another low-income country"), received $616
million (57 percent), and other LICs $302 million (28
percent). Countries that received more than $50 million
were Guinea ($119 million), Zaire ($110 million), Uganda
($78 million), Mali ($74 million), Cameroon ($62 million),
and Senegal ($59 million).

ASSESSMENT OF FINANCIAL FLOWS
FROM ARAB STATES TO SUB-SAHARAN AFRICA

The Sources of Aid to Africa

    Although bilateral aid constituted approximately
two-thirds of total Arab aid to Africa ($2538 million)
in the period 1973-1978,[6] multilateral institutions such
as BADEA, the Special Arab Aid Fund for Africa (SAAFA),
the Fund for Arab-African Technical Assistance (FAATA),
and the IDB continued to play an important role. There
has, however, been a discernible trend toward increases
in the proportion of bilateral flows.
    From 1973 to 1977, $1,731 million in total bilateral
commitments of $2,049 million was made by three coun-
tries--Saudi Arabia ($695 million), Kuwait ($620 million),
and Libya ($416 million). Of the $1,082 million of multilateral commitments in the same period, $544 million was
made by BADEA and SAAFA, $474 million by the IMF Oil
Facility, $38 million by the IDB and the Islamic
Solidarity Fund, $24 million by the Arab-African Inter-
national Bank and Arab International Bank (both of
Cairo), $3 million by FAATA and $0.1 million by the Arab
Fund for Economic and Social Development, which normally
confines its lending to Arab countries. Looking at total
commitments by sector, $1326 million (34 percent) was not
tied to any specific project, with $791 million
committed for balance-of-payments support and $222
million as emergency aid. Of the $866 million (22 per-
cent) for infrastructure, $570 million was for transport
and communications and $295 million for power. Of the
$688 million (18 percent) allocated to services, $337
million was for social services, $240 million for
financial institutions, $59 million for technical
cooperation, and $53 million for trade and tourism.
Commitments to industry ($591 million, or 15 percent)
included $279 million for extractive industries, $172
million for construction, $140 million for processing
industries, and $403 million (10 percent) for agricul-
ture.
    Turning to net flows by donor, of the $710 million

(68 percent) bilateral flows, $570 million came from three countries--Libya ($217 million), Kuwait ($191 million), and Saudi Arabia ($161 million). Of the $255 million (24 percent) bilateral nonconcessional, practically all came from three countries--Libya ($124 million), the UAE ($62 million), and Kuwait ($60 million). Of the $368 million (34 percent) multilateral concessional flows, $183 million came from BADEA and SAAFA, which was taken over by BADEA in 1976, $79 million from the OPEC Special Fund, $5 million from FAATA of Cairo, which is controlled by the Arab League, and $1 million from the Islamic Development Bank. According to UNCTAD, total bilateral flows more than doubled in 1975 (mainly nonconcessional) but increases were less in 1973, 1974, and 1976.

The share and absolute level of aid channeled through multilateral agencies is understated in the figures quoted above. The statistics on financial commitments of Arab states to Africa should include contributions to the World Bank, other U.N. agencies, and other international agencies, but the obvious complexities of separating these contributions preclude this. The figures do, however, include aid channeled through the IMF Oil Facility, calculated on a pro rata basis following the contributions of Arab countries to this facility.

Before we examine the existing level of Arab financial flows to Africa it would be useful to have an overview of the foreign policy issues facing OPEC countries. It may be emphasized once again that the level of OPEC aid must be evaluated differently from that of the DAC countries, simply because the former's aid flows are generated from the "liquidation" of nonrenewable assets. In a sense these funds are "borrowed" from future generations--the responsibility to invest these funds in productive assets naturally inhibits the propensity to give aid to other LDCs. Second, in spite of the 1979 oil price increase, the level of OPEC surpluses will remain below the peak of 1974, mainly because of the increased absorptive capacity of the surplus states. Third, the OPEC states are wary of being drawn into open-ended commitments to fully compensate for the effects that the increased oil prices had on other LDCs and are naturally worried that they may be pressed into a role of replacing aid from other sources.

Finally, it must be noted that the circumstances surrounding the OPEC aid effort are fundamentally different from those of most other donors. Although OPEC aid has helped generate support in international forums for the concerns of donor countries, OPEC countries do not share the strategic concerns of other categories of donors. Moreover, they do not enjoy the gains of DAC donors whose aid generates demand for their exports and expertise. In this sense OPEC aid is

especially desirable, as there is no tying to source.
Hence, the different motivation underlying OPEC aid,
as opposed to DAC aid, should be noted in any discussion
of the role of OPEC aid.

Arab aid to Africa (see Table 7.1) has been in the
form of program as well as project aid, although the
latter constitutes a rising share of total aid. In this,
the Arab countries are following the trend set by the
IBRD and the regional development banks--not too surprising in view of the organizational and technical
assistance given by the IBRD, particularly to the Arab
multilateral organizations. The preference for project
aid is common to other donor groups and stems from the
following factors: the belief that project finance is
less likely to be wasted (the project in question having
been subjected to feasibility studies and cost-benefit
analysis); the desire to see the aid contribution em-
bodied in a visible structure; and finally, the possibility that the recipient country may not have the
technical resources to allocate funds effectively. The
drawbacks to project assistance include a bias toward
large, capital-intensive projects; longer administrative
procedures and lags in the commitment of funds to a
project (although BADEA itself has been improving the
speed of allocation of funds in recent years);[7] and the
danger that there might be a bias against the least
developed countries that may find it difficult to
identify attractive projects because of their inadequate
manpower and technical resources.

In view of the extra costs imposed on the Arab
donors in terms of identifying and evaluating projects,
it seems that there should be a greater emphasis on
straight budgetary assistance. Such assistance would be

TABLE 7.1
MAJOR SOURCES OF FINANCE FOR ARAB AID TO AFRICA

	1973-1977 percentage of total
Saudi Arabia	22.22
Kuwait	19.8
BADEA	13.6
Libya	13.3
UAE	4.7
OPEC Special Fund	3.7
Algeria	2.2

Source: BADEA, Annual Report (Khartoum, 1978).

doubly valuable because the deficits in their external
accounts constitute a major bottleneck to the development programs of African states and because these states
face considerable difficulty in obtaining loans in the
international market. The poorer states are often
effectively barred from obtaining commercial loans and
are reluctant to turn to the IMF because of the imposition of unacceptable constraints on national economic
policy by that organization. Moreover, in spite of
repeated calls for increased program lending by the
Pearson and Brandt commissions,[8] DAC aid remains biased
in favor of project and commodity aid. Some of the drawbacks of project aid are appreciated by Arab donors,
such as the bias toward large-scale projects, as can be
seen in the initial proposals for channeling aid through
national development institutions that would be better
able to identify small- and medium-scale projects.
However, this mechanism for resource transfer has not
been utilized, an issue that will be examined later in
another section.

An important issue in any discussion of OPEC aid is
whether it should be channeled through multilateral
institutions or given on a bilateral basis. The granting of aid is an act of foreign policy--OPEC donors are
naturally concerned about control over the terms, scope,
and direction of their aid effort and about the attribu-
tion of credits by the recipient. The OPEC countries'
wish to control the distribution of their aid also stems
from a realization that an individual donor's interests
may be swamped by the interests of other members of a
multilateral institution. Indeed, there may be widespread dissatisfaction with the policies of an institution, although donors can exercise ultimate control
through refusals to increase the capital base or
replenish capital, as in the case of the Arab Fund for
Economic and Social Development (AFESD) in 1979.[9]

However, while there is an understandable preference
for bilateral aid, there is also an appreciation among
OPEC donors that aid is expected from OPEC as a collective body and that the coincidence of many of the OPEC
countries' foreign policy interests, particularly with
respect to sub-Saharan Africa, renders this practical.
The acceptance of the principle of channeling a major
portion of aid to Africa through multilateral sources
was demonstrated when the BADEA was created in 1973,
soon after the oil price increase, with an initial
endowment of $231 million. This was followed by the
establishment of SAAFA in 1974 under the sponsorship of the League of Arab States, with initial capital
of $200 million. The Arab Fund for Technical Assistance
in Africa (AFTAA) was set up in the same year with
statutory capital of $15 million (later raised to $25
million). The operations of these three institutions,
set up exclusively for the purpose of channeling Arab

aid to Africa, will be examined below, although the
contribution of other Arab multilateral agencies, notably
the Islamic Development Bank, should also be noted.
BADEA was set up to institutionalize African-Arab
cooperation and to coordinate Arab aid with the aid provided to Africa by other multilateral development institutions. The emphasis has been on the provision of
concessionary long-term loans. A sectoral breakdown of
its activities shows that in the period 1975-1978,
BADEA's total commitments for major sectors were as
follows: infrastructure (39.6 percent); agriculture
(2.7 percent); industry (18.6 percent); power (14.8 percent); and emergency aid (5.3 percent). BADEA representatives attend the twice-yearly meetings of the various
Arab funds and coordinate participation by these funds
in the financing of individual projects, as it is better
able to evaluate projects in Africa.[10] Interest rates
charged by BADEA have ranged from 2 percent to 7 percent,
depending upon the overall economic situation of the
recipient country, and the grant element has varied from
28 percent to 57 percent. The majority of loans have a
maturity of twenty-five years, including a grace period
of five years. In this regard it should be noted that
the repayment of loans has been insignificant, so that
transfers made by the bank, unlike the transfers of the
IBRD, so far represent net transfers to Africa.[11]
SAAFA was created to alleviate the balance-of-payments difficulties of African countries after the oil
price rise and to finance the development of oil resources in this region. Its capital base was raised to
$360 million in December 1976, after which its capital
was merged with that of BADEA. SAAFA provided $221.7
million to 35 African countries (mainly most seriously
affected, or MSA, countries) on extremely soft terms--
1 percent per annum, eight years' maturity, three years'
grace period. These terms were later softened even more
to fifteen to thirty-five years' maturity, including
five to ten years' grace period.
After SAAFA merged with BADEA there were two further
increases, of $115 million and $105 million, in BADEA's
capital in 1977. By 1978 the bank's total subscribed
capital stood at $738 million, with paid-up capital of
$590 million and total commitments of $504 million
(representing 68.31 percent of the subscribed capital).[12]
Total commitments had risen to $572 million by March 1980.
Finally, the role of other multilateral agencies set
up by the Arab states should be noted, in particular the
OPEC Special Fund, the Islamic Development Bank, the Arab
International Bank, the Afro-Arab Bank, the Islamic
Solidarity Fund, and AFTAA. Between 1973 and 1977 these
six institutions were responsible for commitments of
$179 million, with $116 million from the OPEC Special
Fund alone, much of it in the form of balance-of-payments
support. The contributions of these institutions have

been important in the area of cofinancing of loans to
Africa, particularly in conjunction with BADEA and Arab
national development institutions, such as the Saudi
Fund, the Kuwait Fund (KFAED), the Iraqi Fund (EIFD),
and the Abu Dhabi Fund (ADFAED). By the end of 1978
BADEA joint financing with other Arab development institutions totalled $378 million, or 31 percent of the total
cost of financed projects.[13] The main focus of the
national development funds remains in the Arab world,
partly because of the difficulties of identifying suitable African projects. However, in recent years they
have extended their commitments to Africa, coordinating
their efforts through the twice-yearly meetings of all
the Arab development funds, where BADEA and other institutions present potential projects and seek to attract
the participation of a number of funds in each project.
Cofinancing appears to be a means of expanding Arab
flows relatively quickly, as the Arab funds do not have
the management resources to undertake project identification and evaluation on their own.

Between 1973 and 1978, if Nigeria and Gabon are
excluded, African oil imports (net of Congo's exports)
rose from 19 percent of their current account deficits
in 1973 to 55 percent in 1974, falling to around 40 percent in 1978, and the total identified Arab commitments
fell from 71 percent of the increase (over 1973) in
African oil imports in 1975 to 26 percent in 1978. Total
(net) current account deficits rose from $1,801 million
(for twenty-six countries) in 1973 to $6,886 million
(for seventeen countries only) in 1978 (of which $3,763
million was accounted for by Nigeria), while total aid
flows to the twenty-six countries (roughly equal to
their current account deficits) rose from $2,448 million
in 1973 to $5,479 million in 1978.

Concessional Flows

Not only was the bulk of Arab aid to Africa in the
period 1973-1978 on concessional terms, but the proportion varied considerably over the period. From a low of
48 percent in 1975, the proportion of total aid had
risen to 82.5 percent by 1978.[14] Over the period 1973-
1978 about $2,530 million (or 65 percent) of total Arab
financial commitments to Africa were in the form of
concessional commitments, which contrasts with Arab
flows to other developing regions, which had a lower
concessional component. The grant element of Arab
concessional aid compares favorably with that of DAC aid,
particularly when one considers that for the former there
is no comparable flow-back of funds and tying of aid
(see Table 7.2).[15]

These concessional flows are a vital component of
the total aid flow, particularly as African countries
face reduced proportions of concessional flows from other

TABLE 7.2
GRANT ELEMENT OF CONCESSIONAL AID FROM OPEC AND DAC COUNTRIES

	1973	1974	1975	1976
OPEC countries	95.3%	81.4%	73.6%	78.8%
DAC countries	87.5%	86%	88.6%	88.5%

Source: OECD, Annual Report (Paris, 1977).

aid sources. Africa's needs in terms of finance for infrastructure have not been adequately met--particularly in the fields of education and skilled manpower, transport and communication, and energy, especially hydroelectric power generation. By their very nature these areas are not amenable to commercial investment, nor are the returns from investment in these sectors quickly realizable. Such investment in infrastructure need not be regarded as "pure aid" by Arab donors--they may make commercial investment in other sectors feasible.

Nonconcessional Flows

The erosion of the oil states' surpluses after 1974 appears to have had its greatest impact on the level of nonconcessional flows to the African countries, which fell from a level of $516 million in 1975 to a low of $39 million in 1977 before recovering to $121 million the next year. Given the temporary nature of the surpluses and the limited capacity of most Arab donors to continue to finance aid to Africa on concessional terms, non-concessional flows would seem to hold the greatest promise for African states in the future. In this re-gard it is vital to effect a reconciliation of the needs of Arab lenders and the African countries. The former desire secure and profitable investments for their assets, and the latter would gain access to funds that would be otherwise unavailable through commercial channels.

There is a need for mechanisms to circumvent the existing process of recycling oil surpluses through the commercial banking system upon which the African coun-tries have increasingly drawn for their investment needs as well as balance-of-payments support. What this mechanism constitutes is a shift in the risk-bearing function attached to financial flows to Africa from the Arab owners of the funds to the commercial banks that re-lend them. The expense of channeling nonconcessional flows through the commercial banks could possibly be reduced through direct lending from the Arab countries to Africa, although there would be the difficulty that the present Arab surplus managers might lack the organizational resources and experience of directly evaluating investment opportunities in Africa on the necessary scale required. However, in recent years Arab funds and private investment institutions have begun to make commercial investments, generally in banking and mineral development.

It is known that Libya has put up a $34 million equity stake in a financial venture in Gabon, committed $20 million in 1976 to pay for Libya's share in a leather industry in Uganda, and lent $101 million to Zaire for a copper-mining project. It has also, through the Libyan Arab Foreign Bank, made commitments for equity shares in the Libyan Arab Uganda Bank, Chad-Arab Development Bank, Arab Libyan Togolese Bank, and Libya-Niger Bank for External Trade and Development. Also on the banking front, the Arab Bank (of Amman) has a minority share in the Arab Bank (Nigeria); the Kuwait Foreign Trading Contracting and Investing Company has a share in Banque Senegalo-Koweitienne; and BCCI Holdings, which has Arab shareholders, has subsidiaries in Nigeria and Swaziland and affiliates in Ghana, Algeria, Djibouti, Egypt, Libya, Mauritania, Morocco, and Somalia. Sudan and Tunisia are members of the African Development Bank, which, together with Kuwait and Saudi Arabia, is also a participant in the African Development Fund (both based in the Ivory Coast). In addition, Algeria has extended a $5 million export credit to Gabon and the UAE has made a commercial loan to Zaire.

The major arguments against increased nonconcessional lending to Africa revolve around the security of these investments and the relative profitability of investment in this region. The first issue will be dealt with in detail in the next section. This desire for security and general willingness to trade off profitability against security has been a major factor in the disposition of the bulk of the surpluses in the developed states. However, the range of investments open to Arab surplus states has in practice been limited to the purchase of government and private securities and real estate. The governments of the United States, West Germany, and Italy, in particular, have actively discouraged large equity investments by the OPEC states in their largest corporations. In a period of rapid inflation in the developed countries, the OPEC surpluses have in effect been channeled into "low-yielding" financial instruments for the most part. The consequent erosion of the surpluses has been accentuated by the depreciation of the dollar over this period; conservative estimates suggest that about one-third of total OPEC surplus holdings were dollar-denominated. These factors were combined with low rates of return from the investment of OPEC surpluses, in the aggregate averaging about 5 percent in 1976 and 1977 and falling to 3.7 percent in

1978.[16] In no year has the rate of return kept pace with
the rate of inflation in OPEC import costs. These
figures on returns, together with estimates of the
corresponding capital depreciation of OPEC assets during
this period, suggest that the costs of security of investment have been very high indeed. There is thus
considerable incentive to turn to more profitable areas
of investment, and Africa, with its large resource base,
could provide a wide range of investment opportunities.
The next section will discuss the ways and means of over-
coming the obstacles to investment in Africa and of
finding channels through which investment funds could
profitably be allocated.

PROSPECTS FOR EXPANSION OF FINANCIAL FLOWS FROM
THE ARAB MIDDLE EAST TO SUB-SAHARAN AFRICA

The current plight of the non-oil-producing, less
developed countries (NOLDCs) cannot be ascribed, as is
often done, simply to the increase in oil prices, because
it also results from the actions of developed countries
that "export" inflation in the form of increases in the
prices of goods they export (particularly finished manu-
factures). This and other points have been well demonstrated by Rehman Sobhan in his draft paper, "Financial
Flows Between Developing Countries: Prospects for
Economic Cooperation Between OPEC and the Third World"
(Centre for the Study of the New International Economic
Order, Oxford, August 1979). Accordingly the developed
countries bear a moral responsibility to assist in
alleviating the plight of the NOLDCs.

Since the 1973 oil price increase, the OPEC group
has established a large number of national and multilateral agencies in order to channel a portion of the surplus to developing countries. The need to stimulate
financial flows to developing African states was under-
lined by the decisions adopted by the Sixth Arab Summit
Conference in Algiers in 1973 regarding the strengthening of Arab economic, financial, and technical cooperation with the African countries. Before turning to the
prospects of expanding the different forms of financial
flows, it would be useful to assess the adequacy of
existing multilateral institutions as instruments for
increasing the level of financial flows.

As has been observed above, of the numerous Arab
multilateral agencies promoting concessional transfers
to the sub-Saharan African states, BADEA, the OPEC
Special Fund, and the IDB have been most important.
The IDB's narrower focus precludes its use as the main
vehicle for increased financial flows to the whole
region. The OPEC Special Fund has been involved in the
following forms of assistance to developing countries:
balance-of-payments support, contributions to international development agencies, and the direct provision

of loans to finance development projects and programs. The fund serves to coordinate the concessional lending programs of the OPEC states and acts as a "think tank" for the aid programs of individual states.

Both BADEA and the IDB have provisions for commercial operations, but they have focused mainly on long-term concessional lending. The low ranges of interest rates charged on loans to this region bear out their concessional character—the weighted average rate of interest of BADEA's financing was only 2.6 percent over the period 1975-1978 (taking into account the interest rates on SAAFA loans). Consequently, although these institutions were set up to channel some of the Arab surplus to developing countries, they have not placed these funds at financially advantageous rates of return for the contributing countries. Hence, while their activity has diversified the distribution of the surplus, these institutions have not sought, by their nature, to compete for the large portion of funds that the Arab countries must seek to invest commercially. Moreover, whatever loans they undertake on nonconcessionary terms serve to increase their capitalization and expand their financing capacity. The nature of their operations so far suggests that these institutions may not be the appropriate channels for commercial placement of Arab surpluses. However, BADEA has been active in promoting commercial investment possibilities among prospective Arab investors, serving as a source of information as well as providing assistance in coordinating lines of credit from other institutional and private sources.[17]

There are a number of commercial ventures, most of them set up with the participation of national governments of surplus states, that are geared to directing Arab commercial investment to this region. The scale of their activity in sub-Saharan Africa has been small so far, but they could form the basis for channeling much higher levels of commercial investment. These investment institutions have in the main been formed at a national level; it is suggested here that multilateral investment institutions would have considerable advantages in terms of greater spreading of risks. It would be useful at this stage to examine briefly the activities of some of the Arab investment institutions operating in Africa.

The Kuwait Foreign Trading, Contracting and Investment Company (KFTCIC) was established in 1965 to invest its assets in the form of loans and equity participation in investment mainly in Arab and African countries. A number of subsidiary companies and banks were set up to facilitate investment in different regions, although only a small proportion of investments were in Africa. The Libyan Arab Foreign Bank (LAFB) has been active in establishing small-scale joint ventures in African countries, particularly in the banking sector.

Of the multinational Arab investment institutions, the Arab-African Bank has been in operation since 1964, financing foreign trade and development projects in Arab and African countries. However, both this institution and the Afro-Arab Company for Investment and International Trade (AFARCO) have devoted only a small fraction of their resources to non-Arab Africa.[18] Some Arab financial institutions that have hitherto concentrated their activities on the Arab world could extend their activities to sub-Saharan Africa--the Arab Investment Corporation (AIC), the Kuwaiti Real Estate Investment Corporation (KREIC), the Saudi Arabian Real Estate Corporation (SAREC), and the Arab International Bank. The level of commercial investments could be greatly augmented if the numerous Arab companies concentrating on commercial investment in the Arab and Western world could be induced to invest in the sub-Saharan region. There is a need for a multilateral Arab investment company concentrating on sub-Saharan Africa alone. Initially there would have to be considerable commitments made by Arab governments, as the reluctance of private Arab investors to invest in a hitherto unfamiliar region of investment possibilities would have to be overcome. Such an institution should not be regarded as another means of extending aid to developing Africa--rather, it should constitute a profitable outlet for the disposition of the surplus currently invested in Western capital markets. Participation would be extended to private companies, which would by themselves be unwilling to accept the risks and administrative difficulties of investing in Africa.

A range of projects suitable for commercial investment will be briefly examined in the following section. An alternative to forming a large multilateral investment institution would be to encourage numerous national investment companies. However, some form of guarantees would be needed to overcome the reluctance to invest in Africa, possibly through the creation of an institution along the lines of the Inter-Arab Investment and Guarantee Corporation (IAIGC). The IAIGC, set up in 1971, operates only in the Arab world and covers the following types of risks: nationalization and confiscation; transferability of dividends and principal; and, finally, losses caused by war or internal disturbances.[19]

The establishment of a similar institution for Arab investment in Africa could be a powerful catalyst in stimulating private commercial investment. However, some of the larger private investment companies such as the First Arabian Corporation (FAC) have already made limited investments in developing Africa. The FAC has set up a joint venture with the government of the Central African Republic that will operate through a number of subsidiaries, including a diamond-mining and -export company, a large-scale agricultural company, an

international bank, and a trade and transportation
company. However, the number and scale of such private
commercial investments is small and could be greatly
expanded.

Public-sector funds from the Arab countries could be
used in joint ventures with private concerns, as they
have been in the Arab world. A major problem, however,
is that although Arab governments have the necessary
funds, they generally lack the technical expertise with
which to develop industries. This could be solved either
by investing in Africa in partnership with foreign or
transnational companies that have the necessary technological "know-how" or by developing Arab domestic industries
and transferring the newly acquired expertise abroad
(perhaps following the Indian example of consultancies).

In this connection it is worth referring to a con-
fidential briefing document prepared by Professor Zuhair
Mikdashi for a meeting of the Arab-European Business
Council held at Cologny, near Geneva, on November 11,
1979. This document lists the following constraints on
direct investment by OPEC in the Third World: (1) the
limited number of entrepreneurs and financiers in the
OPEC capital-surplus countries able to identify and
consummate investment opportunities; (2) the inadequacy
of information on investment projects, legislative and
administrative frameworks, and the sociopolitical
environment; (3) the narrowness of areas of interdependence (e.g., trade) among developing countries
(OPEC and non-OPEC); (4) the need to involve several
parties in the realization of investment projects,
especially advanced enterprises from the technologically
advanced countries; and (5) the comparative ease of
investing or disinvesting in Western financial markets,
which enjoy greater transference of information and
rapid communications. Arab governments might, however,
attempt to reduce investment risks in developing countries through wider distribution of lending.

A major bottleneck in the flow of funds to projects
in the sub-Saharan countries has been the difficulty
involved in identifying and evaluating a large number of
alternative investment projects, particularly where
commercial investment is concerned. It is frequently
suggested that there should be increased emphasis on the
operations of development finance companies in individual
countries that could carry out the functions now undertaken by regional and multilateral institutions. These
national development banks could coordinate lines of
credit from regional, international, and other institutions and identify and finance projects in line with
national development goals. Extending Arab aid to such
institutions could be important in relieving the donors

of much of the burden of administering aid for an unfamiliar region, particularly in view of the strain on resources of trained personnel that an aid program involves. Aid channeled through such national development banks could take various forms: equity participation, the provision of long-term credit lines, the provision of trust funds for specified uses, or cofinancing in various forms. The problem with this whole approach has been the weakness of the institutional structure of existing development finance institutions in the countries of this region, particularly in terms of skilled and experienced personnel. It was only in 1978 that BADEA first assisted a development finance corporation--the Development Bank of Central African States (BDEAC)--that specializes in promoting medium- and small-scale projects as part of a program for regional economic integration.

Arab assistance could be invaluable to the sub-Saharan developing countries in the field of borrowing in international capital markets. Some African states that have been unable to tap commercial sources of credit could do so given Arab sponsorship of their bond issues. This possibility assumes added relevance given the increasing willingness of Arab investment funds and banks to act as managers and comanagers for major loans in the Eurocurrency market. In this way the commitment of a limited amount of Arab funds could serve as a catalyst to substantially increase the flow of commercial credits to the region.

Another method of improving the access of the sub-Saharan states to capital markets is by influencing the policies of the commercial banks with which the Arab states are major depositors. However, once OPEC governments have made their deposits in the commercial banking system, they have no control over the subsequent use of the funds. One solution might be for Arab governments to direct a larger proportion of their deposits to banks in which they themselves have a share (especially those that have connections in Africa), e.g., Arab International Bank (Cairo), Arab-African International Bank (Cairo), Arab Bank for Investment and Foreign Trade (Abu Dhabi), Gulf International Bank (Bahrain), Saudi International Bank (London), United Bank of Kuwait (London), Banque Arabe Internationale d'Investissements (BAII) (Paris), Union de Banques Arabes et Françaises (UBAF) (Paris), Banque Franco-Arabe d'Investissements Internationaux (FRAB) (Paris), European Arab Bank (Luxembourg), Bank of Credit and Commerce International (BCCI) (Luxembourg), National Bank of Abu Dhabi, National Bank of Dubai, Qatar National Bank, and National Bank of Bahrain. The Arab governments might then have greater control over the subsequent use of their funds. On the noncommercial side, Arab co-financing of loans to sub-Saharan Africa has assumed significant proportions--by the end of 1978 BADEA's co-financing with Arab funds and the Islamic Development Bank involved total commitments of $378 million. BADEA's cofinancing with other institutions has also been impor-tant and has had several advantages in terms of spreading risk for large projects and economizing on administrative resources in the evaluation and monitoring of projects.

Before we examine investment possibilities with potentially high yields, it might be useful to assess the potential positive impact (in terms of promotion of commercial investment in Africa by both Arab funds and private companies) of devising effective frameworks to legally protect foreign investments in sub-Saharan African countries (consistent, of course, with the goals of these countries' national economies).

The legal framework governing foreign investment needs to be reappraised in each of the countries of the region to determine whether it can be redesigned to provide certain basic safeguards that investors seek. Investors attach importance to stability of contractual relations, the right to repatriate the profits earned on their investments, and assurance of compensation in the event of nationalization. At the same time, states, conscious of the need to secure permanent sovereignty over natural resources and other national objectives, are prone to attach importance to retaining the sovereign power to take action that may be considered necessary to protect the national interest. It would, however, be counterproductive to devise a legal framework for foreign investment if its provisions were totally un-acceptable to foreign investors. The essential point is to know where to draw the line--or to strike the balance--so that capital, technology, and management skills can be secured for national development on the best possible terms. The capacity to exercise fine judgment in this area would be enhanced by an under-standing of the global investment environment and the conditions prevailing in the industry or sector con-cerned. New approaches to devising mining legislation and minerals resource agreements compatible with the principle of permanent sovereignty over resources merit careful study.[20]

OPPORTUNITIES FOR INVESTMENT OF THE ARAB SURPLUS

In the preceding two sections we have discussed the broad orders of magnitude of the flows of finance from the Middle East to various countries in Africa and made an assessment of the way in which these flows might develop in the years ahead. Before discussing any specific opportunities in particular countries it would

be useful to say something of general relevance to the
LDCs in Africa as a whole.

According to the forecast of the Economic Commission
for Africa, the rate of growth of GDP (at 1980 prices)
in the group of twenty African LDCs will average around
3 percent per annum in the decade 1980-1990. Slow growth
is particularly evident in agriculture, which is forecast to grow by less than 2 percent during this period;
industry is also forecast to grow relatively slowly, at
an average annual rate of around 4.5 percent. Total
investment is forecast to grow by less than 5 percent
annually without a commensurate increase in output because of inefficient capital utilization; the savings gap
is expected to grow to around 4 percent of GDP by 1990
while (based on current trends) imports are expected to
grow nearly 1 percent per annum faster than exports over
the decade as a whole. The net result therefore will be
a growing savings gap and a growing trade gap with little
or no impact on current levels of per capita income.

It is obvious, therefore, that a continuation of
past trends would be disastrous for the LDCs and that
almost all of them would be faced with mounting mass
poverty and unemployment. To alleviate these problems,
it would be necessary for these countries to aim for and
achieve a significantly higher rate of economic growth.
But to attain such growth would imply faster rates of
growth in agriculture and industry, improved capital
efficiency, and increased labor and land productivity.
All of this would require an investment growth rate of
around 7 percent in real terms throughout the 1980s, but,
more crucially, an increase in both the savings gap and
the foreign trade gap. All in all, therefore, the international community will have to sustain a minimum level
of capital assistance of around 6 percent of GDP if these
countries are to make a breakthrough from the low
(historical) rates of GDP growth; the countries themselves will have to adopt appropriate policies to make
such growth possible.

Although international assistance will be needed on
a large scale, this should be combined with an increased
level of commercial investment. The next section will
examine possibilities for commercial investment in
different sectors, with particular reference to removing
the obstacles to commercial placement of the Arab
surpluses in this region.

We have been talking generally of the opportunities
and requirements for accelerating economic development
in sub-Saharan Africa without drawing attention to the
fact that we are talking about a group of forty less
developed countries of varying sizes, of varying geographical characteristics, and of sharply differing
potential. In the earlier sections of this chapter we
have sought to provide a national classification according to existing level of development and recent economic

performance. We have thus had to lump together in our discussion countries of the Sahel with countries like Nigeria, Gabon, and Ivory Coast. These countries have problems and hence opportunities that are very different indeed. In a study of this length we cannot go into a detailed assessment of the potential of individual countries in sub-Saharan Africa.

Mineral and Petroleum Development

After gaining independence in the postwar period, most states of the region adopted a policy of encouraging foreign capital inflows in the form of direct investment in the mineral and petroleum sector. The foreign mining companies' disregard of national development goals and the mounting evidence that host governments were deriving minimal benefits from the operation of these companies led to disillusionment and ultimate rejection of this policy. This change in policy manifested itself in the wave of nationalizations and takeovers of mining interests in the mid-1960s. The mining companies reacted by redirecting their investments toward the white-ruled states of Southern Africa, and other regions deemed less politically risky.[21] This has been part of a worldwide shift in mineral and oil exploration and activity away from the LDCs. The Brandt Commission pointed out that the drilling density in prospective oil areas in industrialized countries is about forty times that in those of the oil-importing developing countries and that in recent years as much as 80 to 90 percent of spending on exploration has been concentrated in the developed and richer developing countries.[22]

Thus, significant gaps have emerged in the financing of mineral and petroleum development. In the petroleum sector, this is seen in the reluctance of the large oil companies to make any substantial commitment in countries believed to have large deposits of oil, such as Niger, Ghana, and Guinea-Bissau.[23] Another gap in financing that has been identified is in the development of small but economically viable deposits in some other states; the size of these deposits does not attract foreign oil companies seeking exportable supplies. In the interests of reducing the region's dependence on imports of oil, such deposits need to be developed. Finally, there is inadequate financing for exploration activities in the region. The governments of most states are not in a position to undertake the risks of exploration activity (which on average accounts for about 5 percent of the total cost of investment in nonfuel minerals and 25 percent for oil); the IBRD and regional banks have concentrated their financing in areas of proven deposits; and the U.N. Revolving Fund for Natural Resource Exploration has so far proved inadequate.

There appears to be scope for Arab financing in this

sector, but some of the problems that have been responsible for limiting investment by Western companies must
still be faced. There is bound to be some uncertainty
about the potential value and size of mineral and oil
deposits when concessions are negotiated, and this may
render such agreements inherently unstable. As the
Brandt Commission indicated, although investors must feel
there is a possibility of high returns from their capital
if they are to undertake very risky exploration activity,
"whenever a really rich deposit is discovered, a country's nonrenewable resources will appear in retrospect
to have been signed away too cheaply and the popular
demand for renegotiation will be irresistible."[24] To
alleviate this problem, financing could be arranged
through a multilateral financing institution or host
governments could be invited to take up major shares in
every project. (However, here again the Brandt Commission identified inadequacies in the level of financing
of the equity contribution of host-country governments
in joint ventures.)

The Arab surplus states could help not only with the
financing of mineral and oil exploration and development,
but also in the establishment of facilities for the
processing of mineral and oil products. Given the
potential profitability of such activities, these
financial flows could take the form of commercial investments, if the appropriate legal safeguards for foreign
investments existed. Moreover, in areas where foreign
companies are unwilling to participate in the development of a country's resources, Arab private and national
corporations might be able to provide the required
technical expertise--this is particularly true of
development of oil and gas resources.

Agriculture

The opportunities for large-scale investment, with
the prospects of high rates of return, make this one of
the more attractive areas of investment. In view of the
professed desire to attain self-sufficiency in food
production among the nations of the South, investment in
African land resources is vital, as the intensity of land
use is among the lowest of all developing regions. Out
of 191 million hectares of arable land in sub-Saharan
Africa in 1975, only 93 million hectares were cropped.
The use of fertilizers has always been inadequate, and
it decreased when fertilizer prices rose after 1973.
Moreover, Africa is the only developing region that
decreased its volume of tractor imports between 1971 and
1976. These factors indicate why this region has become
more dependent on food imports in this period and suffered
a fall in per capita food production during the 1970s.
If this process of agricultural stagnation were reversed,
it could considerably benefit both Arab donor countries

and the nations of sub-Saharan Africa; moreover, the
financial flows to agriculture in this region could take
the form of nonconcessional flows, possibly from Arab
private investors, a suggestion that we will examine
below.

In most countries of the region, agriculture's share
of GDP is in excess of 30 percent, whereas this sector
in most countries received 10-20 percent or less of
gross investment in the 1960s and early 1970s.
Plans for the 1980s call for increased investment, but
such investment will concentrate on the production of
cash crops. Overseas development assistance (ODA)
represents 50 percent of total investment in food production and hence plays a role in the food sector out of
proportion to its share of total investment in the
region.[25] However, the needs of the region in terms of
agricultural investment will require substantial increases in foreign resource flows. The Regional Food
Plan for Africa adopted at Arusha in 1978 calls for
direct investment expenditure of $27 billion in the
period 1975-1990, with a foreign exchange component of
about one-half. However, the Arab states may not be in
a position to make substantial contributions to this program on nonconcessional terms.

The Arab states import the bulk of their food requirements from outside the region, and although they
have made massive investments in Sudan and Egypt to
achieve regional self-sufficiency in food, they could
find it profitable to diversify their sources of supply.
Small-scale agricultural projects--in cereal, fruit,
vegetable, and livestock production--could be financed
in Africa, with the returns being realized in terms of
exports to the Arab states. There are problems with
developing appropriate technologies for sustained
intensive production in both the semiarid and high-
rainfall areas, as well as weaknesses of infrastructure,
particularly a research and development infrastructure.
This may constitute a promising field for the much-
discussed trilateral approach, in that the developed
countries could contribute trained personnel and research and development efforts. The problem with
attracting private Arab investors into this area is
that, although they may be able easily to identify markets for agricultural products in the Arab world, they
may not be willing to assume the problems of directly
administering such projects. This difficulty might be
dealt with through greater involvement by national
development banks in the region as well as the inter-
mediation of institutions such as BADEA in identifying investment opportunities and communicating them to
the private sector in the Arab countries. Such investments could become a reality if an investment guarantee
system along the lines of IAIGC were established and
there were improved legal protection for foreign investors

in Africa. The large investments that are being made in
infrastructure--particularly in soil reclamation and
irrigation (such as the Senegal River Basin Project, the
Niger River Basin Project)--will increase the number of
feasible commercial investment projects. The weakness of
the transport system could act as a major obstacle; however, the emphasis by the Economic Commission for Africa
(ECA) on investment in this sector suggests that this
problem will also be alleviated.

Industry

The forty countries of sub-Saharan Africa constitute
the least industrialized part of the Third World. In
general, the economies of this region have remained at
the primary stage. On the one hand, a large part of
their agriculture is still at a traditional subsistence
level; on the other hand, the production of tropical
agriculture or forest products--mostly in the raw state
or barely processed--and mining, sometimes followed by
the extraction of concentrates or refining, are almost
exclusively for export. Manufacturing industry, either
for import substitution or for export, is as yet
generally little developed. It is hardly surprising
therefore that Africa contributed in the 1970s less than
10 percent of the total industrial production of the
Third World, compared with 55 percent and 38 percent
for Latin America and Asia respectively. In fact, more
than half of the 10 percent was accounted for by Egypt,
Algeria, Morocco, and Tunisia, countries not falling
within the purview of this study. This should indicate,
on the face of it, a considerable untapped potential for
industrial development in sub-Saharan Africa, but
serious impediments heavily qualify this potential.
There is no doubt that Africa's principal asset
for industrialization is its abundance of natural resources. This is true even today, when little prospecting has been carried out, as is indicated by its
rich endowment in minerals, energy (both hydroelectricity
and oil), and forest. However, Africa's problems are
enormous and are far more serious than those confronting
other continents. For example, Africa has a low level
of economic development to start from; an extremely weak
agricultural base generating resources extremely slowly
or not at all; a vast continental mass, long distances,
and an inadequate transport infrastructure; an inadequate
supply of qualified staff; restricted domestic markets;
virtually no regional economic integration; and--above
all else--a scarcity of capital.
African countries have three central concerns:
(1) to accelerate development in order to improve
standards of living; (2) to diversify the economic base
and render it less vulnerable to outside forces; and
(3) to accelerate and achieve within a short span of time

the "Africanization" of their commercial life. It has accordingly been realized that small- and medium-sized industry will play an essential role in this process.

The essential role of such industry follows from these facts: (1) these enterprises produce diversity and balance in African economies that are otherwise dominated by a few large foreign enterprises; (2) they help make the economy more independent of foreign influences by generating internal patterns of trade; (3) they play a vital role in changing socioeconomic attitudes and in the emergence of a domestic managerial class; and (4) they create job opportunities because their shortage of capital forces them to be more labor-intensive. Unfortunately, few African countries have very successfully organized industrial development along these lines. Most African governments have seemed to be more concerned with relatively large projects, usually requiring both foreign assistance and foreign expertise. Although this has, to some extent, been unavoidable, especially in such fields as energy and mining and in infrastructure (without which no development can take place anyway), more could have been done. Indeed, the more successful African economies, such as Ivory Coast, Senegal, Cameroon, Gabon, and (in a different way) Tanzania, have all attempted to foster small- and medium-sized industry on an organized basis with substantial state support.

The two constraints on directing the location of light industry toward sub-Saharan Africa are the shortage of skilled labor and the lack of supporting domestic markets. These factors have been responsible for the concentration of industrial investment in the larger and richer countries. The second problem could be tackled either by greater integration of regional African markets or by planning production mainly for export. There seems to be considerable scope for Arab investment in the food- and mineral-processing industries in this region. Such investment would involve substantial gains to both parties if the share of processing costs in the final prices of most commodities is as high as is believed. For example, rather than purchasing tea, coffee, and cocoa from multinational corporations operating in Africa, Arab companies could undertake the necessary processing and marketing arrangements themselves. Where the processing of particular commodities requires substantial energy inputs, Arab countries could find that they have a previously ignored comparative advantage. Whereas the technology and skilled-manpower requirements might be greater than the Arab investors themselves possess, they could draw on other developing countries for complementary inputs.

Moreover, Africa itself may have some advantages in its endowment of energy resources and potential sources of hydroelectric power. The comparative advantage of African producers of minerals such as bauxite (the processing of which requires large energy inputs) has not been exploited, mainly for lack of financial support. The participation of private Arab investors as well as the Arab funds in commercial-industrial projects would have the additional advantage of attracting Western capital that would otherwise view the political risks and the level of total financial risks as unacceptably high. Before such investments become a reality there is a need for the Arab multi-lateral and other institutions to devote more resources to identifying and publicizing private investment projects. Agencies such as the Fund for Research and Investment for the Development of Africa (FRIDA), and to some degree BADEA, are at present partially performing this function. FRIDA was set up to promote labor-intensive, export-oriented projects in industry and handicrafts. It investigated export-oriented activities in the sub-Saharan African countries and found that there were attractive investment possibilities in cloth-ing, leather products, toys, wood products, and ceramics, among others. FRIDA developed its own channels of dis-tribution in these sectors and after identifying viable projects sought financial, technical, and marketing partners in the developed countries. More organizations established on similar lines could play an important role in alerting Arab investors to potential areas of commercial investment in Africa.

NOTES

1. The country groupings are based on pp. 172-173 of Organisation for Economic Co-operation and Development, Development Co-operation, 1979 Review (Paris, 1979).
2. Arab Bank for Economic Development in Africa, Afro-Arab Co-operation (Khartoum, 1979).
3. OECD, Development Co-operation, 1979 Review.
4. BADEA, Afro-Arab Co-operation, 1979.
5. BADEA, Afro-Arab Co-operation (Khartoum, 1978), Table 3, p. 18.
6. BADEA, Afro-Arab Co-operation, 1979.
7. Middle East (London), August 1978, p. 95. See also BADEA, Annual Report 1978 (Khartoum, 1978), p. 19.
8. Brandt Commission, North-South: A Programme for Survival (London: Pan, 1980), p. 222; Partners in Development: Report of the Commission on International Development, Lester Pearson, Chairman (New York: Praeger Publishers, 1969).
9. Middle East, July 1979, No. 57, p. 84.
10. "Setting Afro-Arab Ties on Solid Ground," interview with Dr. Chedley Ayari, chairman of the board, BADEA, Middle East, August 1978, No. 46.
11. OECD, Development Co-operation, 1978 Review (Paris, 1978), p. 23.
12. BADEA, Annual Report 1978, p. 17.

13. Ibid., Annex 5, p. 59.

14. BADEA, Annual Report 1979 (Khartoum, 1979).

15. United Nations Conference on Trade and Development, Annual Report (Geneva, 1979).

16. Centre for Research on the NIEO, Financial Flows Between Developing Countries (Oxford, 1980). See also Euromoney (London), May 1978; Middle East Economic Survey (London, Vol. 21, No. 30, 14 May 1978).

17. Middle East Journal, August 1978, p. 96.

18. T. Scharf, Trilateral Co-operation, Vol. 1 (Paris: OECD Development Centre, 1978), p. 179.

19. Ibid., pp. 32-33.

20. M. Faber and F. R. Brown, Changing the Rules of the Game (Report of Workshop on Mining Legislation and Minerals Resource Agreements--Gaberone, Botswana, 9 October-13 October 1978) (Gaberone: Commonwealth Secretariat/U.N. Centre on Transnational Corporations, 1978).

21. G. Lanning and M. Mueller, Mining Companies and the Underdevelopment of Africa (London: Penguin Books, 1979), pp. 20-27.

22. Brandt Commission, North-South, pp. 155, 164.

23. International Bank for Reconstruction and Development, A Programme to Accelerate Petroleum Production in the Developing Countries (Washington, D.C., 1978).

24. Brandt Commission, North-South, p. 156.

25. OECD, Interfutures (Paris, 1978), p. 127.

8
Arab Aid to Black Africa:
Myth Versus Reality

Michael Lyall

*The problem we have [in Tanzania] now, really
is the problem of the international community.
This year we are consuming less oil than we
consumed in 1972, but we are paying nine times
as much for it. You can't call a country
"developing" when today it is consuming less
oil than it was seven years ago.*

*The only reason we're not collapsing is
because of some of our agricultural successes.
Otherwise, quite frankly, a country like this
could just collapse. This year I am going to
spend half of our export earnings on oil.*

--President Julius Nyerere, 1979

In 1973 the petroleum products import bill of sub-
Saharan, nonoil-producing African countries (except
South Africa and Zimbabwe-Rhodesia) exceeded $284
million. In 1979 it is estimated to have exceeded $1.7
billion, and it was projected to exceed $2.7 billion in
1980, that is to say ten times, or 1,000 percent, more
than it was in 1973 (Table 8.1). In 1973 a barrel of
Saudi Arabian light crude oil sold at $3 a barrel; in
early 1980 the price was $26 a barrel, and the OPEC
average was more than $30 a barrel--i.e., in seven years
crude petroleum prices had increased between 800 and
1,000 percent. Put differently, Black Africa's consumption of petroleum products by volume has barely increased, although in a developing region it would have
every justification for increasing. In the same seven
years the inflation rate (as measured by the consumer
price indices) in all OECD countries averaged 10 percent
per annum; that is to say, as a rough measurement, the
cost of vital goods and services imported from them by
developing countries would have increased by some 77 percent since 1973.

From 1974 to 1978 inclusive, total Arab aid (including OPEC Special Fund) to all non-Arab African
countries is estimated to have amounted to $1.4 billion

181

TABLE 8.1
PETROLEUM IMPORTS FOR REPORTING AFRICAN COUNTRIES ($ MILLIONS)

	1973	1974	1975	1976
Burundi	1.63	2.62	3.30	4.25
Ethiopia	20.10	49.13	68.45	53.62
Ivory Coast	25.27	129.06	145.96	149.33
Kenya	46.71	190.96	236.40	223.37
Madagascar	14.91	44.79	68.22	52.17
Malawi	8.95	14.80	17.78	21.95
Mauritania	6.49	12.86	20.56	19.66
Mauritius	11.50	27.97	31.97	30.87
Niger	6.68	13.05	12.83	14.75
Rwanda	2.25	4.89	8.03	9.64
Senegal	21.15	58.25	60.15	71.13
Sierra Leone	9.23	25.23	22.37	11.21
Sudan	24.57	85.64	95.77	89.31
Tanzania	48.14	140.56	79.58	94.16
Togo	4.84	10.98	13.00	12.78
Upper Volta	--	9.40	13.36	10.75
Zambia	31.62	89.43	93.71	108.35
TOTAL	284.04	909.62	991.44	977.30

	1977	1978	est. 1979	proj. 1980
Burundi	5.56	6.67	9.65	15.25
Ethiopia	75.70	62.66	90.85	143.50
Ivory Coast	169.54	171.15	248.15	392.00
Kenya	242.01	238.96	346.50	547.50
Madagascar	44.16	52.80	76.55	121.00
Malawi	23.69	30.18	43.75	69.00
Mauritania	9.50	13.13	19.00	30.00
Mauritius	40.97	45.71	66.30	105.00
Niger	18.40	22.08	32.00	50.00
Rwanda	12.23	14.80	21.50	34.00
Senegal	85.01	102.00	148.00	234.00
Sierra Leone	25.47	33.33	48.30	76.00
Sudan	127.28	133.10	193.00	305.00
Tanzania	101.89	135.25	196.00	310.00
Togo	20.38	13.37	19.40	30.00
Upper Volta	17.75	21.30	30.90	49.00
Zambia	104.03	102.11	148.00	234.00
TOTAL	1,123.57	1,198.60	1,737.85 (+44%)	2,745.25 (+58%)

Source: Chase Manhattan Bank, N.A., Economics Department.

in commitments, of which $800 million had actually been disbursed (Table 8.2). In the four years from 1975 to 1978 the total aid received from all sources by sub-Saharan African countries was $25.4 billion, of which $4.0 billion was disbursed by multilateral organizations, $16 billion under bilateral or public assistance programs, and the balance of $5.4 billion by unclassified or private sources.[1] (It should be stated that these figures do not include guaranteed and subsidized export credits, which can be said to equally benefit the exporting and importing countries concerned.) In the same period 1975-1978, $640 million was actually disbursed by Arab countries and the OPEC Special Fund to the same sub-Saharan countries. These disbursements are included in the figures cited above and represent 2.5 percent of total aid disbursed. Some, but not many, would argue with the empirical observation that the major part of the remaining $24.7 billion will have been derived from the World Bank-IMF and from OECD states.

TABLE 8.2
ARAB AID TO NON-ARAB AFRICAN COUNTRIES

	1974	1975	1976	1977	1978
Commitments ($m)					
Bilateral donors	132.1	194.9	140.6	200.1	199.5
Multilateral institutions*	85.0	64.2	140.1	157.7	79.1
TOTAL	217.1	259.1	280.7	357.8	278.6
Net disbursements ($m)					
Bilateral donors	129.9	128.7	70.9	53.4	93.0
Multilateral institutions*	31.1	109.8	35.2	80.7	65.9
TOTAL	161.0	238.5	106.1	134.1	158.9

*Including OPEC Special Fund.

Source: OECD, Annual Review (Paris, 1979).

In the period 1975-1977, the most recent period for which statistics are available, total OECD public aid to all developing countries amounted to $42 billion, while total Arab-OPEC aid for the same period amounted to $16.8 billion (Table 8.3). Expressed as a percentage of GNP, these aid flows averaged 0.34 percent in OECD countries, and 3.2 percent in OPEC countries, although it should be stated that for OPEC countries the average is dramatically increased by Kuwait and the United Arab Emirates, where the percentages are 10.18 and 10.97, respectively. Excluding these states, the OPEC average drops to 1.4 percent of GNP.

Although it is not within the scope of this chapter, it is somewhat instructive to contrast all these figures with those for financial aid by so-called Communist countries. In the years 1954-1978 (i.e., over a twenty-five year period) sub-Saharan Africa received a total of $4.8 billion from all Communist countries, of which $1.1 billion was supplied by the USSR, $1.4 billion by East European states, and the balance of $2.3 billion by the People's Republic of China.[2]

Imprecise as some of these statistics may be, the enormous disparities recorded at least give some sense of dimension as to who is really doing what for whom. Leaving aside the paucity of the Communist world's contribution to the economic, as opposed to the military, development of Black Africa, one is forced to note the yawning quantitative gap between the rhetoric and the reality of Arab aid to Black African states. In fact, the vast majority of direct Arab economic aid has gone to the Islamic states of North Africa, the Middle East, and Asia. Between 1975 and 1977 the Arab members of OPEC disbursed $16.4 billion, of which $480 million, or 2.9 percent, ended up in Black Africa. It is obvious from both statistical and empirical evidence that Islamic states, or states with substantial Muslim populations, have benefited disproportionately from Arab economic aid. This is not to deny the developmental needs of the Islamic states that have benefited from Arab-OPEC aid or the generosity of the donor nations concerned; rather, it is intended to give the lie to the alleged amplitude of the Arab-OPEC response to the equally pressing needs of Black Africa.

There has been, and continues to be, a mutually deceptive arrangement, tacit or otherwise, between OPEC and the Third World to present First World (or OECD) countries as the sole villains of inflation and Third World misery (e.g., the OPEC secretary general's recent comments that the problems of developing countries were due to inflation in the industrial countries and to "other endemic economic problems" that caused an "atmosphere of economic injustice").[3] This artifice has the convenient effect of removing the spotlight from the

TABLE 8.3
OPEC AND OECD DEVELOPMENT AID, 1975-1977

OPEC ($ millions)	1975	1976	1977
Nigeria	14	83	64
Algeria	41	54	47
Iraq	218	232	53
Iran	593	753	202
Venezuela	31	96	72
Saudi Arabia	1,997	2,407	2,373
Libya	261	94	109
Kuwait	975	614	1,442
Qatar	339	195	118
United Arab Emirates	1,046	1,060	1,262
TOTAL	5,515	5,588	5,742

OECD ($ millions)	1975	1976	1977
Italy	182	226	186
New Zealand	66	53	53
United Kingdom	863	835	914
Japan	1,148	1,105	1,424
Austria	64	48	118
Finland	48	51	49
Netherlands	604	720	900
France	2,093	2,146	2,267
Australia	507	385	427
Belgium	378	340	371
Denmark	205	214	258
West Germany	1,689	1,384	1,386
Canada	880	887	992
United States	4,007	4,334	4,159
Norway	184	218	295
Sweden	566	608	779
Switzerland	104	112	119
TOTAL	13,588	13,666	14,697

Source: World Bank, World Development Report 1979 (Washington, D.C., 1979).

primary source of misery (studiously avoided in all
international forums by participating game-players in the
name of "economic solidarity"), while doubtless appealing
to the Third World's sense of schadenfreude. Whereas
Black Africa may have derived vicarious gratification
from the discomfiture of its erstwhile "oppressors," its
own intellectual and political dishonesty, which, with a
few honorable exceptions, continues to this day, has
helped lead many African states to an economic impasse,
with dimensions that are only now (if at all) beginning
to be appreciated.

For although it is clear that the majority of OPEC
states give not a fig for the protestations of the First
World at ratcheting petroleum price increases, it has
shown itself remarkably sensitive to any hint of public
criticism from the ranks of the "oppressed." Thus Black
Africa's acquiescence was "purchased" at the first Afro-
Arab Summit Meeting in Cairo in March 1977 with extravagant pledges of $1.45 billion ($1,002 million from Saudi
Arabia, $241 million from Kuwait, $137 million from the
United Arab Emirates, and $77 million from Qatar). Then
at the 1979 OAU Summit Meeting in Monrovia, when
rumblings of discontent were again to be heard (coupled
with threats to resume diplomatic relations with the
state of Israel), Dr. Chedly Ayari of BADEA rushed
to the scene to assure participants that 82.5 percent
of the $1.45 billion pledged in Cairo had been effec-
tively committed by June 1979. (To arrive at this
percentage, BADEA had simply added up all commitments to
African countries by bilateral and multilateral Arab aid
agencies since the inception of their respective aid
programs, i.e., including commitments prior to the Cairo
summit meeting.) As usual reality has fallen far behind
the public relations mythology, and the Cairo meeting
has resulted, so far, only in $51 million additional
aid to Africa. [4]

In the 1980s, however, it is likely that the curtain
will be rung down in no uncertain manner on this Arab-
African charade. For too many years OPEC has been able
to avoid the consequences of its actions because Western
(i.e., OECD) financial institutions have effectively
acted as intermediators between OPEC surpluses on the
one hand and Third World deficits on the other. The
majority of developing countries have thereby avoided,
at least in the short term, the immense structural
dislocation implicitly caused to their development by
the OPEC cartel and, not incidentally, the more search-
ing and baleful gaze of that lender of last resort:
the IMF. For reasons of profit and politics (e.g., by
plugging Third World deficits they have permitted their
First World clientele continued export earnings),
commercial banks have actively connived at this
expedient recycling, assuming credit risks that, at the
very least, should have been shared with their OPEC

depositors. Or, to put the matter in vulgar perspective:
What are the relative risk assets of OPEC and OECD institutions in Black Africa? The answers are near-zero and
billions, respectively. It is the contention of this chapter that the 1979
oil price increases will prove to be the straw that
breaks the Third World's back, unless the Third World
(primarily Black Africa) finally develops the political
courage to raise such a clamor that the primary source
of its present afflictions is shamed into some more
effective form of relief than another round of empty
pledges. In 1980 oil imports will average 17.5 percent
of Black Africa's total imports; in 1973 they averaged
6.5 percent (Table 8.4). External debt service ratios,
in most cases, have doubled or tripled since 1973
(Table 8.5), the consequence of borrowing OPEC surpluses
from commercial banks on short terms at high interest
rates to cover earlier oil-induced deficits (on both
current and capital-spending accounts). Under such

TABLE 8.4
OIL IMPORTS AS A PERCENTAGE OF TOTAL C.I.F. IMPORTS, SELECTED
SUB-SAHARAN AFRICAN COUNTRIES

	1973	1978	est. 1980*
Burundi	5	7	11
Ethiopia	9	14	22
Gambia	6	10	16
Ghana	n.a.	11	17
Ivory Coast	4	8	13
Kenya	9	16	25
Liberia	n.a.	16	25
Madagascar	7	17	27
Malawi	6	9	14
Mauritania	5	7	11
Mauritius	7	9	14
Niger	8	12	19
Rwanda	7	8	13
Senegal	6	11	17
Sierra Leone	6	12	19
Sudan	6	11	17
Tanzania	10	11	17
Upper Volta	n.a.	8	13
Zambia	5	14	22

*Assumptions: 20 percent p.a. import growth, resulting in 1980
imports 44 percent above 1978. Oil import bill is assumed to
have risen 44 percent in 1979 and 58 percent in 1980, resulting
in a 128 percent rise over the two-year period. As a result,
oil imports in 1980, as percent of total imports, should be 58
percent above 1978.
Source: Chase Manhattan Bank, N.A., Economics Department.

TABLE 8.5
EXTERNAL DEBT SERVICE RATIO,* SELECTED SUB-SAHARAN
AFRICAN COUNTRIES

	1973	1978	est. 1980
Burundi	2.7	4.6	
Ethiopia	6.5	n.c.**	
Gambia	1.3	1.0	
Ghana	3.6	4.0	
Ivory Coast	7.2	16.0	22.0
Kenya	5.6	9.5	12.2
Liberia	5.2	6.4	11.5
Madagascar	5.1	3.4	7.0
Malawi	7.6	8.0	
Mauritania	5.5	6.0	
Mauritius	1.7	2.3	
Niger	2.1	5.5	
Rwanda	0.3	0.9	
Senegal	8.0	21.9	19.4
Sierra Leone	8.6	15.3	
Sudan	11.4	31.0	35.0
Tanzania	7.7	7.5	
Upper Volta	5.6	8.0	
Zambia	28.8	26.0	18.0

*As percentage of exports of goods and nonfactor services.

**Not calculated. The heavy indebtedness to the Soviet Union renders computation of the debt service ratio, based on World Bank figures, meaningless.

Source: Chase Manhattan Bank, N.A., Economics Department.

conditions simple banking prudence eventually rears its head in the banking parlors of the colossi of London and New York, and recycling, via commercial banks, comes to an abrupt and conclusive halt. In this context one is forced to remark that at the end of 1980 at least nine Black African nations were finally face to face with the IMF,[5] whose painful cures (which this writer and others view as frequently impractical)[6] had been so assiduously avoided for so long by courtesy of the commercial banks.[7] Less encouraging, in the long term, is the attempt by the World Bank to administer an emergency balance-of-payments support fund of several billion dollars for the Third World, for the World Bank's relative "leniency," if put into practice, will once again permit OPEC to avoid the Third World question.

The question to be addressed, quite simply, is what mechanism or mechanisms (if any) do Arab-OPEC states propose to alleviate the debilitating effects of inflation-recession ("stagflation") in developing countries,

of which one of the prime components is the price of oil?
Black Africa is effectively impacted in three ways
by the surging price of petroleum: first, by the direct
cost of oil imports (an increase of 1,000 percent in
seven years); second, by the inflationary element of such
increases in the ultimate landed cost of goods and services imported from the First World (an increase of 77
percent between 1973 and 1979); and third, by declining
demand, and hence revenues, for its primary products
(its principal exports) in the First World, as OPEC
petroleum and First World economic imcompetence combine
to produce a delayed but consequential recession in the
First World, thereby tipping the Third World into
recession as well. To this vicious cycle, the OPEC
response to date has been tacitly to proclaim, by its
pricing decisions, that it shall itself be immune to the
inflation it induces, by indulging in a game of leap-frog
that can and does lead only to beggar-my-neighbor.
The industrialized nations of the world have
sufficient political, social, and economic depth to with-
stand, painful as they may be, the readjustments required
by the end of an era of cheap energy. Demand in such
nations, and the very patterns of demand, are finally
showing themselves to be price-elastic and, over the
long term, susceptible to technological intervention.
Not so in the developing countries, where the only
elasticity that realistically faces the respective
authorities is an implied halt to development. In
developing nations, where energy consumption is already
pared to the bone, a fundamental restructuring of consumer habits, and consequent industrial and technological
responses, is a luxury that is not even there to be
afforded in the first place. Therefore, unless there is
a genuine effort by both Arab-OPEC states and OECD
states to ameliorate the present lot of the Third World,
the consequential dashing of expectations could result
in the very political instability that the maturer members of OPEC claim to abhor.
In view of the relative austerity now being
preached, and in some cases even practiced, in the
industrialized world, it would be unrealistic to expect
much additional financial contribution from that
particular quarter, although the World Bank is fore-
casting real growth in development aid flows between
now and 1990 (Table 8.6). Those observers uninfected
by North-South rhetoric might even suggest that with
respect to Black Africa, the OECD aid contribution
compares very favorably with that of Arab-OPEC states.
With OPEC's 1980 surplus estimated to exceed $120
billion,[8] most of it to be concentrated in Arab states
whose absorptive capacity is now strictly limited, Black
Africa could rightfully expect some part to be put to
more productive use than driving the price of gold sky-
high (to the enormous benefit of South Africa).

TABLE 8.6
DEVELOPMENT AID FLOWS BY DONOR CATEGORY, 1979-1990

	In billions of dollars				Average annual percentage growth at 1975 prices	
	1975	1977	1985	1990	1975-1977	1977-1990
OECD	13.6	14.7	41.8	69.0	-1.9	4.8
OPEC	5.5	5.7	9.4	12.4	-3.7	-1.2
Other donors	0.5	--	1.3	1.9		
TOTAL	19.6	--	52.5	83.3		
TOTAL at 1975 prices	19.6	--	24.7	29.4		

Source: World Bank, World Development Report 1979 (Washington, D.C., 1979).

The alleviation of the impending plight of much of Black Africa requires a more imaginative cooperative effort than the hitherto ponderous parallel and co-financing exercises conducted by Arab and Western institutions. The hallmarks of such programs have been bureaucratic delays and institutional inertia compounded by governmental confusion and conflict on the African side. (The basic concept of "time equals money"--particularly in an inflationary world--seems to be largely absent in public institutions.) The present situation requires programs remarkable for their speed and simplicity, coupled with a radical but long-term restructuring of African nations' debt profiles and of their development mechanisms. More in hope than with any expectation that this hope might be fulfilled, the basic structures of some suggested programs and mechanisms are considered below.

1. The capital-surplus Arab-OPEC states should provide funds for a special and conditional facility to be administered by either the IMF or their own watchdog body. The object of such a facility should be to permit the reorganization of external debt structures on a long-term basis, which implies the provision of long-term, lower-cost funds. It means the prepayment (or in many cases the repayment of defaulted loans) to commercial banks of short-term (i.e., ten years or less) debt, much of which was provided with OPEC deposits in the first place. This reverse recycling will also leave part of the credit risk where it should properly rest, i.e., in OPEC hands. (The idea of "bailing out" commercial

banks has been popularly presented as anathema--
usually by those most interested in a collapse of the
Western financial system on which the rest of the world
perforce depends.)

The provision of such a facility should be conditional not on the adoption and implementation of the
IMF's customary deflationary policies, but rather on
policies that promote economic growth. "So long as OPEC
can price-fix itself a large surplus, the health of the
world financial system needs economies that grow fast
enough to service their foreign debts, not ones that
deflate far enough to throw off deficits."[9] It should
also be conditional in the sense that it does not reward
or assist instances of gross economic mismanagement or
of government officials' and their cronies' treating the
national treasury as their private Swiss bank account.

2. Capital-surplus OPEC states finally should
resolve to grant certain categories of nonoil LDCs some
constructive relief from their monopolistic price-fixing--
not by price cutting, against which they have firmly
set their faces, but by development deposits.

- Surplus OPEC nations should permit nonoil LDCs
  with per capita GNP below a predetermined level
  to purchase petroleum products with 50 percent
  foreign currency and 50 percent local currency.
- The local-currency payment would be deposited
  in the name of the petroleum-vending country in
  the local national development bank or similar
  institution[10] on a long-term basis (fifteen to
  twenty-five years with a minimum of five years'
  grace before any principal repayments) and
  bearing the same rate of interest as that offered
  by the IMF on SDR deposits.
- These deposits would be guaranteed as to payment
  of principal, interest, and convertibility by the
  IMF, and the rate of convertibility into SDRs
  would be fixed at the time of each deposit.
- All interest and principal payment by the LDC
  would be made in foreign exchange. In the event
  of default, the IMF as guarantor would debit
  the appropriate drawing account of the LDC,
  throwing the LDC into an IMF stabilization program
  if a higher drawing level was encroached.
- The local-currency deposits would be used
  strictly for valid development purposes, under
  the supervision of the World Bank or a similar
  institution if requested by the OPEC depositor.
- If the deposits needed to be utilized for foreign
  purchases (e.g., machinery, equipment), the LDC
  should be able to sell the local currency to the
  IMF for the appropriate foreign currency on a
  long-term repurchase agreement.

The adoption of such a development deposit scheme would open mutually agreeable vistas for both OPEC nations and nonoil LDCs, as well as having the beneficial side effect of partially reducing the volatility of excess OPEC liquidity.

For OPEC surplus states it would provide an investment vehicle that could be considered equal to or even better than an investment in short-term Eurodollar deposits or U.S. government bonds and that certainly would be put to more productive and humanitarian use than subsidizing inflationary U.S. government deficits.

For nonoil LDCs it would diminish in dramatic fashion their current foreign exchange deficits, at the same time assuring them of long-term development funds on terms and conditions appropriate to the magnitude of the task (which is certainly not the case with commercial bank loans). If an LDC was foolish enough to print the requisite local currency, the consequent inflation would be on its own head; and the IMF could always withdraw its guarantee of any future development deposits, thereby halting incremental development, if not the printing presses.

3. All aid organizations--Arab, OECD and multilateral--would greatly facilitate project implementation and funds disbursement if the many organizations concerned were to desist from bureaucratic duplication and self-justification. In major development projects, in which a multiplicity of development institutions are inevitably concerned, each institution (with the honorable exception of the OPEC Special Fund) has usually insisted on executing its own feasibility study and on mounting its own reconnaissance missions (normally at least two or three per institution per project). This duplication and waste of time, money, and effort would be considered ludicrous, were its delaying effects not so harmful. There are no rational reasons, apart from bureaucratic and chauvinistic self-justification, why a single Arab institution and a single OECD-multilateral institution should not be designated to act on behalf of all interested parties on a project-by-project basis.

4. Last, but by no means least, many Black African nations need to rapidly and radically restructure the bureaucratic face that they present to the outside world in matters concerning development and aid. There is nothing more calculated to frustrate and delay the outside world's efforts to assist in development than to be caught, as is far too often the case, between conflicting ministerial or departmental priorities and prejudices. Those intragovernmental disputes need to be resolved within the government (not played out in cat-and-mouse games with potential external assistance), and authority to execute without delay should then be confided to a single arm of government that subsequently conducts all development relationships (technical, legal,

financial, etc.) with all external bodies. This clearly
implies the establishment of a minuscule, but mighty,
development committee (certainly not another department
or ministry), staffed by a country's best brains and
answerable only to prime minister or president. Such
committees will require a clear legal mandate to cut
through any and all bureaucratic impediments that
threaten the orderly and swift development process.
The establishment of such powerful national development
committees will clearly offend multitudes of bureaucratic
mini-power centers. No matter. Given their advanced
industrialized state, bureaucratic inertia, obstruction,
corruption, and waste can arguably be afforded by OECD
nations; not, however, by the nations of Black Africa,
where bureaucracy has to date been the greatest growth
industry.
    None of this is likely to come to pass until such
time as Black Africa eschews the simplistic delights of
"chip-on-the-shoulder" rhetoric for the substance of
economic and hence political reality. In a world of pro-
claimed and allegedly perceived interdependencies,
there can be no new economic order so long as one part
of the equation is falsified (deliberately or unwittingly)
by the present fictional convenience of Arab-African
political and economic solidarity. Nor will it be
achieved without a clearing of the Augean stables of
African bureaucracy.
    If politics and economics are indeed indivisible,
then Black Africa has many of its own political shibbo-
leths to blame for its economic shortchanging. Either
these must be cast out of the temple, or the rest of the
world may gladly pick over the corpse, all the while
murmuring like Shakespeare's Richard II when summoned
to John of Gaunt's deathbed:

            "Pray God we may make haste
            And come too late."

NOTES

    1. The figures are these: 1975, $6,635 million; 1976,
$5,847 million; 1977, $6,885 million; 1978, $6,188 million.
Marchés Tropicaux et Méditerranéens, 16 November 1979.
    2. Financial Times, Editorial, 4 March 1980.
    3. Financial Times, 15 July 1980, and Dr. Ibrahim F. I.
Shibata's letter of reply.
    4. Of the $1.45 billion pledged at Cairo, more than 80 per-
cent was to be committed bilaterally through the respective
national aid funds, $180 million was pledged to BADEA, and $35
million to the ADF.
    The bilateral aid was to be administered by the national
funds on behalf of the governments that had made the Cairo
commitments, which were to receive special additional resources
from their respective governments. At year end 1979, none of the

national aid funds had received these additional resources. (They had continued, however, to make project commitments to Black Africa, but these were financed out of ordinary existing capital and cannot be considered "additional.")

With respect to the $180 million for BADEA, Arab countries had decided prior to the Cairo summit to increase its capital by 50 percent. Prior to the summit meeting, BADEA's subscribed or "pledged" capital was $707 million. At year end 1979 it amounted to $738 million, i.e., an additional $31 million.

Insofar as the $35 million for the ADF is concerned, only Kuwait has honored its commitment in full; the UAE paid part of its pledge in 1979. Saudi Arabia's $11 million contribution in 1978 cannot be considered "additional," as this amount had been pledged prior to the Cairo summit. Qatar, so far, had not contributed.

5. Benin, Congo, Liberia, Senegal, Sierra Leone, Sudan, Tanzania, Zambia, Zaire. The Ivory Coast and Kenya were being "advised" by the World Bank.

6. From the Economist, 15-21 March 1980:

Ask any of those finance ministers what to expect inside [the IMF], and he will mutter glumly that he expects he will be forced to deflate. That is the strongest image the IMF has. It is the main reason why so few countries have borrowed from it (in the past three years it has actually been a net borrower itself), and why those that do borrow have often first procrastinated themselves deep into an economic bog.

Straight deflation—cutting demand for goods and services—will cut imports; so will that other favourite IMF recommendation, devaluation, which will also boost exports. There is hardly a country in the world where these prescriptions will not turn deficit into surplus. But what one deficit country can do, all cannot. They cannot all simultaneously boost exports and cut imports; cannot all devalue; cannot all shed their deficits, unless OPEC's cartel is broken and its surplus wiped out.

As president of the world economy, the IMF knows that. As local policeman, it believes that offenders must be brought to book. That schizophrenia was sensible when deficits were small and not caused primarily by a cartel. In the 1980s it is harmful, especially for the many countries that would benefit from the IMF's advice (and, to a lesser extent, its money) if the advice was different.

7. Here one should also note the lamentable lack of cooperation between African states, the IMF, and commercial banks. For a number of years the IMF has berated commercial banks for their lack of "prudence" in lending to Third World countries (and there are many cases in which ignorance and greed indeed predominated), at the same time denying them the very documentation that might have induced such prudence—the IMF country reports. Commercial banks have pleaded for these reports to no avail, both the IMF and

member states claiming "confidentiality"--the IMF presumably because it believes that it will no longer receive the requisite statistical information from the member state if it subsequently imparts such information to other more accommodating lenders; the member state presumably because it knows full well that commercial banks would become much less accommodating if they laid their hands on the "goodies." Only in "rescheduling" (i.e., too late) have commercial banks been able to exact IMF country reports as the price of their continued cooperation.

8. U.S. Treasury Department.

9. _Economist_, 15-21 March 1980.

10. For a number of years Venezuela and Mexico had in effect a somewhat similar program with certain Caribbean countries.

9
The Legal Framework
for Transnational Investment
and Lending in Sub-Saharan Africa

A. O. Adede

INTRODUCTION

Three basic assumptions provide the context of this
chapter. They are

- that a number of African countries possess
  investment potential for the improvement of
  their agricultural production for both domestic
  consumption and trade and others have mineral
  resources that could be more vigorously explored
  and substantially developed, but that they lack
  the capital, technology, and trained manpower
  necessary for the rational development of such
  resource potentials;
- that some Arab oil-producing countries have
  surplus petrofunds but are disadvantaged
  by other factors such as the lack of suitable
  agricultural land, the development of which could
  increase their capacity to diversify their
  economies and ability to absorb domestically
  more of the petrofunds generated from the
  exploitation of their petroleum resources; and
- that OECD member states--the Western developed
  market economies--have technology, the manpower, the capital, and the banking facilities,
  all of which are essential for facilitating the
  achievement of the development goals of a
  modern state.

The basic thesis is, therefore, that those who have
natural resources and agricultural potential but lack
the technology, capital, and manpower necessary for
rational exploitation of such resources; those who predominantly have only the surplus capital and need investment outlets abroad; and those who have a combination of

---

The views expressed in this paper are those of the author and are
not to be attributed in any way to the United Nations.

all these factors, should seek to explore and establish
means by which their various endowments may complement
each other on the basis of demonstrable mutual interdependence.

I intend first to deal with the legal framework for
investment. I have chosen to focus upon the emerging
trends in the state contracts for natural resources
development between African countries and foreign multinationals. The analysis points out which old practices
in the concession agreements must be abandoned, as they
were designed to offer full legal protection only to the
rights and interests of the alien concessionaires, with
little regard to the various rights and interests of the
host developing countries. The new trends illustrate a
more balanced approach to the legal relationship between
an African country and a foreign company under a modern
state contract for natural resources development.

In the second part of the chapter I will examine the
legal framework for transnational lending in Africa, including loan contracts between African countries and
foreign commercial banks and loan contracts between
African countries and international lending institutions.
Here again the rights and interests of the African countries as borrowers and those of the lending parties are
identified and examined in the context of the specific
economic, political, and social realities that suggest a
particular approach to loan agreements as instruments
for establishing relationships between the parties in a
manner consistent with mutual interdependence.

In the third part, I will survey bilateral agreements for economic and technical cooperation between the
African countries and the developed countries, on the
one hand, and similar agreements between African states
and the other developing countries of the Third World,
on the other hand. The analysis in this part discloses,
inter alia, that the old bilateral agreements of friendship, commerce, and navigation (FCN) seem to have dis-
appeared and are replaced by a new breed of bilateral
agreements on specific fields of cooperation. The inclusion of the consideration of the question of technical
cooperation among the developing countries (TCDC) and
economic cooperation among the developing countries
(ECDC) is an indication of my personal conviction of the
role such cooperation could play within the context of
the theme of African-Arab-OECD triangular cooperation.
Bilateral loan agreements between developing and
developed countries are examined in this part.

What emerges is a suggestion for legal frameworks
producing instruments in which all the parties are
called upon to assess real trade-offs of rights and
interests in the process of giving legal effect to
aspects of the New International Economic Order.[1] In
making suggestions for such legal frameworks I am reminded, as a lawyer who may be involved in the preparation

of such contracts and agreements, to exercise caution not to turn the identifiable bargaining positions of a client into a demonstration of toughness and also to avoid the tendency of reaching only for the too technical concepts for inclusion in the agreement in the hope of "pulling a fast one." I am also reminded of the fact that, in the process of negotiating and reaching legitimate trade-offs, the short-term rights and interests of a client must be properly balanced against the long-term advantages. In sum, the legal framework should create a relationship between the parties that is intended to work.

TRENDS IN AGREEMENTS FOR NATURAL RESOURCES DEVELOPMENT BETWEEN AFRICAN COUNTRIES AND MULTINATIONALS

The development of the old concession agreements for minerals exploitation--from documents that protected predominantly the rights and interests of the alien concessionaires to modern instruments for rational development of such natural resources that offer protection for both the developing host country and the foreign multinational--serves as a useful illustration of the desired legal framework for the area of foreign investment in Africa. The basic idea behind the legal framework is to designate new areas of mutual trade-offs between the parties to mineral resources agreements while rejecting the one-sided protection of the multinationals that is said to have characterized the concession agreements of the nineteenth and early twentieth centuries.

There has evidently emerged a trend in which the developing countries generally, including those in Africa, have sought to increase their benefits from the exploration and exploitation of their natural resources by the OECD multinationals. In the wake of the concept of permanent sovereignty over natural resources, given clear expression in the United Nations,[2] the African countries have enacted domestic laws attempting to govern comprehensively foreign investments in the area of natural resources development. By this trend, the African countries seek to continue moving further away from the old practice of negotiating individual and non-uniform concession agreements for a particular mining activity. The comprehensive national laws, whether called mining code or foreign investment law, however, provide only a general framework on the basis of which negotiations with multinationals are to be conducted. The specific terms of the agreement are thus left for the government negotiators to hammer out with the multinationals within the framework of the provisions of the applicable domestic laws, which may include the constitution of the state itself.

It is useful to discuss briefly the basic features of the old concession agreements so as to ascertain what specific areas require changes in order for there to be

a more balanced protection of the parties within the
meaning of mutual interdependence.

The Basic Features of the Old Concession Agreements

The traditional concession agreements concluded in
the nineteenth century had certain basic features that
have been abandoned since the beginning of the second
half of the twentieth century. The old-regime concession agreements were based on royalty payment as the
financial obligation of the concessionaire; the concessionaire was often given more land than he could be
expected to develop within a reasonable period and the
concession agreements were normally designed to last for
a very long time--usually more than fifty years. The
host government seldom interfered in the operation of
the concessionaire, who was thus left to determine everything, including the marketing and the price of the
minerals. As historically significant illustrations,
I offer below some of the African concessions of the old
regime that reflect such practices.

From royalties on the basis of volume of output
to income taxation. In the concession agreement between
the government of Liberia and the Liberian Mining Company
Ltd. (LMC) of 27 August 1945, there was a basic royalty
of 5 cents per ton on all iron ore shipped by the company.
This same system was also used in the concession agreements for oil exploration that relied on payments of
royalties based on the tonnage of crude oil produced--a
practice that remained undisturbed from 1900 to 1950,
when the change from royalty to income taxation occurred.
The practice reflected in the LMC agreement is
central to our present analysis for two basic reasons.
First, it portrays an African experience immediately
relevant to our discussion of the legal framework for the
multinationals in Africa. Second, and most important,
the subsequent developments in its operation clearly
illustrate the stages of evolution that have occurred in
this specific question of fixing the financial obligations for the concessionaires in terms other than
royalties based on the volume of output. The LMC first
departed from its original fixed royalties of 1945 as
the sole basis for government's revenue to the system of
income taxation that allowed the government's "participation in profits" after a certain point. As has been
cogently observed:

> Participation was to begin when LMC had liqui-
> dated its debts and had brought its "recovery
> investment" to $4 billion, or by 1957, which-
> ever came first. Thereafter, it was to receive
> 50 percent of profits. The income tax was to
> supplement the royalty payments which could

continue. In 1965 the basic agreement was
further amended to provide that the 50 percent participation rate would take effect as
of 1 January 1965 and participation was to be
in lieu of royalty payment.[3]

The change from fixed royalties to income taxation,
coupled with the acceptance of government participation,
is a significant attribute of the modern concession of
which more will be said presently.
The study of this trend throughout the Third World
discloses that there was a shift from purely fixed
royalties to some formulas using both the income tax
and royalty in a more refined way, as summarized below:

A further step in this process was the introduction of the idea of giving the producing
country a share in the profits from exploitation. This profit-sharing was achieved by
replacing the royalty system with a system of
taxes on the concession. Royalties were not
actually abolished but were now credited against
the tax, in other words, the Government continued to receive royalties originally con-
tracted for and then increased the amount
payable until it equalled the percentage of
profits which had been agreed on (usually 50
percent), the difference being paid in the
form of taxes. The next step was taken in
1965, when the producing countries succeeded
in having royalties treated not as a credit
against the taxes, but as an expense to be
deducted before the tax rate was applied.[4]

The final step the host governments took to increase their financial benefits from the extraction of
their natural resources was therefore the introduction
of taxation as the principal source of revenue. The
shift from reliance on royalties to the use of income
taxation, in the form of participation in the company's
profits, took place by stages. Using the LMC example,
we observe that the government initially received 25 percent of profits. This was later increased to 35 percent and finally to 50 percent of profits. When the
"fifty-fifty" profit-sharing formula was established,
royalties were abandoned as the basis of calculating
the financial obligations of alien concessionaires.
The pioneers of this final shift to fifty-fifty profit-
sharing were the oil concessions in the Middle East and
North Africa.[5]

Complete control of large areas of land leased over
long periods. Another characteristic of the old concession agreements is that they usually granted

concessionaires larger areas of land than the foreign
investor could actually develop within a reasonable time.
Apart from granting large areas of land under such circumstances, the traditional concessions also lasted too
long. An example in this connection may be cited of the
1926 agreement between the Firestone Company and the
government of Liberia. The agreement was to last for
ninety-nine years and covered one million acres of land
at an annual rental of six cents an acre. The area was
used to grow rubber, for which the Firestone Plantation
Company was established. Of the million acres given
under the agreement of 1926, the largest area developed
and put into immediate use by 1953 was 100,000 acres,
representing the Cavalla plantation and 90,000 acres of
the Harbel plantation.[6] Thus, almost thirty years after
the million acres were granted, the company was not able
to use even half of it.

   Minimum host government participation and establishment of enclaves. Another basic feature of the old
concession agreements is that the concessionaires were
assured of no governmental interference with the management of the operation. Under the agreements, the foreign
company completely assumed all risks and ran the show in
the concession areas, which virtually became enclaves
"governed" by the foreign company. An example of such an
enclave is the 1906 concession grant by the Congo Comité
Special du Katanga to a Belgian company, the Union
Minière du Haut Katanga. Under the agreement, the
company (Union Minière) virtually had sovereignty over
the concession area. Commenting on the agreement, two
authors made the following observation: "The company's
rights were as extensive as to partake of quasi-
governmental powers."[7]
   Generally, the concessionaires provided plant and
equipment, public roads, port facilities, townships,
power, and water supplies, constituting a complete
infrastructure run solely for the benefit of the foreign
company. All these became the property of the foreign
company and were not usually available to the general
public in the host country, unless excess capacity
existed and access was consequently given to the host
country on terms specified and dictated by the foreign
company. The host governments were accordingly compelled
to take a passive attitude, which reduced their participation to nothing more than that of collectors of revenues
in the form of royalties and other types of financial
considerations. They did not involve themselves in the
operation of the company to gain access to other economic
and technical benefits related to the exploration and
exploitation of the natural resources in question.
Playing such a role, the developing host governments left
it to the foreign concessionaires to determine how the
mineral in question would be mined and the rate of

output; the cutoff grade; whether or not the minerals would be processed, to what extent, and where; the price at which the minerals were to be sold and where; and the places where the profits gained from the operation were to be invested, including the terms and conditions of such investment.

Secrecy surrounding the old concession agreements. Most of the traditional concession agreements between a particular investor and a host country were kept secret between the parties and were not generally available except when the foreign companies used them as a guide to their negotiations and conclusion of similar agreements with other host governments. This situation constituted a serious handicap for the negotiators from the newly independent countries, who found it difficult to obtain information on questions of law, technology, economics, and other important issues related to concession agreements. Thus, it was hard for them to evaluate the proposals of the foreign companies that had at their disposal all the information contained in agreements concluded elsewhere.

This situation changed, however, when copies of concession agreements became increasingly available to host governments. The credit for breaking the secrecy surrounding the traditional concession agreements goes to the members of OPEC, who were the first to publicize their negotiating positions and the terms of their agreements.

The availability of the OPEC agreements in the oil sector of mineral resources increased the chances for developing host countries to learn from each other and to adopt whatever was relevant in the publicized agreements to their local situations and needs. The suggested changes introduced by OPEC, which influenced the development of new approaches found in modern agreements, include, for example, active state participation in the operation of the mining company, maximization of government revenues through carefully negotiated financial obligations, stricter control of the activities of the foreign companies, and the setting up of national oil companies as appropriate.

It will become evident in this discussion that much experience gained in the petroleum sector was useful to the African countries, which were thus able to apply the techniques used in that sector, with necessary adjustments, to the hard minerals sector in negotiating a modern state contract for natural resources development.

Having regard, therefore, to the foregoing basic features of the old concession agreements, it is easily understood why changes were necessary to achieve a more balanced protection of the rights and interests of the host governments, as the owners of the natural resources, and the multinationals, with the capacity to explore and exploit the resources in question. The changes have been increasingly inspired by the concepts of both permanent sovereignty over natural resources[8] and the New International Economic Order.[9]

Illustrative Elements of Modern Agreements for Natural Resources Development

The basic features of modern contracts for mineral resources development are reflected in clauses that address issues that can be clearly delineated. Let us take first, for example, those provisions of a modern contract that are aimed at expanding benefits for the citizens and the local business community and increasing the host government's capacity to exercise sovereignty over the country's natural resources. The illustrative clauses address issues that clearly demonstrate new legal obligations establishing a more balanced framework for cooperation between the parties to the contract, as summarized below.

● Modern state contracts for mineral resources development between African countries and foreign countries now contain clauses requiring the multinational to provide technical training and experience for the citizens of the host country. Apart from the training clause, there is also a provision requiring the multinational to give employment to the local trained personnel. The degree to which these requirements are negotiated in contract terms differ. But it must be appreciated that training and employment of local personnel is a significant aspect of transfer of the necessary mining technology. The transfer of technology does not mean only the machinery and other producer goods and blueprints; it includes the availability of skilled manpower.[10]

● There are also clauses in modern mineral contracts that obligate the foreign company contractor to rely on local materials and to use local business enterprises in carrying out the activities. Here again, specific clauses differ in terms of the extent to which the foreign company is allowed discretion in these matters and the extent to which the encouragement of local business is made mandatory. The availability of the materials in question, their conditions and terms of delivery, and their cost as compared with the imported ones are always taken into account.[11]

● Certain modern contracts now address the question of assisting the host government to construct local refineries to increase the availability of petroleum for domestic consumption and possibly for export. Others simply include clauses obligating the company to ensure, during the contract, that there is enough petroleum supply for domestic consumption of the host country.[12]

• In response to the old practice of allowing concessionaires to hold large tracts of land for long
periods, modern contracts now have provisions for both
voluntary and mandatory relinquishment of contract land
area not needed by the company at various stages of its
activities. The surrender and relinquishment terms are
thus aimed at ensuring that the company holds only the
portion of land that it can put to active use. This
lessens the company's financial burden of annual rent per
unit of land held and also makes it possible for the host
government to get the land back for other uses.[13]

• In order to protect the interests of the host
government, it is now common for the contracting foreign
company to accept the obligation to supply the host
country with as accurate information as possible on the
various stages of mining activities conducted by the
company. The notification requirements deal with records
of operation and their inspection and verification by the
host government to ensure that the company is complying
with its obligation under the contract.[14]

• Apart from the obligation to supply data for
verification by the host government, a foreign company,
under modern mineral contracts, is now obliged to spend
a certain specified sum of money with respect to a
specific stage of activity. The minimum investment
requirements are usually contained in the work plan
negotiated, detailing the expectation of the parties at
each stage of exploration or exploitation, and providing
for liquidated damages for failure on the part of the
company to fulfill the contract terms at any stage. All
these are aimed at ensuring diligent performance in the
process of natural resources development.[15]

• Modern contracts for mineral resources development
also demonstrate the parties' awareness of the problems
that may occur from mining activities carried out without
due regard to environmental damage. Thus such contracts
now contain clauses requiring the company to avoid
damage to the environment, to avoid and minimize waste,
and to ensure the use of up-to-date equipment.[16]

The above elements of modern state contracts for
natural resources development indicate a clear difference
from the old concession agreements in taking into account
the interests of the host countries. The other basic
features of the modern contracts are reflected in the
various options open to the governments in their participation in the mining operation and their choices for
maximizing financial and other benefits from the
development of the natural resources in question. The
options that a government may exercise reflect a
deliberate decision by that government as to the role to
be played by a particular mining industry in the overall
development scheme of the country. Three basic
approaches seem to have been followed by the African

countries, as demonstrated by their contract terms with
foreign companies. Once again, I offer a summary of the
essential elements of these approaches:

 • There are clauses in modern contracts that reflect
the government's emphasis upon maximization of revenue
without the desire to control the management and operations of the foreign company in connection with the mining activity under contract. Under such an approach the
host government assumes the role of a passive revenue
collector, relying upon receipts from taxes, royalties,
bonuses, rents, and other forms of payments detailed in
the contract. A revenue-oriented contract may, nevertheless, contain all the other elements of a modern
contract summarized above. But since the host government is interested in the maximization of revenue and
less managerial control over the affairs of the foreign
company, the scope of those other clauses and the degree
of their enforcement become the areas of trade-offs.
This approach is now clearly in the minority. But it is
still an available option, and only the government itself
may reject it, in full knowledge of its economic
priorities.[17]

 • The second approach reflected in modern contracts
between African countries and foreign companies is
characterized by an orientation toward effective participation in and control of the operations of the mining
company by the host country. Participation by the
government of the African host country may be achieved
by means of joint ventures: equity joint ventures, in
which the host government purchases agreed numbers of
shares of the foreign company contractor; or contractual
joint ventures, in which the host government and the
foreign company establish a new, separate company to
undertake the actual mining activities under the contract. Under these joint ventures, the government may
opt for a minority equity participation, majority equity
participation, or a fifty-fifty equity participation.
These degrees of government participation are distinguishable from the option of complete ownership of
the mining operation.[18]

 • The third option, then, is one characterized by
complete government control of the mining operation
through ownership of 100 percent of the resources produced. Such complete government control may be achieved
through an option for concluding a service contract with
a foreign company,[19] a management contract,[20] or a
production sharing contract.[21] Whatever may be the
terminology used for these types of contracts, they share
a basic element: Title to the resources and the right to
exploit them are retained by the host government; the
foreign company assumes the responsibility for the
exploration expenses and gets its return either in fees
or by way of the right to a share of the production.

The foreign company is required to operate through
locally constituted subsidiaries and plays the role of a
hired operator or contractor rather than that of a
partner in a joint venture with the host government.
But it must be observed also that some of these arrangements include provisions under which the host government
undertakes to sell to the contracting company a portion
of the mineral produced at an agreed price. Such a
clause may be said to create an obligation upon the host
government, thereby establishing a form of association
that is not strictly that of an employer (host government) and a supplier of services (the contracting foreign
company). The ability of a particular host country to
exercise the options included in these types of contracts depends on the availability of skilled manpower
and the existence of a well-established national company
capable of assuming the responsibility of operating the
mining industry in question. Lack of such desiderata
would lead to the conclusion of a management contract or
a contract for specific tasks such as exploration only,
production only, or marketing only.[22]

With respect to the last two approaches, which rely
upon various degrees of government participation in or
full control of the mining company, care must be taken
to agree on certain fundamental issues; an arrangement
based on profit-sharing must grapple with the definition
of the concept of reasonable rate of return on investment
for the company, which would affect the amount of profit
to be shared. Here the host government must look out
for problems of transfer-pricing and the high ratio of
debt in the capital brought in by the foreign company as
its equity participation, which would enable it to repatriate lots of funds in the name of legitimate payment
of the principal and interest on such debt. In the
production-sharing arrangements and other arrangements
for payment in kind, the host government should ensure
that it would be able to market successfully its portion
of the production. Inability to secure the market for
the host country's share of the production could prevent
the country's receiving any of the benefits it expected
to gain from such arrangements. With respect to management contracts, again the host government must take care
to avoid arrangements by which the contracting foreign
company siphons the profits from the operations in the
form of disguised, exorbitant salaries paid to individual
experts, while the management contract fee itself is
kept visibly low.
In order to deal with all these problems modern
contracts have included detailed clauses relating to the
accounting and profits-reporting procedures.[23] Again,
to enforce intricate accounting procedures the host
country needs skilled local manpower. It is thus easy to
see why the training clauses of the modern contracts for

natural resources development have become so important. A balanced protection of the interest of the parties requires that the legitimate profits earned by the company, and the salaries paid to its foreign personnel, be enjoyed by the company and such employees under clearly defined conditions. Modern contracts have commonly contained clauses that deal with the following:

- exchange-control provisions aimed at facilitating the repatriation of the company's profit from the local operations;[24]
- exchange-control clauses dealing with the manner in which foreign personnel of the company could repatriate their salaries and other emoluments generated while serving the company in the host country;[25]
- taxation provisions aimed at inducing the foreign company to invest in the host country by either granting tax holidays[26] or agreeing to taxation arrangements that would enable the foreign company also to take advantage of the tax laws of the foreign company's home government.

The foregoing examples of issues addressed by modern contracts for natural resources development between African states and multinationals demonstrate one set of areas in which trade-offs between the negotiators may occur. An illustration of such trade-offs, showing the bargaining strength of the parties, may be found in the treatment of certain legal matters in the contract. I now turn briefly to such legal questions.

Provisions on Settlement of Disputes, Applicable Law, Stabilization of the Contract Regime, and Force Majeure

In this section I will attempt to give examples of modern contract provisions relating to the stated legal issues and to show how the relevant clauses reflect the ability of the parties to balance the protection of their various interests under the contract. Certain points need emphasis at the outset. There must be a proper interplay between the settlement-of-dispute clause and those applicable law clauses that seek to "freeze" the contracts by providing that their provisions must not be changed through executive or legislative action by a host state, come what may. Such clauses present a too rigid approach and a too extreme method of protecting the interest of the foreign company. All that being said, it is interesting to find that such clauses, aimed at creating "legal enclaves" in the form of unchanged contract terms to "stabilize the contract regime" for the benefit of the alien contractor, are included in certain modern agreements for mineral resources

development in African countries. A survey of the provisions with regard to these legal issues thus provides
an opportunity to demonstrate whether the host country
made a clear choice or whether it was in a weak bargaining position vis-à-vis the foreign company.

• A survey of the disputes-settlement clauses
discloses three major approaches with minor variations.[27]
There is the approach reflected in clauses stipulating
that disputes arising under the contract are to be
settled by the competent local courts that have final
jurisdiction on all matters. The second approach favors
settlement of contract disputes through preconstituted
international forums such as the International Centre for
Settlement of Investment Disputes (ICSID) and the International Chamber of Commerce (ICC). The third approach
favors settlement of contract disputes through ad hoc
arbitral tribunals to be established in a manner provided for under the contract itself. The foreign
companies predominantly prefer the second or the third
approaches, both of which rely upon international forums
to provide the third-party settlement procedures. The
host governments generally prefer the first approach--
settlement through competent local courts.[28]

• Invariably, all the contracts provide that they
are to be interpreted in accordance with the domestic
laws of the African host state in question. Stipulation
that the contracting state's law is the applicable law
can be rendered illusory if the contract itself has an
arbitration clause stipulating that different procedures
can be applied that, in effect, take the substantive
terms of the contract out of reach of the originally
stipulated applicable law. Thus, there must be a proper
interplay between the settlement-of-disputes clause and
the applicable law clause of the contract.[29] The
temptation to stipulate some law other than the law of
the contracting state,[30] especially the insistence of the
foreign company on making the law of its home country
the proper law of the contract, may be interpreted as a
vote of no confidence in the local African law by the
foreign company or may be simply the tendency of the
foreign company's lawyers to stipulate the law with
which they are familiar--their own country's law.[31]

• In response to the prevalent practice of stipulating the law of the host state as the proper law of
contract, foreign companies have sought to include
protective clauses that obligate the host state not to
take any actions that would affect any of the terms of
the contracts during the contract period. Thus, the
applicable law becomes the law at the time the contract
was concluded, and where changes are later introduced
into that law, the contract itself would remain a legal
enclave, based on the old law frozen at the point of the
agreement.[32]

• Under the force majeure clauses, also found in
certain contracts, any failures on the part of the
government or any of its instrumentalities on the one
hand or the foreign company on the other to fulfill any
of the obligations assumed under the contract are not to
be considered as a breach of the contract or actionable
default if such failures are caused by force majeure.
In order to have a clear understanding as to what
constitutes force majeure for the purpose of the clause,
certain contracts have included a definition.[33]

I have attempted to summarize trends in modern
mineral contracts with African governments that distinguish them from the old concessions whose basic
features I discussed earlier. It is now possible to
suggest that the term "modern contract" is used here, not
to denote the particular time period in which it was
concluded, but to acknowledge the degree to which the
contract embodies the new approaches.

My intention was to show that a modern state contract for natural resources development in Africa
combines various contractual obligations aimed at allowing all parties the options for securing maximum mutual
benefits arising from the rational utilization and
development of the resources in question. As the contracts themselves establish long-term relations between
the parties, it is necessary that they recognize that
technical, economic, or political changes may occur that
could unavoidably affect their terms. Accordingly, a
flexible approach to their interpretation and the possibility of their renegotiation, modification, and
adjustment, as appropriate, must be envisaged by the
parties.

LEGAL AND ECONOMIC ASPECTS OF TRANSNATIONAL LOAN
CONTRACTS WITH FOREIGN COMMERCIAL BANKS

Identification of Rights and Interest
of the Parties For a Balanced Protection

I would like to introduce this section with the
following anecdote. "When a retired sea captain's
sister-in-law came to join his household, a Cape Cod
story goes, the old salt demanded $10 a week from the
lady for room and board. Her sister, the captain's wife,
agreed to the arrangements, provided the captain gave
the $10 to her. Without telling her husband, she
routinely returned the money to her relative, thereby
assuring the financial satisfaction of all parties."[34]

This story is said to have been cited as a rough
parallel to what has been happening to the petrodollars
accumulated by the Arab oil producers. The surplus funds
have been channeled to the consuming countries by international banks playing the role of the sea captain's

wife. Part of the surplus petrodollars has been used
to pay for the oil producer's massive imports from the
industrialized countries. Part of that surplus revenue
is being loaned by the banks to the Third World countries that have thereby accumulated oppressive debts,
for the servicing of which they are compelled to borrow
further.

The debt burden of the nonoil developing countries
and therefore those in sub-Saharan Africa is a subject
about which the United Nations has expressed concern
and for which certain remedial actions have been
suggested.[35] I mention the subject here only to indicate
the economic foundations of various interests the parties
have when they seek protection through the legal framework under discussion. I intend to identify certain
economic aspects of the problem that merit consideration
in discussing the legal framework in a realistic context.
This will enable me to demonstrate, at least, how the
nonoil African members of the Third World are caught in
the middle as the least powerful of the unequal partners
in the envisaged triangle.

● Every time OPEC increases the price of oil, either
by raising the price per barrel of the crude produced
or by deliberately cutting back production of the crude
(thereby pushing the price up as a result of unadjusted
demand), the nonoil developing countries feel a double
pinch: one directly and another indirectly. In the
first place, they have to borrow the funds to foot the
high oil bills. This directly increases their indebtedness. In the second place, the higher oil costs may slow
economic growth in the industrialized world and affect
its ability to buy the exports of the nonoil developing
countries. Loss of exports earnings from trade with
the industrialized world thus becomes the indirect pinch
felt by the nonoil developing countries as a result of
high oil prices. For the OPEC countries, it means more
surplus funds for investment. They seem to have preferred to invest in real estate in the OECD countries or
to deposit funds in the commercial banks of the Western
world, instead of directly investing in projects in
sub-Saharan Africa. For the Western commercial banks,
it means more petrodollars to recycle, for which they
must find clients.
● The increase in borrowing from foreign commercial
banks by the nonoil African countries has been due to a
vigorous campaign by the banks. Faced with the buildup
of OPEC deposits and a decline in loan demands from
traditional domestic borrowers, foreign commercial banks
have been desperate to find "offshore" outlets, which
they have found in the Third World. Some of the Third
World countries have been compelled by certain conditions
not to go to international lending institutions like the
IMF for help with their balance of payments or to the

World Bank for project loans and have found the foreign
commercial banks to be a willing alternative source.
The foreign commercial banks approach lending activity
to their African clients with the usual business expectation of making profits. There is no reason to suggest
that they lend to African clients out of sympathy with
the clients' chronic problem with balance-of-payments
deficits. Accordingly, the relationship being established
between the banks and their clients is somewhat symbiotic:
The lender and the borrower need each other. It is
therefore imprudent to insist upon developing a legal
framework to offer more protection of the rights and
interests of one party than those of the other. A loan
contract should therefore strive toward a balanced
protection of the rights and interests of both the
borrower and the lender.
    ● The Arab petrofunds are in the form of short-term
deposits that, in turn, constrain the commercial banks
that recycle them to offer only comparable short-term
loans (three years) to their Third World clients. This
presents a real problem for the borrowers, who are
consequently faced with huge, high-interest loans carrying short maturity periods and also are therefore not
amenable to an arrangement for repayment through funds
generated from the operation of the loan project. A
suggestion readily comes to mind: Commercial banks
could consider means of offering loans to their Third
World clients that have longer, but still reasonable,
maturity periods and that would be more conducive to
payment through funds generated from the loan project.
It is clear that the primary interest of lenders is in
getting their money back, and enjoying reasonable
interest on it. They would accordingly attempt to avoid
default situations that could adversely affect these
expectations. The borrowers also have an interest in
maintaining credit-worthiness with the commercial banks
as alternative sources of the needed funds when the IMF
proves difficult and the World Bank cannot be tapped.
Third World borrowers would, accordingly, avoid actions
that could tarnish their credit rating with the foreign
commercial banks and would strive toward efficient dis-
charge of their loan obligations under the contract.
    ● Where the magnitude of the loan required by a
client is beyond the level of the amount U.S. law permits
a U.S. bank to extend to a single client, there may be
a syndicated loan. Because of the possible competition
in the syndicated loan, the borrower may be able to
negotiate better terms, including, for example, longer
maturity rates and a lower figure for the "spread,"
which is the profit margin in the form of a difference
between the London Interbank Rate (LIBOR) and the fixed
interest charged by the banks in the Eurocredit arrangement. Specific features of syndicated loans, such as
cross-default clauses, will be subject to further

discussion in the context of the actual loan agreements provision.

• The syndicated loans may also include the participation of international lending institutions such as the IMF, for financing of balance-of-payments problems, and the World Bank, for financing development projects. The foreign commercial banks gain two advantages by inviting the World Bank, for example, to join them in a loan transaction. First, the commercial banks may have the legitimate desire to monitor the economic performance of the borrower so as to ensure that conditions are conducive to the success of the loan project, which enhances the chances of repayment of the loan. But they would find it politically unwise or merely impractical to be directly involved in the actual monitoring and supervising of the utilization of every loan they extend to a sovereign state. Accordingly, they prefer leaving monitoring and supervision to either the IMF or the World Bank, as the case may be, which have the machinery and a long tradition of monitoring the utilization of their loans. Second, the participation of the IMF or the World Bank in a single loan transaction with the commercial banks may be said to give the commercial banks comfort. As noted earlier, the syndicated loans usually have cross-default clauses. The commercial bank is comforted, then, by its belief that Third World borrowers would avoid default on the commercial loan at all costs, because the cross-default clause means that the borrower defaulting on the commercial loan defaults also on the IMF loan involved. Being in the bad books of the IMF and the World Bank is something no African state borrower would want.

• Participation of the foreign commercial banks in syndicated loans with the IMF or the World Bank also became necessary as a practical matter, when it was obvious that the two international lending institutions did not have enough liquidity to meet the rising demands from clients faced with rising costs of development resulting from increasing oil prices. The petrofunds from the commercial banks thus provided the additional finance. For this reason, going to the commercial banks to borrow funds carrying high interest rates and shorter maturities became an unavoidable alternative for the Third World. But the decision to approach the commercial banks in certain cases was more of a choice to avoid the stringent borrowing conditions that the IMF imposes upon its clients, especially those who are borrowing on their later tranches.[36] Certain new developments have recently occurred that could give the Third World a "break" from the situation. First, there has been a more vigorous campaign to increase the liquidity of both the World Bank and the IMF so as to make them more capable of financing Third World debts or deficits on terms comparatively better than those the commercial banks

offer. The IMF has also recently decided to relax its
stringent conditions and may, accordingly, become a more
active financial source for project financing. The consequences of these developments are readily distinguishable
from those that may occur when the commercial banks decide
to give up their sea captain's wife's role of recycling
the petrodollars. There have been reports that some of
the banks want to stop recycling, although others still
want to continue with the business.

The foregoing has been an attempt to provide some
economic and other relevant reasons for the kinds of
rights and interests of parties that are expressed in
loan agreements. Proper balancing of the identified
interests of the parties is, accordingly, a challenge to
those who negotiate loan contracts. The lenders may
take the position that, once the funds have been re-
leased to the borrowers, a condition is created in which
the borrower has everything (the money) and the lender
is left with nothing but the piece of paper in the form
of a loan agreement. Thus the lender may want the legal
instrument to be more favorable to the lender than to
the borrower. This, in my view, would be a dangerous
approach to loan agreements and should not be encouraged.
In concluding this discussion, let me revert to two
points relating to the rights and interests of the oil
producers in this triangle. Earlier I mentioned that the
Arab oil producers have clearly preferred to invest their
surplus funds in the OECD countries rather than in the
Third World--in particular, sub-Saharan Africa. This may
reflect the oil producers' belief that their investments
demonstrably receive better protection in the OECD
countries than they could receive in the seemingly
unfavorable investment climate of sub-Saharan Africa.
The onus, on the one hand, is on the countries of sub-
Saharan Africa to demonstrate their willingness to
attract such investments. On the other hand, the Arab
oil producers should also attempt to abandon their too
generalized fear of investment in Africa. They may
initiate direct investment in sub-Saharan Africa by,
for example, establishing a direct-lending vehicle for
specific projects--for which they can compete by offering
more concessionary terms than either the foreign
commercial banks or the international lending institutions. To guarantee their protection, they could work
with an OECD consortium that would also be willing to act
as collateral for the African borrower for the clearly
defined development project.
The possibility has been raised that the OPEC
countries may decide, because of their reading of the
market situation, to curtail crude oil production. If
they did so, however, it would be imprudent to say that
the so-called Seven Sisters (Exxon, Royal Dutch Shell,
British Petroleum, Mobil, Texaco, Gulf Oil, and Standard

Oil of California) have more right to that crude in the
soil than the owners of the natural resources in
question.[37] The oil-producing countries may legitimately
fear that their nonrenewable resource will be depleted
through extravagant consumption by the OECD states or by
the OECD countries' decision to stockpile the oil to
build their reserves. The possibility that oil-producing
countries might decide to keep the crude in the soil may
effectively force the industrial countries to initiate
and/or strengthen energy conservation policies or look
for alternative, nonpetroleum sources of energy. For the
Third World and sub-Saharan Africa, however, such a
decision would result in the double pinch explained
earlier, emphasizing again their position as the least
powerful of the unequal partners of the triangle.

Survey of the Standard Clauses of Loan Agreements

The purpose clause. This clause is intended to
state clearly the purpose or purposes for which the loan
is required. From the lender's viewpoint, the clause
must be unambiguous so that it can easily be used to
determine the nature of the economic performance expected
of the borrower and the "economic effects"[38] of the loan
itself. From the borrower's viewpoint, the purpose
clause of the loan agreement must necessarily reflect the
discretion that a sovereign state is usually allowed to
exercise in the use of resources in the manner it deems
fit for its national development. In this context, the
purpose clause must be flexible enough to allow the
borrower to make necessary adjustments. The relationship
must be allowed to work, and any reasonable flexibility
in the application of the loan is desirable.

Repayment clause. This must be carefully drafted
to protect the interest of the lender in achieving repayment as stipulated, as well as the interest of the
borrower in being able to reasonably vary the repayment
schedule because of unforeseen circumstances. This
clause should include an allowance for renegotiation
of the loan-repayment schedule and terms for the purpose of avoiding default situations. Renegotiation
clauses in loan agreements have, however, been found
undesirable by international bankers. They feel that
the needed flexibility may be achieved and the technical
defaults avoided by mutual trust and understanding between the lender and the borrower. Renegotiation
remains a distinct possibility, but one that need not
be spelled out at the start. The point being emphasized
here, however, is that it seems unreasonable to compel
the developing-country borrowers to tighten their belts
to the extent of cutting their waists in an attempt to
live up to rigid repayment terms. Flexibility must be
seen as a benefit for both lender and borrower, both of

whom should be interested in the survival of the money
market. The approach is to maintain the relationship
the agreement created between the two and to avoid a premature termination of that relationship on technical
grounds that pay no attention to the economic problems
of one of the parties.

Representation and warranties clauses. These include statements made by the borrower as to financial and
other pertinent considerations; the confirmation that the
obligation being assumed under the loan agreement is
proper under the relevant domestic laws of the borrower;
and recognition of reciprocal enforceability of judgments rendered in the courts of the country of the lender
and of the borrower in cases arising out of the loan
agreement.

Covenants clauses. These are usually affirmative
covenants in the form of promises by the borrower to per-
form certain actions either automatically or at the
request of the lender. Their principal purpose is to
provide the lender, at the outset of the agreement and
during its course, with information indicating the
general credit-worthiness of the borrower. They also
include negative covenants such as restrictions on
working capital, additional borrowing, guarantees,
dividends, and cross-default clauses in syndicated
loans, all of which basically aim at tightening the
control of the lender over the actions of the borrower.
Taken together, both the affirmative and the negative
covenant clauses are clearly restrictive. But the
extent to which they are to be applied in any individual
case is practically a matter of discretion on the part
of the bank. The borrower is thus left with the promise
that the bank would not insist on enforcing terms of
the loan that are so harsh as to be unconscionable.

Event-of-default clauses. These clauses refer to
defaults that could occur and spell out remedies in the
event that any should occur. For the syndicated loans
there is the cross-default clause, which merely states
that a default on one of the loans is a default on all
the other loans. The usual cause of the breaking of
covenants is default; loan agreements will generally
stipulate that the bank notify the borrower and, in
certain instances, allow a grace period for correction,
or they might provide that appropriate remedial action
go into force at the moment of default. Such practices
seem to enforce the notion that, despite the restrictive
nature of the covenants, banks tend to apply them in
such a way as to avoid engaging in what may plainly be
called irrational or counterproductive behavior.

Additional burdens clause. This clause protects the bank against subsequent events that may change the interpretation of the agreement, either actions of the borrowing state or events in the country of the lender. The clause usually provides that where such actions create additional financial burdens upon the bank or prevent the bank from fulfilling its obligations, resulting in loss of earnings, the following sanction is stipulated: The bank may cancel the loan or the borrower is required to compensate the bank for the increased cost or reduced amount receivable due to the changed circumstances. A typical provision, which merits reproduction in its entirety, reads as follows:

Notwithstanding any other provision herein, if any applicable law, treaty, regulation, or directive, or any change therein or in the interpretation or application thereof, shall make it unlawful for the Bank to maintain or give effect to its obligations as contemplated by this Agreement, the Commitment of the Bank hereunder shall forthwith be cancelled and the Borrower shall prepay to the Bank, upon its demand, the entire unpaid principal amount of the Notes together with all accrued interest thereon from the last day of the previous Interest Period to the date of such prepayment. If such prepayment is made on a day which is not the last day of an Interest Period, the Borrower shall pay to the Bank, upon the Bank's request, such amount or amounts as will compensate the Bank for any loss or expense incurred by the Bank in the re-employment of funds obtained by the Bank for the purpose of maintaining the loans hereunder. A certificate as to any additional amounts payable pursuant to the foregoing sentence submitted by the Bank to the Borrower shall be conclusive absent manifest error.

In the event that any applicable law, treaty, regulation or directive, or any change therein or in the interpretation or application thereof, or compliance by the Bank with any request (whether or not having the force of law) of any relevant central bank or other comparable agency, shall subject the Bank to any tax of any kind whatsoever with respect to this Agreement, the Notes or the Guarantee or acquisitions of debt obligations of obligors outside [the country of the lender] or change the basis of taxation of payments to the Bank of principal, interest or any other amount payable under this Agreement or the Notes or under the Guarantee (except for changes in

the rate of tax on the overall net income of
the Bank imposed in [the country of the lender]),
or shall impose, modify or deem applicable
any reserve, special deposit or similar
requirements against foreign assets held by,
or deposits in or for the account of, or
advances or loans by, or any other acquisition
of funds by, any office of the Bank, or shall
impose upon the Bank any other condition with
respect to the eurodollar market or to this
Agreement, the Notes, the Guarantee or the
loans hereunder, and the result of any of the
foregoing is to increase the cost to the Bank
of making or maintaining the loans hereunder
or to reduce any amount receivable by the
Bank under this Agreement or the Notes or
under the Guarantee, then the Borrower shall
pay to the Bank, upon its demand, additional
amounts which will compensate the Bank for such
increased cost or reduced amount receivable.
A certificate as to any additional amounts
payable pursuant to the foregoing sentence
submitted by the Bank to the Borrower shall
be conclusive absent manifest error.

If the Borrower cannot lawfully pay such
increased amounts and cannot or does not
obtain an exoneration from any such condition
the Bank may, by telex or cable notice to
the Borrower, declare the Note to be due and
payable as of the date of such notice.[39]

It is fair to observe that the borrower should pay
careful attention to the above provision, as it implies
that the lender seeks to protect its interest against
subsequent events affecting the loan agreement without
offering a corresponding protection to the borrower.
It would be, in my view, useful to ascertain which of
the clauses protecting the interest of the lender could
also be used as vehicles for protecting legitimate,
corresponding interest of the borrower. A provision
with additional burdens such as the one above could, for
example, be counterbalanced by including a clause dealing
with the consequences of the lender's failure to fulfill
its obligation under the loan as a result of subsequent
events that are in no way connected with the joint or
separate conduct of the borrower, or the borrower's
failure to fulfill its obligation as a result of subsequent events brought about by external economic forces
that the borrower has no power to prevent or mitigate.

It also seems reasonable that covenant clauses
that include only provisions for certain automatic
performance on the part of the borrower for the lender's
benefit could be drafted to recognize events requiring
automatic performance on the part of the lender for the

borrower's benefit. Most of these clauses seem to
proceed on the assumption that only the borrower may have
difficulties and that only the lender must be protected
against the consequences of such difficulties. This
assumption may not be correct in all cases.

As noted in the comment on the repayment clause, it
also seems reasonable that the clause should specifically
recognize the possibility that a loan may be renegotiated
and rescheduled so as to avoid default. The point here
is that both the borrower and the lender have a keen
interest in avoiding default. The borrower seeks to
avoid default on loans so as to maintain its credit-
worthiness with the bankers. The bankers also seek to
avoid defaults because they might have a snowballing
effect that could interfere with the international money
market. It is my view then, that the payment and event-
of-default clauses should recognize the mutual interest
of the parties and include provisions that reasonably
protect the interests of both the lender and the
borrower.

The foregoing observations are part of my basic
approach to loan agreements, negotiated in the spirit
of mutual interdependence in which a balanced protection
of the legitimate rights and interests of the parties
is the rule.

Settlement-of-disputes clauses. As this question is
also dealt with in the discussion of mining agreements,
it is necessary only to touch upon those aspects that
directly concern loan agreements.

Settlement of disputes of loan agreements between
governments and foreign commercial banks remains an
issue with respect to which no uniform practice may be
said to have emerged. Two approaches may, however, be
identified. There is the view that such disputes should
be settled through arbitration, created by the will of
the parties and relying upon lex arbitrii enshrined in
the loan agreement itself. The lex arbitrii would thus
deal with questions of the submission of the disputes;
the constitution of the tribunal; the validity of the
award--its enforcement, interpretation, revision,
annulment, and so on; the procedure to be followed; and
the applicable law as stipulated in the contract. On
this latter point, it is important to reiterate that
negotiators must, accordingly, strive to achieve a proper
interplay between the applicable law clause and the
settlement-of-disputes clause so as to avoid complicated
conflicts of law. The practice of the International
Centre for the Settlement of Investment Disputes between
States and Nationals of Other States, under the World
Bank, has attempted to facilitate the use of such
arbitration and now contains a mature jurisprudence that
establishes a useful interplay between the applicable
law clause and the clause dealing with the jurisdiction

of the Centre. Thus, settlement of disputes under a
loan agreement between states and foreign commercial
banks may draw on that practice. Unless, however, a
particular loan agreement confers jurisdiction upon the
World Bank's Centre, the arbitration contemplated in
the agreement must be ad hoc.

Foreign commercial banks have, however, been
demonstrably unenthusiastic about using arbitration to
settle loan agreements disputes. They seem to prefer
to settle such disputes through competent local courts
of law, stipulated specifically in the contract as the
proper forum. The commercial bankers adduce two arguments against arbitration as a mode of settlement.
First, they point out that the constitution of an ad hoc
arbitration is a slow process and for that reason prefer
proceedings before an existing and competent court of
law. Second, the banks seem to hold the view that, in
a dispute arising out of the nonpayment of the loan,
there is really nothing to arbitrate. Either the borrower
pays the loan as required by the terms of the loan agreement or the consequences of such failure to pay must be
allowed to operate in a manner determined by a judge in
a court of law. An ad hoc arbitration whose functions
rely upon the will of the parties would, in the bankers'
view, tend to take into account questions of equity, thus
going beyond the terms of the agreement as originally
accepted by the parties and departing from considering
only the immediate interest of the bank to secure payment
of the loan.

It may be observed, then, that from the point of
view of the borrower, arbitration that is capable of
applying the principle of equity--understood in this
context to mean what is fair and reasonable--would be a
preferable forum for settlement of loan disputes requiring third-party procedures. But the bankers may also
weigh the ability to secure enforcement of an arbitral
award against that of securing enforcement of local
court judgments, where there are no applicable instruments between the parties concerning reciprocal enforcement of such awards or judgments. Accordingly, the banks
may also find it advantageous to accept, for reasons of
enforcement, arbitration as a mode of settlement of loan
disputes. It must be emphasized, however, that a loan
agreement is distinguishable from other state contracts
for economic development. Therefore, it is not easy to
generalize that arbitration is an effective approach to
resolution in all cases of economic disputes encountered
by multinationals.

As noted earlier, with respect to concession
agreements settlement by courts of the host government
is now the common practice. With respect to loan agreements, however, the choice is still between settlement
before the competent courts (usually of the lender) and
settlement through arbitration.

Applicable law clauses. In the case of loan agreements with international lending institutions, I should
mention the initial practice by which the IBRD made the
interpretation of loan agreements with member governments
subject to the law of New York State. This practice was
soon discontinued. The present IBRD practice is now contained in the general conditions clause, which reads as
follows:

> The rights and obligations of the Bank, the
> Borrower and the Guarantor under the Loan
> Agreement and the Guarantee Agreement shall
> be valid and enforceable in accordance with
> their terms notwithstanding the law of any
> State or political subdivision thereof, to
> the contrary. Neither the Bank nor the
> Borrower nor the Guarantor shall be entitled
> in any proceeding under this Article to
> assert any claim that provisions of these
> General Conditions of the Loan Agreement or
> the Guarantee Agreement is . . . un-
> enforceable because of any provision of the
> Articles of Agreement of the Bank.[40]

The object of the above provision is not only to
remove the loan agreement and the guarantee agreement
from municipal systems of law but, effectively, to make
the agreements subject to international law. The current
IBRD general conditions, by which it abandons its initial
practice of "commercialization" of international agreements (making them subject to the laws of New York) and
by which it now applies international law, introduces
the next important point in the development of the law
in this area. What has emerged is not a uniform
applicable law rule, but an assertion of parties'
autonomy. Under the system of parties' autonomy, which
may permit designation of international law as the proper
law of state contract, a process called "internationalization of state contracts" is said to have occurred. It
has been expressed authoritatively as follows: "It is
now possible to suggest the prevailing view that a
contract between a State and a foreigner may be subject
to 'internationalization' in the sense that, if the
parties so intend, it is governed by public internationalization law."[41]

The real consequences of "internationalization" of
state contracts are yet to be fully grasped. Simply
agreeing to make a contract with a foreign company
subject to international law ought not to be construed
to mean that the state has thereby assumed the same kind
of international obligation it would have under a treaty.
The breach of an "internationalized" state contract
would not engage an international responsibility for a
state.[42]

The scope of "internationalization" of state contracts may, however, be complicated by the exercise of parties' autonomy in adopting, from municipal contract law, the technique of dépaçage (segregation of issues), according to which the parties may decide to stipulate not one but two or more applicable laws in a single loan agreement. Using this technique, the parties may, for example, stipulate international law as the proper law of the contract governing the validity of the agreement, while segregating certain specific issues that, for reasons of practicability, are to be governed by designated municipal laws. This could be the case of a loan agreement on the basis of which bonds are issued for various capital markets; such a case might require the stipulation of relevant local laws to govern the various issues related to the bond transactions, even though the main loan agreement remains subject to international law. This technique of dépaçage and its implications signal the need to elucidate further the possibility of maintaining a distinction between the law governing the validity of a contract and the legal regime relating to the interpretation and application of its terms and other obligations derived from it.

BILATERAL AGREEMENTS FOR ECONOMIC AND TECHNICAL
COOPERATION AND LOAN AGREEMENTS BETWEEN GOVERNMENTS

This section is designed to survey briefly the legal framework reflected in the bilateral agreements for economic and technical cooperation between developed and developing countries, on the one hand, and those among the developing countries themselves, on the other hand. I will also consider the basic features of bilateral loan agreements between developed and developing countries.

Bilateral Agreements for Economic Cooperation

The available examples disclose a practice in which the modern bilateral agreements for economic cooperation usually take the form of very short and less detailed instruments dealing with broad outlines. They all have a standard preamble in which the parties assert, inter alia, their determination to establish or strengthen economic cooperation between them, based on the concepts of sovereign equality and mutual respect.

The substantive articles then proceed to give the general framework for achieving the stated goal of strengthening economic cooperation. In these articles it becomes clear that economic cooperation cannot be discussed without reference to technical cooperation and that parties must address the questions of economic and technical cooperation in the same agreement. Thus, whether the instrument is called an "Economic Cooperation Agreement" or an "Economic and Technical Cooperation

Agreement," certain supportive measures are usually
included to deal, in general terms, with cooperation in
the spheres of industry, mining, agriculture, trade,
transport and communication, public works, and the like.
No specific articles are drafted to deal with these
issues in the general agreement, except to refer to the
fact that, for example, the nature and operational details of such activities may include transfer of knowledge and technique of research work and educational
programs.

By reserving detailed provisions on such supportive
activities for later, separate agreements, the bilateral
agreements for economic cooperation accordingly differ
from the traditional treaties for friendship, commerce,
and navigation. The FCN treaties, which seem not to be
much in vogue now, were comprehensive instruments in
which detailed provisions on all relevant activities of
cooperation between the parties were included. But some
of the issues covered by the FCN treaties--such as
reciprocal treatment of nationals, protection of the
parties' foreign investments, the most-favored-nation
clause in trade and commerce, the avoidance of double tax-
ation--have either become subject to standard regulation
by domestic legislation or been comprehensively treated
in multilateral global, regional, or subregional treaties
to which the parties may be signatories. The result
then is the general economic and/or technical cooperation
agreements that provide only a broad framework, but call
for additional protocols and more detailed agreements on
specific spheres of cooperation to be concluded between
the parties later. In the broad framework, the agreements tend to stress, among other things, the need to pay
attention to the developmental objectives and priorities
established by the developing country that is party to
the agreement. They also establish joint commissions
whose basic function is to supervise the implementation
of the agreement and the identification of specific
projects and spheres of cooperation with respect to
which additional specific agreements between the parties
would be necessary.

This practice encourages closer examination of the
rights and interests of the parties for the purpose of
balancing them properly in the instrument. The approach
of recognizing and respecting the rights and interests
of both parties is also the guiding principle in the
negotiation of such economic cooperation agreements as
are emphasized by the work of UNCTAD.[43]

Bilateral Agreements for Technical Cooperation and
the Preoccupation with the Protection of Experts

When an instrument bears the heading "Agreement for
Technical Cooperation," it may be in itself a major
independent agreement between the parties, or it may be

a specific agreement on the particular subject of
technical cooperation, concluded to implement the terms
of a prior general agreement on economic cooperation in
force between the same parties as observed above. Thus
it becomes a supportive measure for the economic cooperation agreement. Whatever its nature, an agreement for
technical cooperation is a little more detailed in its
provisions in certain aspects and may, as appropriate,
also leave options for the conclusion of additional
protocols to enforce some of its terms. As a general
rule, most agreements are in the form of independent
general agreements contemplating such further elaboration.
There is evidence that such agreements have shown a
marked degree of concern with the protection of foreign
experts. Examination of the development of the law in
this area is of special interest in the light of the
United Nations resolutions on Technical Cooperation
among the Developing Countries and specific actions that
have been taken to encourage such cooperation.[44] The
treatment of experts under such agreements differs:

• In a TCDC agreement between an African country
and a Latin American country, no elaborate provisions
exist giving foreign experts elaborate protection by way
of privileges and immunities. The relevant article
merely states that the contracting parties undertake to
provide the experts with the necessary facilities to
ensure the satisfactory completion of their work under
the agreement and that official visas will be granted to
nationals of each party free of charge.[45]
• The above contrasts sharply with the terms of
another agreement between two other states from the
developing countries of Africa and Latin America, in
which the subject of privileges of experts received more
detailed treatment. Detailed provisions are included
specifying that experts and members of their households
will enjoy the same privileges and immunities as U.N.
personnel in the respective territories.[46] This approach
also differs from one in which the parties merely agree
to extend such privileges as may be in force in
accordance with the domestic laws of each state party.[47]
• The TCDC agreements deal with a two-way flow of
experts. In the technical cooperation agreements between
a developing country and an industrial state, the movement of experts is one-way--to the developing country.
Industrialized states thus demand even more complete
protection for their nationals abroad. Clauses include
those ensuring the foreign experts the right to repatriate a fixed amount of their salaries; the right to
import duty-free certain household effects, including
foodstuffs; and the right to be held harmless in cases
of local proceedings brought against them for alleged
harm done in the course of duty.
• Invariably, the agreements for technical

cooperation between an African and an industrialized, developed country extend the following privileges and immunities: to exempt the experts from taxes or any fiscal charges in respect to all remunerations paid by the experts' home government; grant the experts immunity from legal actions in respect of any words spoken or written and in respect of any acts performed in an official capacity; give protection to the person and property of the experts; provide experts with necessary work permits and exempt them from normal immigration regulations or travel restrictions subject to the requirement that the expert be given an identity card, register with the local police and obtain a residence permit; exempt the experts from local national service obligations; and effect repatriation of the experts in time of national or international crises.

The lesson one learns from the agreements whose terms I have briefly analyzed is that drafters should spend more time developing the substantive law under which technical exchange and cooperation may be achieved rather than continuing this preoccupation with protection of experts. I grant that the experts should be allowed to carry out their work under conditions conducive to successful completion of the specific project agreement. But that should not be the main point of agreements.

Bilateral Loan Agreements for Development Projects
_____

This last section focuses on some legal and economic considerations in bilateral loan agreements between industrialized and developing countries. Such loan agreements are to be distinguished, first, from the general agreements for economic cooperation covering foreign public grants and other forms of official assistance to developing countries, and second, from the credit lines opened for the borrower, specifically offered to enable the developing country to buy particular goods and services from the lender; no money flows from the lender to the borrower. Thus the borrower has no choice but to secure such goods and services from the country supplying the credit. Agreements for credit lines are thus usually brief; they may include an approved list of items covered under the terms of credit.

Loan agreements concluded to finance specific projects or for general economic development are, by contrast, more detailed. They usually contain, at the least, clauses dealing with such issues as: the conditions under which further contracts may be concluded by the borrower for executing aspects of a project being financed by the loan; repayment schedules for both the principal and interest when the loan is interest-bearing; detailed warranty clauses protecting the

interests of the lender in case of default on the part
of the borrower; privileges and immunities for the experts
from the lending country working under a loan project;
and other issues, including settlement of disputes and
applicable law. Certain basic ideas merit emphasis at
the outset to form the rationale behind the legal framework being suggested. Once again, the idea is to
ascertain what legitimate interests of the parties require a balanced protection by the loan agreement. Here
then are some of my views on this question:

• It is prudent to avoid clauses in bilateral loan
agreements that encourage the tendency to regard such
loans as outright favors offered by the lending states,
which are then entitled to dictate the terms of the loans
for all time.

• A bilateral loan, whether interest-free or otherwise, creates an obligation upon the borrower to repay
the loan. Consequently, serious consideration should be
given to allowing the borrower enough discretion to apply
the loan to securing goods and services, either from the
lender or in the open market, whichever is more
economically feasible.

• Where, therefore, the execution of a project loan
calls for further negotiation of additional specific
contracts for the supply of goods and services, the
borrower would exercise the discretion of entering into
such additional contracts, to be financed by the project
loan, without being compelled by the agreement to secure
prior formal approval of the lender, preventing the
borrower from using its own economic judgment to get
goods and services at a competitive market price. This
is an argument about tied loans[48] and a call for depar-
ture from the rigidity of such loans.[49]

• The lender obviously has an interest in ensuring
that it gets the money back. It may legitimately seek
to ascertain that conditions existing in the borrowing
country are conducive to the repayment of the project
loan. Nevertheless, this does not mean that the lender
is entitled to exercise onerous surveillance of the
borrower in the form of endless tie-in contracts.

• A bilateral loan agreement should, accordingly,
reflect a more balanced consideration of the interest
of both the borrower and the lender. An effort to
achieve such a balance would discourage the inclusion in
a bilateral loan agreement of complicated and detailed
covenants and warranties aimed primarily at protecting
the interest of the lender in securing, in addition,
markets for its goods and services in the borrowing
country, beyond the interest of securing the eventual
repayment of the loan itself under the agreed terms.

• As I argued in connection with loans from
commercial banks, the conditions of repayment of bilateral loans should also be flexible. Possibilities

for renegotiation of payment terms should be envisaged
in cases in which unforeseen circumstances create super-
vening impossibility of performance for the borrower, such
as unfavorable domestic economic conditions, caused and
aggravated by external economic factors beyond the control of the borrower.

• Only in the absence of another legal instrument
in force between the parties, such as agreements for
economic cooperation or for promotion of foreign investment in general, should a bilateral loan agreement be
burdened with clauses dealing with issues such as
expropriation,[50] or protection of the foreign experts.

The foregoing are some of the basic ideas I wished
to put forth for providing a bilateral loan agreement
with the necessary economic and political foundation,
taking into account the obvious inequality between the
borrower and the lender. Having sought to establish a
legal relationship between the parties to the loan
agreement along the lines suggested here, the negotiators
may hope that the relationship will work smoothly and,
consequently, decide to remain silent on the question of
settlement of disputes. But they may also address the
question in several ways. Provisions exist in which the
negotiators include a clause simply stating that disputes
arising under the loan agreement shall be settled by
consultations, or by any other means mutually agreed
upon by the parties, or through a compromisory clause
naming a particular third-party procedure. Most of the
agreements provide for dispute settlement by ad hoc
arbitral tribunal to be established in accordance with
the terms of the loan agreement itself. The settlement-
of-dispute clause invariably touches upon the applicable
law, with respect to which a tendency has existed to
stipulate the law of the lender as the governing law.[51]
The idea of making an international agreement between
two sovereign states subject to the municipal law of one
of the states creates jurisprudential problems, the
discussion of which is beyond the scope of this chapter.
Suffice it to observe that international law should be
the proper law for determining the validity of a bilateral loan agreement as well as its interpretation
and application. But, as I have just hinted, there are
certain controversies about this.

CONCLUSIONS

One of the basic concerns of those engaged in the
process of developing the law is the proper identification of the rights and interests of all participants
whose conduct and acts are to be governed by the law.
Throughout this chapter, I have attempted to focus on the
identification of the rights and interests of parties
to agreements for natural resources development, loan

contracts, and other agreements of cooperation. The
legal framework herein suggested also includes procedures
through which the legal rights and interests of the
parties could be vindicated in case of disputes.

In order, therefore, to provide appropriate economic,
political, and social contexts in which the law among
unequal partners should be fashioned, it has been
necessary to touch briefly upon such issues. But there
are those who would give more details about the international monetary system in general and how it affects
the rights and interests of the partners in the
triangle;[52] about the present situation of financing
Third World debt;[53] and about the intricacies of the
Eurobond market.[54] The legal framework analyzed in this
chapter must thus be tested against the other realities.

If all of us agree that the oil-producing countries,
the nonoil African countries, and the members of the
OECD need to revise their expectations of how they can
mutually benefit from their specific endowments, then it
would seem that changes must be made in an orderly way.
Bringing about orderly change is within the province and
function of the law. The development from the old concession agreements to modern agreements for natural
resources development presents one example of using
the law to redefine priorities, rights and interests,
and other legitimate expectations of all the actors in
the world arena in a more balanced manner.

The evidence may be overwhelming in the direction
of giving the Third World "a break." This is just to
confirm that earlier legal relationships overwhelmingly
tended to favor the industrialized countries and their
transnational companies. The pendulum should be returned
to the middle, and this is the struggle evidenced by the
new approaches to the breed of contracts and agreements
examined in this chapter. Where the pendulum swings
completely the other way, past the middle from its
original position favoring the members of the OECD, it
may be an indication that the imbalance was of a magnitude requiring nothing short of that. The legal framework must thus be flexible enough to allow the assertion
and vindication of the recognized rights of all the
would-be parties to the triangle, commensurate with the
relevant political and economic realities of each
particular situation.

NOTES

1. See General Assembly Resolutions 3201 and 3203, 6th Special
Session, GAOR Supp. 1 (A/9559). The series of United Nations
resolutions on this issue is conveniently documented in
E. Laszlo et al., eds., The Objectives of the New International
Economic Order (1977). See also S. Bagwat, ed., The New International Economic Order (1976); M. Bedjaoui, Toward a New International Economic Order (1979).

2. United Nations General Assembly Resolution 1803 (XVII), GA Supp. No. 17 (A/5217). For a background analysis of the resolution see, e.g., Schwebel, "The Story of the UN: Declaration on Permanent Sovereignty over Natural Resources," 49 ABAJ 463 (1963). For recent analysis of similar subsequent resolutions see, e.g., Adede, "International Law and the Property of Aliens, The Old Order Changeth," 19 Malaya L. Rev. 175, at 184-191 (1977); Onejeme, "The Law of Natural Resources Development," 5 Syracuse J. Int'l L. and Commerce 1 (1977).

3. See discussion in D. Smith and T. Wells, Negotiating Third World Mineral Agreements: Promises and Prologues 32 (1975).

4. Ibid.

5. See generally H. Cattan, The Evolution of Oil Concession Agreements in the Middle East and North Africa (1967).

6. W. Taylor, The Firestone Operations in Liberia (1956).

7. Wetter and Schwebel, "Some Little Known Cases on Concessions," 40 Brit. Y.B. Int'l L. 143 (1964).

8. Supra note 2.

9. Supra note 1.

10. See, e.g., 1970 Nigerian Oil Mining Lease (Land and Territorial Water Areas), para. 17; Agreement between the Imperial Ethiopian Government and the Louisiana Land Exploration Company, and Whitestone International Inc. of Dallas 1973 (hereafter cited as Ethiopian-Whitestone Agreement); Agreement between Egypt and ESSO Company 1974; Agreement between Ivory Coast and ESSO, 1970; Agreement between Mauritania and AGIP, 1971; Agreement between Mali and Texaco, 1970.

11. Compare, e.g., provisions in Ethiopian-Whitestone Agreement supra note 10; Egypt-Esso Agreement supra note 10; and Madagascar-AGIP Agreement 1968.

12. Compare, e.g., provisions in the Nigerian Oil Mining Lease, supra note 10, requiring building of local refinery, and agreements between Mauritania and Texaco and between Mauritania and AGIP--both stipulating the obligation to ensure domestic supply and no local refinery.

13. Compare, e.g., Ethiopian-Whitestone Agreement for mandatory surrender clause and Ivory Coast-ESSO Agreement for voluntary relinquishment clause.

14. See, e.g., Egypt-ESSO Agreement, Nigerian Oil Mining Lease.

15. See, e.g., the work plan in the Ethiopian-Whitestone Agreement and Egypt-ESSO Agreement.

16. See Nigerian Oil Mining Lease.

17. For further discussion see Asante, "Restructuring Transnational Mineral Agreements," 73 AJIAL 335 (1979).

18. For a background study, especially tracing the emergence of the fifty-fifty profit sharing, see Cattan, The Evolution of Oil Concession Agreements in the Middle East and North Africa (1967).

19. For further discussions on these terms, see, e.g., Adede, "A Profile of Trends in the State Contracts for Natural Resources Development Between African Countries and Foreign Companies," 13 N.Y.U. Int'l L.J. (1980).

20. Ibid.

21. Ibid.

22. Ibid.

23. See, e.g., the 1975 Egypt-Esso Agreement.
24. See, e.g., the 1968 Agreement between Mauritania and Esso.
25. See, e.g., the 1972 Agreement between Madagascar and Chevron.
26. See, e.g., the Zambian Agreement on the Acquisition of the Copper Mines.
27. See, e.g., the 1974 Egypt-Esso Agreement, the 1973 Ethiopia-Whitestone Agreement, 1974 Libya-Occidental Agreement, Nigeria Mining Lease, the 1970 Mali-Texaco Agreement, Kenya (ICDC)-Romania (Geomin) Agreement, and the Zambian Agreement on the Acquisition of the Copper Mines.
28. This is consistent with paragraph 2(c) of Article 2 of the Charter of Economic Rights and Interests of States.
29. Where the law of the contracting state is stipulated as the proper law, the real effect of such a provision depends primarily upon the extent to which the conflict-of-law rules, to be observed by the forum for the settlement of disputes provided for in another article of the contract, would permit reference to the law of the contracting state.
30. Let it be observed that the World Bank had a practice, now abandoned, of making all loan contracts with governments subject to New York State law. But see text in relation to note 40 _infra_.
31. The extent of the role played by either the "no confidence in the law of the developing country" or "the choice of the familiar law" in the choice of the applicable law provision is not, however, easy to determine.
32. For examples of such freezing clauses, see the Libya-Texaco Agreement, 1971; Mali-Texaco Agreement, 1970; Mauritania-S.P.M. Petroleum Co., 1967.
33. See, e.g., Egypt-Esso Agreement, 1974; Madagascar Chevron Agreement, 1965; and Mauritania-S.P.M. Petroleum Co., 1967.
34. _New York Times_, 24 June 1979, p. 1. "Managing OPEC Money."
35. See, e.g., the suggestions made at the 4th Meeting of UNCTAD in Nairobi and the 5th Meeting in Manila in response to U.N. resolution 3362, 29 GAOR, Seventh Special Sess. Supp. no. 1, U.N. Doc. A/10301(1975).
36. The recent case of Zaire, in which the IMF has taken a direct role in supervising the country's internal financial affairs, is a case in point. Consider also the austerity programs initiated by Egypt in 1978 at the instigation of the IMF as a precondition for receiving an IMF loan.
37. A summary of the step-by-step approach followed by the OPEC members to gain control of all aspects of the petroleum industry, thereby reducing the powers of the foreign oil companies, is found, for example, in "OPEC Tells the Oilmen the Party's Over," _Economist_, 16-22 February 1980, pp. 81-82. See also _New York Times_, 26 February 1980, pp. D1 and D12.
38. See Widdicombe, "The Effects of International Lending Programmes in Developing Nations," 7 _Vanderbilt J. Transnational L._ 593 at 603 (1974). See also Adede, "Loan Agreements between Developing Countries and Foreign Commercial Banks," 2 _Syracuse J. Int'l L. and Commerce_ 235, note 37 at 244 (1974).
39. Text of a loan agreement between an African country and a foreign commercial bank, supplied in confidence. Unpublished.

40. See Section 701 of IBRD Loan Regulation No. 3.

41. F. Man, "About the Proper Law of Contracts Between States," Studies in International Law 241 (1973).

42. The law of state responsibility has been in the process of codification by the International Law Commission of the United Nations for the past twenty-six years. For the latest position on the effort to produce a multilateral convention on the subject, see Report of the International Law Commission at Its Thirty-first Session, U.N. Doc. supp. No. 10 (A/34/10) at 228-369 (1979).

43. While the work on the TCDC is being done by the United Nations Office of Technical Cooperation in New York, the question of ECDC is being tackled by UNCTAD in Geneva.

44. See U.N. General Assembly Resolution 3461 (XXX).

45. See the 1974 Agreement on Technical and Scientific Cooperation between Egypt and Brazil.

46. See the 1973 Agreement between Kenya and Brazil.

47. See the 1973 Agreement between Cameroon and Brazil.

48. For comments see DeSoto, "How to Untie Tied Loans," 1 Africa: International Perspective (January-December 1975-1976).

49. See, e.g., the 1974 loan agreement between Denmark and Tanzania, which allows Tanzania to use a portion not exceeding 25 percent of the loan to secure goods and services in the open market.

50. For a loan agreement containing an expropriation clause, in which the borrower agrees not to take any action of expropriation or nationalization, see the 1971 agreement between Denmark and Malawi.

51. See, e.g., discussion in Adede, "Approaches to Bilateral Loan Agreements Between Developed and Developing Countries: Some Lessons from the Practice of Denmark, the United Kingdom and United States," 5 Dalhousie L. J. 121, at 124-128 (1979).

52. See, e.g., M. Mendelsohn, Money on the Move: The Modern International Capital Market (1980).

53. See, e.g., C. Davis, Financing Third World Debt (1970).

54. See Silkenat, "Eurodollar Borrowings by Developing States: Trends and Negotiating Problems," 20 Harv. Int'l L.J. 89 (1979).

Abbreviations

ACP	African, Caribbean, and Pacific
ADFAED	Abu Dhabi Fund
ADF	African Development Fund
ADIC	Abu Dhabi Investment Company
AFARCO	Afro-Arab Company for Investment and International Trade
AFESD	Arab Fund for Economic and Social Development
AFTAA	Arab Fund for Technical Assistance in Africa
AIC	Arab Investment Corporation
AOI	Arab Organisation for Industrialisation
BADEA	Arab Bank for Economic Development in Africa
BAII	Banque Arabe Internationale d'Investissements
BCCI	Bank of Credit and Commerce International
BDEAC	Development Bank of Central African States
Btu	British thermal unit
CIA	Central Intelligence Agency
COMECON	Council of Mutual Economic Assistance
DAC	Development Assistance Committee
ECA	Economic Commission for Africa
ECDC	Economic cooperation among the developing countries
ECOWAS	Economic Community of West African States
EDF	European Development Fund
EEC	European Economic Community
EFTA	European Free Trade Area
EIFD	Iraqi Fund
ELF	Eritrean Liberation Front
EPLF	Eritrean People's Liberation Front
FAATA	Fund for Arab-African Technical Assistance

FAC	First Arabian Corporation
FAO	Food and Agricultural Organization
FCN	Friendship, commerce, and navigation
FRAB	Banque Franco-Arabe d'Investissements Internationaux
FRELIMO	Front for the Liberation of Mozambique
FRIDA	Fund for Research and Investment for the Development of Africa
FROLINAT	National Liberation Front
GDP	Gross domestic product
GNP	Gross national product
IAIGC	Inter-Arab Investment and Guarantee Corporation
IBRD	International Bank for Reconstruction and Development
ICC	International Chamber of Commerce
ICDC	Investment cooperation development company
ICSID	International Centre for Settlement of Investment Disputes
IDA	International Development Association
IDB	Islamic Development Bank
IMF	International Monetary Fund
KGB	Soviet secret police
KFAED	Kuwait Fund
KFTCIC	Kuwait Foreign Trading, Contracting and Investing Company
KIC	Kuwait Investment Company
KIIC	Kuwait International Investment Company
KREIC	Kuwaiti Real Estate Investment Corporation
LAFB	Libyan Arab Foreign Bank
LAFTA	Latin America Free Trade Area
LDCs	Least developed countries
LICs	Low-income countries
LMC	Liberian Mining Company
MSA	Most seriously affected
NATO	North Atlantic Treaty Organization
NIEO	New International Economic Order
NOLDCs	Non-oil-producing, less developed countries
NOPEC	Non-oil-producing and exporting countries
NRER	Nonrenewable resources

OAPEC	Organization of Arab Oil Producing and Exporting Countries
OAU	Organization of African Unity
ODA	Overseas Development Assistance
OECD	Organisation for Economic Co-operation and Development
Onersol	Office de l'Energie Solaire du Niger
OPEC	Organization of Petroleum Exporting Countries
RPI	Regional petroleum importer
SAAFA	Special Arab Fund for Africa
SALT	Strategic Arms Limitation Talks
SAREC	Saudi Arabian Real Estate Corporation
SAVAK	Iranian Secret Police
SDR	Special drawing right
SITC	Standard International Trade Classification
TCDC	Technical cooperation among the developing countries
UAE	United Arab Emirates
UBAF	Unions de Banques Arabes et Francaises
UDC	Underdeveloped country
U.N.	United Nations
UNCTAD	United Nations Conference on Trade and Development
UDEAO	Customs Union of West African States
UNESCO	United Nations Educational, Scientific and Cultural Organization
ZANLA	Zimbabwe African National Liberation Army
ZIPRA	Zimbabwe Independence People's Revolutionary Army

About the Editor and Contributors

Dunstan M. Wai. M.A. (Oxon.), M.A., Ph.D. (Harvard), was born in Kajokaji, Southern Region, Sudan, and has been a visiting research fellow in the International Relations Division of the Rockefeller Foundation (1977-80), New York, and a fellow of the Woodrow Wilson International Center for Scholars. He is now a consultant for private foundations and the United Nations.

A. O. Adede. LL.B. (Boston University), Ph.D. (Fletcher School of Law and Diplomacy), legal officer, Legal Division, United Nations Secretariat, New York.

Kamal Hossain. LL.B., B.C.L., D. Phil. (Oxon.), former director, Centre for Research on the New International Economic Order, Queen Elizabeth House, Oxford; head, Awami League Party, Bangladesh.

Suleiman I. Kiggundu. B.A. (UEA), M.A. (Strathclyde), M.A. (Purdue), Ph.D. (Boston University), senior lecturer and head of the Department of Economics, Makerere University, Kampala.

Robin Luckham. M.A. (Oxon.), Ph.D. (Chicago), research fellow, Institute of Development Studies, Sussex University.

Michael Lyall. M.A. (Oxon.), M.B.A. (Harvard), managing director, Laidlow, Adams and Peck, Inc., New York.

Ali A. Mazrui. B.A. (Manchester), M.A. (Columbia), D. Phil. (Oxon.), professor of political science, University of Michigan, Ann Arbor, and B.B.C. Reith Lecturer, 1979.

Frank A. Ocwieja. M.A., M.A.L.D. (Fletcher School of Law and Diplomacy), vice-president and senior project manager, Chase Trade Information Corporation, New York.

Ernest J. Wilson III. B.A. (Harvard), M.A., Ph.D. (Berkeley), assistant professor of political science, University of Michigan, Ann Arbor.

Index